MAKING TELEVISION PROGRAMS

A PROFESSIONAL APPROACH

Second Edition

RICHARD BREYER
Syracuse University

PETER MOLLER
Syracuse University

with

MICHAEL SCHOONMAKER
Syracuse University

WAVELAND

PRESS, INC.

Prospect Heights, Illinois

Making Television Programs was created on the Macintosh computers in the Newhouse School's Communications Graphics Lab. Design and layout were done in PageMaker 4.0; graphics were created in FreeHand 2.02. Proofs were printed on a LaserWriter II and final output was printed on a Linotronic 200 at 1270 dpi. Text was set in the Futura Condensed and ITC Garamond Condensed families, both from Adobe. Photos and some graphics were stripped in using traditional methods.

For information about this book, write or call:

Waveland Press, Inc.
P.O. Box 400
Prospect Heights, Illinois 60070
(708) 634-0081

Graphic Design and Illustrations: Rik Ahlberg
Cover: Rik Ahlberg

Photo credits: pp. 43, 71, courtesy MacNeil/Lehrer Productions; pp. 56-58, courtesy Grey Advertising; p. 162, courtesy CNN.

This book is dedicated to Jenifer Breyer and Sharon Schoonmaker. They worked overtime at their jobs so their husbands could work on this book.

ACKNOWLEDGEMENTS

We believe this second edition of *Making Television Programs* is unique among television and film production texts because of the way it combines theory and practice. Using case studies we attempt to actively involve the reader in the step-by-step details of the production process. When you finish this book we expect that you will feel like you have been behind the scenes with professional production teams.

If *Making Television Programs* does this, if it takes you to script conferences, editing suites, studios and productions being shot on location, a great deal of credit goes to Michael Schoonmaker. Michael designed the text and layout. We are grateful for his hard work and vision.

Rik Ahlberg was responsible for the graphic design, illustrations and cover of the book. As you read the text, you will see how much Rik's work adds to both readability and realism. We are grateful for his dedication and unique design touch.

Thanks also to Greg Waldt, Corey Watson and Alex Bhargava for their photographs and to Don Diefenback for his help on the glossary.

Two of the chapters in Unit Two analyze a commercial for a Proctor and Gamble product. We are indebted to this company and the Grey Advertising Agency for making themselves and their commercial available to us.

Also we express our thanks to Steve Kent of *Santa Barbara*, Ed Gabriel of Eric Mower Associates, Sam Nassar of Montage Productions, Dean Walters of WSTM, *The MacNeil/Lehrer News Hour*, Turner Broadcasting System, Lenweaver Design, Stan Alten, Don Edwards, Marshall Matlock, and Lisa Mignacca of The Newhouse School at Syracuse University.

Laurie Prossnitz, our editor at Waveland Press, is another person who has our gratitude. She has kept our team on course; not always an easy task.

Contents

Introduction

Making Television Programs' emphasis on the process rather than the technology of producing television programs distinguishes it from most other books on the subject. We believe cameras, recorders, microphones, editing suites, and character generators are no more important to students of television production than pencils, typewriters, or word processors are to students of writing. Knowing how to use a pencil does not make a writer any more than knowing how to use a camera makes a television producer. But, because there are so many costly and complicated devices required to express ourselves with television, there is a tendency to confuse learning how to operate television equipment with learning how to communicate.

For example, we believe the first step toward learning how to communicate with television is becoming "television literate"; that is, learning how to watch television with a critical eye. When we began writing this book we spent a considerable amount of time deciding what to call it. While we are reasonably pleased with *Making Television Programs: A Professional Approach*, it does not tell the whole story. This book is also about watching television.

Another issue we discussed when selecting the title of this book is whether or not to include the word film. *Making Television and Film Programs: A Professional Approach*, in many ways, is a more accurate description of the content of this book. Distinctions between film and television production processes and techniques are disappearing. Professional production teams using single video cam-

eras and video editing equipment are employing many of the same lighting, shooting and editing techniques used in film production. Many made-for-television movies are shot on film and edited on videotape; others are produced completely on videotape. In homes, schools, and businesses, videotape playback units are replacing film projectors. For this reason more and more producers are making educational, industrial and even entertainment films on videotape.

This blending of television and film into one medium has resulted in less specialization. Very few professional producers, directors, camera operators, lighting designers or editors work only in television or only in film. In schools like the one in which we teach, there are no longer curricula that concentrate just on film or just on television. Students learn to work in both media.

In the end we did not add the word film to the title of the book because we were concerned that it would confuse any reader who is new to our field. However, the way of thinking, designing, writing and producing we describe in this book applies to both film and television.

Making Television Programs: A Professional Approach is used for courses in production, writing, and production design. It is also meant for the professional person responsible for designing, writing or producing programs.

Ideally, the book should be read through once before any specific application of the process is attempted. The reader will then have an overall view of a complex process. We expect the reader will return to specific portions of the book to review topics of concern when the need arises. For example, when a student needs to complete a class project on lighting, he or she will turn to those pages in the book which deal with light and its use in television. Or as someone begins the work of producing a television program, the chapter on the Commitment Stage should be reviewed.

A unique feature of television production is the way collaborators work with one another. Television production is not a one-person show, nor is it the work of a committee. It falls somewhere between the two. The case studies in this edition give detailed examples of this unique interaction. These examples come from different types of television: commercial, public/educational, institutional/corporate, and cassette television.

Throughout this book we use terms which are likely to be unfamiliar to you. We have chosen not to define these terms in footnotes because we feel that would impair the readability of the book. For this reason, there is a glossary at the end of the book. We encourage you to refer to it whenever necessary.

Near the end of the book, in Appendix A, there are samples of many of the documents and forms used in television production. Releases, edit decision lists, lighting plans, facility request forms, storyboards, treatments and scripts are some of the materials found there. They should be useful for both students and professionals.

There are no simple rules which describe how to make television programs. It would be misleading to suggest that there were. But there are methods of conceiving and expressing ideas, collaborating, and exploiting technology which form the foundations of a professional approach to television production.

Those who succeed in this profession are well aware of these foundations. The intention of this book is to help you join their ranks.

UNIT 1

The Contemporary Production Environment

Marshall McLuhan described technologies as extensions of the human hand and mind. The human race's first technologies—the stick, fire, and the wheel—transformed the world as they extended mankind's reach and power. Technologies like photography, radio and television define twentieth century civilization and characterize our world of instant and ubiquitous communication.

In the last twenty years, these technologies have changed dramatically. As a result, the institutions and industries which use these technologies have also changed. Charlie Chaplin would have difficulty finding his way around the film studios of modern Hollywood. What would Fibber MaGee and Molly think of today's stereophonic radio which we wear on our head? Could such early pioneers of television as Jackie Gleason and Lucille Ball have ever imagined today's couch potatoes watching MTV or the latest release from the video store?

The change from analog to digital recording and editing of the television image is just one of the many innovations which have had an impact on the production environment. The successful producer, director, writer and designer understand this new environment and how to work within it. In the next three chapters, we will review these changes and suggest how they have transformed both the form and content of what appears on the television screens in American living rooms, dorm rooms, classrooms, board rooms, and the like.

Chapter 1

An Evolving Tradition

Suppose you're sitting in front of your television set with the remote control in your hand. You watch a few minutes of a basketball game and then switch to the news. After the news you watch part of a *Magnum P.I.* rerun and then turn to a made-for-TV movie, *Clean But Dead*. This movie fails to hold your interest so you pop a cassette of Hitchcock's classic, *Rear Window*, into your VCR.

Everything you have watched came to you through your television set. With the exception of the Hitchcock film, all the programs were listed in *T.V. Guide*. Yet, only a portion of the news was produced in a television studio. And only this studio segment of the news and the "live" portions of the basketball game were produced in the traditional television style of production.

What is clear from these examples and the following discussion is that the term "television" no longer refers to a single type of production. Television production, as well as the programs themselves, have evolved significantly since TV was first introduced in the mid-1940s, and continue to evolve.

STYLES OF TELEVISION PRODUCTION

The basketball game was shot with four cameras placed around the court, each showing a small part of the entire event. One camera had a wide shot of the court, another showed the fans, another the coaches and players on the bench, and the fourth was on the edge of the court, mounted on the shoulder of a camera operator, for close-ups of the action under the net.

In a van parked just outside the stadium, a director sat in front of a bank of monitors where the shots from the four cameras were displayed.

Using a device called a video switcher, the director edited or selected shots from the four cameras and added prerecorded material and graphics.

DIRECTOR
Take camera four!

ASSISTANT DIRECTOR
Ready CG. Three...you have the long shot...two, close up of the ball in Jenkins' hand.

DIRECTOR
Key in CG! I need a wide shot of the scorer's table...something's going on there.

ASSISTANT DIRECTOR
One, can you get the scorer's table? Good, hold it.

DIRECTOR
CG out. Take one.

ASSISTANT DIRECTOR
Ready four...

This twenty-five second portion and the game was sent through a satellite dish placed near the remote van where the director edited the game. From the dish it was sent to a satellite which in turn relayed the program to television stations, cable companies and individually owned satellite dishes. Some stations immediately rebroadcast the program. Other stations and cable companies recorded the game for future broadcast.

This television style of production is also used for programs that are scripted and performed by actors. For example, soap operas, sitcoms and many of the series on *Masterpiece Theater* are produced in this multi-camera, television style. Directors and their staffs rehearse actors, cameras operators, and lighting and sound technicians before production. Then, when the episode is performed, as when the curtain rises in the theater, the action proceeds on its own. However, unlike the theater, because the program is being recorded on videotape, portions of it can be redone and edited into the program before it is aired.

During production, directors of television drama, like directors of basketball games, communicate with their camera operators and other members of the crew through microphones and headsets.

The studio portions of the news you watched were broadcast as they were produced, "live" in the television style. It was done in a television studio where three cameras took three different shots of the news team sitting behind their desks: camera #1, the anchor; camera #2, the weather person; and camera #3, the sports person. The director and her staff, in a control room next to the studio, selected which shots to use and in what order. In addition, she coordinated the "rolling-in" of prerecorded news stories shot on location.

These prerecorded stories were produced film style, using a single video camera. That is, one camera recorded a variety of angles and perspectives of a traffic accident, political rally, and parade. Later, with the help of an editing machine, some—not all—of these single shots were shortened, reordered and edited into the news.

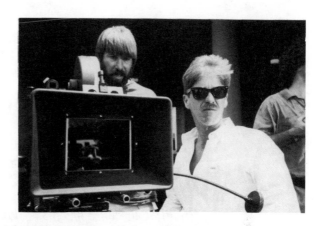

Made-for-TV movies, commercials, documentaries, and music videos typically use the film tradition of shooting with one camera and editing after production. These types of programs tend to be faster paced and appear more polished and more controlled than programs produced in the television style. During production in the film style, images and sounds are recorded individually and out of sequence. This gives production teams opportunities to closely control light, sound, action, camera movement, and delivery of the actors' lines.

Here is an example of how the climactic scene from the made-for-TV movie *Clean But Dead* was produced film style.

(DETECTIVE ANNE MASON ENTERS THE LAUNDROMAT AS THE KILLER IS ABOUT TO DROWN HIS FOURTEENTH VICTIM IN THE SOAPY WATERS OF THE RINSE CYCLE.)

ASSISTANT DIRECTOR
Ok, everyone, check your script...this is shot #33.

DIRECTOR
I think I'll change it slightly from what's on paper. I want to see the detective through the pile of laundry....more from this angle.

(DIRECTOR BENDS DOWN AND SHOWS WHERE THE CAMERA SHOULD BE PLACED.)

VIDEOGRAPHER
How about from here...with a touch of the washing
machine blocking the killer's vision.

DIRECTOR
Ok...but just on the edge of the frame...no more.
Sandy, lighting is too high key. I need more shadows
in the corner.

(LIGHTING DESIGNER HAS HIS ASSISTANT MOVE A
LIGHT)

DIRECTOR
Good. Thanks.

ASSISTANT DIRECTOR
Can we get the actor in please?

(ACTOR ENTERS THE SCENE.)

DIRECTOR
Ok, Fran, stand next to the door and look around,
until you see the killer, then run for it. You'll run out
of frame. We're shooting this in close up so you don't
need to give us too much. Ready?

ACTOR
Yes.

ASSISTANT DIRECTOR
Quiet on the set...sound...

SOUND PERSON
Check...

ASSISTANT DIRECTOR
Camera...

VIDEOGRAPHER
Speed...

DIRECTOR
Action...

After an hour and a half and fourteen versions or "takes" of this ten second shot, the director is satisfied and the lighting designer, sound operator and videographer move their equipment to the other side of the laundromat for another shot.

When this scene is edited and its sound track mixed, it will appear as if all the action took place at one time. However, it will not have the same quality or "feel" as the studio portion of the evening news or the basketball game. Material produced film style like news stories, commercials, MTV videos, and made-for-television movies have a composed, controlled quality to them as compared to the spontaneous, real-life quality of programs produced in the multi-camera television style.

In television's early days, during the 1940s and early 1950s, even though there was a film process called *kinescope* to record programs, most television was broadcast "live" from a studio. Three or four bulky cameras were rolled into the studio to broadcast interviews, dramas and variety shows. Once in a while a television station might produce a *remote* (shot on location), although this was much more

CHANGES IN TELEVISION PRODUCTION

expensive. Vans carrying a portable control room and the same bulky cameras used in the studio were set up at county fairs, sporting events, or political rallies. Because there were no satellites then, telephone wires carried remote programs back to the home station where they were broadcast or stored with kinescope for future use.

Even though videotape replaced film as a method of storing and rebroadcasting programs, film continued to be used for single camera productions. Documentaries, news segments, commercials, and dramas continued to be shot and edited on film.

In the mid-1970s, videotape editing equipment became available which made it possible for the single camera, film style of production to be performed with video equipment. For the first time producers could shoot and edit film style on videotape or film.

Most news departments immediately switched to video-tape for their location shots. The tight deadlines in news production made videotape ideal for their purposes.

Some documentary producers began shooting and editing on videotape at about the same time. However, the quality of the image, the bulky video cameras, and the unreliable video editing systems of the 1970s kept most documentarians working in film. Also, in the mid-1970s most audiences viewed documentaries on movie screens, not on television sets. This kept documentary producers working primarily in film.

In the mid-1980s, when video cameras became smaller, (lighter and more durable), editing easier, and videotape the primary way of seeing documentaries, more producers turned to video.

Before the 1980s, all prime-time entertainment programs shot on location were produced on film. For example, episodes of *Magnum, P.I.* were produced on film and transferred to videotape for distribution to television. Today, with improvements in the quality of the video image plus the significantly lower costs of producing on videotape, more and more entertainment programs are being produced on videotape. *Clean But Dead*, was shot and edited on videotape; if it had been made ten years ago it would have been shot on film.

Many commercials for national audiences continue to be produced on film. However, virtually all regional and local commercials are produced on videotape using the film style of production.

Rear Window was made long before films became available on videocassettes. This new way of distributing feature films is not only changing the way films are seen, it is also changing the way they are made. Some filmmakers shoot on film and immediately transfer it to videotape for editing, post production and distribution. Shooting a feature length film in this manner is significantly cheaper than working totally in film. Others produce "films" totally on videotape. High Definition Television (HDTV) and large, wall size television screens for home or theater use make it even more feasible for "films" to be shot and distributed on videotape.

When discussing film and television production, we cannot ignore the technical differences between the film and television image. Film renders much more detail than video and has a wider tolerance for extremes of dark and light. However, as video cameras improve in quality and sensitivity, these technical differences will become less pronounced. High Definition Television, for example, has twice the number of scan lines and twice the picture information as a normal television image, and more closely approximates the image quality of film.

As a result of all these changes and the new ways we are using our television sets, the word "television" does not mean the same as it did in the past. It has become more than a medium of news, sitcoms, soap operas, action serials, and sports. It is also a medium for contemporary and classic films.

This overlapping of television and film has also caused an overlapping of the professions in those mediums. Not very long ago, writers, designers, producers, and directors worked only in film or only in television; seldom in both. Those who worked in film usually knew nothing about television and those who worked in television knew nothing about film. Today, professional producers, writers, directors and designers must be "fluent" in both traditions. Many are involved in producing programs which contain both the live, immediate quality of multi-camera television and the "painted," composed quality of single-camera programs produced in the film style.

Chapter 2

The Types of TV

Until the mid-1970s, television served three broad categories of audiences: the general "mass" audience of commercial television; pre-school, elementary, and secondary students who watched afternoon educational programs; and well-educated adults who watched public television. With the introduction of satellites, cable television, and videocassettes in the 1970s, television now serves a much wider variety of audiences.

For example, there are programs distributed on videocassette for opera devotees, employees of IBM, visitors to the Smithsonian Institution, dermatologists, skiers, stamp collectors, and aerobic dancers. There are also programs distributed on cable networks for relatively small audiences with specific interests, such as arts (A&E); sports (ESPN, SPORTS Channel); and current affairs (C-SPAN). Still other networks provide programming for audiences defined by race or heritage (BET, Univision).

This new environment has affected everyone working in television production. The challenge of communicating to, educating, and entertaining viewers who have more choices and a broader set of expectations means that production teams must be much more inventive than in the past.

For most producers, a *key* first step is to answer such questions as "What's the purpose of this program?", "Who is the audience?", "How long should it be?", "In what form?", and "Is there a need for supplementary materials?" The answers they come up with affect everything from whether to launch a project to budgeting and casting a production once it has begun.

For purposes of discussion, it will be helpful to group television programming into four broad categories: 1) commercial, 2) corporate/institutional, 3) cassette television, and 4) public/educational. Each of these will be discussed in the following sections.

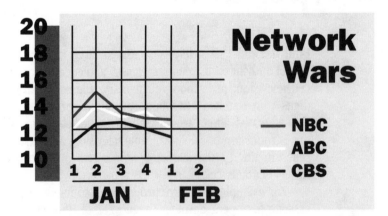

COMMERCIAL TELEVISION The single most distinguishing feature of commercial television is ratings. In most cases, they are the measure of success in this category of television. The exceptions are programs produced as public services and these are normally a very small percentage of the total amount of programming hours produced by a commercial station.

The higher the ratings, the more income earned from the sale of time slots before, during, and after programs. For example, it would be difficult to sell a thirty-second time slot to a national sponsor—a sponsor who wants to reach a national audience—for $100,000 if the time slot were located in the middle of a program with 100,000 viewers. Each viewer would cost the sponsor a dollar. Most advertisers would find this too expensive. On the other hand, $100,000 for a thirty-second time slot in the middle of a program with an audience of 20 million would be relatively easy to sell to an advertiser because each viewer would cost an inexpensive one-half cent.

Sponsors have the options of buying time and having their commercials shown locally as well as nationally. Because of the relatively small number of viewers who watch a local station, the cost for local time is much less than a time slot on a national network. Instead of many thousands of dollars for twenty seconds on a network, a few hundred may be all that a sponsor has to pay a local station to have its commercial shown.

In the mid-1970s, satellites and cable television brought more players into an area that has traditionally been dominated by the three major commercial networks, ABC, CBS, and NBC. These relative newcomers included FOX, HBO, Nickelodeon, and the Turner networks(CNN & TNT); also "super stations" (stations that serve both local and national audiences) like WOR and WPIX in New York and WGN in Chicago.

This increased competition is one of the reasons that, in the 1980s, the percentage of viewers who tuned to ABC, CBS, and NBC dropped from 90 percent to about 60 percent. However, even though these networks do not dominate television production and distribution as they did in the past, they are still very important contributors to television programming. The three primary networks produce, with their own staff and facilities, the more popular evening newscasts, morning talk shows of national interest (*Today*, *Good Morning America*), and major sports events (the World Series, the Olympics, the Super Bowl). In addition, they hire or co-produce with production companies the bulk of prime-time programming: sitcoms, variety shows, adventure shows, mini-series, and made-for-TV movies. Many of these programs are broadcast elsewhere as reruns after premiering on the commercial networks. For example, *Cagney & Lacey*, *Hill Street Blues*, and *The Jeffersons* are now seen on cable networks and independent stations, but were produced and initially distributed by a major network.

The phrase "nothing breeds success like success" has particular relevance to commercial television. A show that is a hit with viewers (and advertisers) tends to breed imitators. Many kinds of shows are based on formats that have proved successful in the past. For example, most sitcoms have flat lighting, a laugh track, and word-based jokes; news programs are based in studio news rooms and hosted by one or two anchors; and adventure programs typically begin with a fast-paced montage that is edited to the program's theme music. These familiar forms tend to interest large numbers of viewers and get high ratings.

CORPORATE/ INSTITUTIONAL TELEVISION

There are no ratings in what we call corporate/institutional television. Even if there were, they would be of little use. Popularity is normally not a useful means of judging a program produced in this type of television. Such a program is effective when it teaches, trains, or motivates the audience for which it was intended—whether this is the employees of an insurance company, the students of a school district or university, the visitors to a museum, or the patients, nurses, and doctors of a hospital.

There are a number of ways to deliver programs to these specialized audiences: videocassette or video discs, satellites, and local cable connections. For example, an international brokerage firm mails videocassette programs to employees located on three continents. A high school distributes regularly scheduled programs through wires inside the school's two buildings. A state health department rents two hours of satellite time to distribute an in-service training course to hospitals around the state.

There are a variety of ways production teams are hired in this type of television. Many large corporations, hospitals, and school districts employ an in-house staff, including producers, writers, directors, camera operators, sound people and engineers. Smaller institutions—small businesses, locally administered federal or state agencies, colleges—normally hire production teams on a free-lance or job-by-job basis.

However they are hired, production teams must observe and understand the institution they serve. Knowledge of everything from the long-term goals to the unwritten dress code of the business, school, or hospital for which a team works is as essential as knowing how to write a script or edit film or videotape.

This does not mean production teams simply find out what the corporation or institution wants and delivers it to them. Those who do this usually produce uninspired programs that, in the long run, do not serve the client or further the careers of the members of the production team. Production teams in all types of television, but especially corporate/institutional, must lead, not follow.

Let's listen in on a luncheon conversation between two producers.

PRODUCER #1
You really have to get pushy sometimes, for the client's own good.

PRODUCER #2
Tell me about it! If you're doing print they usually leave you alone and let you be the expert. But if it's television or video, everyone thinks he's an expert. Maybe it's because they watch so much of it?

PRODUCER #1
Whatever the reason...I'd say eight out of ten of my clients, smart people I genuinely respect, go a little crazy when they hear the word video or television. And when they see a camera...they really go bananas. Some even begin to take over writing the script and start telling me how to shoot.

PRODUCER #2
And we both know that leads to disaster.

PRODUCER #1
Yes, like the time I was told to adapt Man of La Mancha for a sales meeting of an underwear company.

PRODUCER #2
Very tasteful. "To Dream the Impossible Dream" must have been a knockout.

PRODUCER #1
That's exactly what it was, they fired me. Can you believe it? They fired me because I did exactly what they told me to do.

PRODUCER #2
Yes, I can believe it because the same thing happened to me. Except you had more fun. I got burned because I produced a television adaptation of, are you ready, a fifty-page training manual...made great TV. I warned them, told them it wasn't right for television. They said, "No, it's just what we want." Then when it was finished and they saw it, they asked why I did such a stupid thing...right before they told me they would not need my services anymore.

This conversation points out two common problems with programs in corporate/institutional television. First, programs often fail because their structure or "vehicle" has nothing to do with the educational, training, or motivational objectives of the program. No matter how well produced the version of *Man of La Mancha* might have been, it is the wrong structure for a training program. The story of a classic knight involved in the underwear business might have worked as a sequence in a comedy for late night commercial television but as part of a sales meeting for serious, hard nosed business people it was a disaster.

Second, training or educational programs may fail

because production teams do not use television appropriately. Most viewers, no matter how sophisticated, have difficulty comprehending and retaining the content of a training program unless they see the "lesson" demonstrated within some kind of "story." An example of this problem is the 50-page manual that is made into a television presentation. A television program could never replace a well written training manual. There is too much detailed information in a written text of this type. Television works best when it demonstrates how ideas, or rules are applied. A more effective approach would have been to tell the "story," in a documentary style, of a new employee who used the training manual to solve some of the problems he or she faced the first month on the job. This would have demonstrated how to use the manual.

So, no matter how well done the adaptation of *Man of La Mancha* or the television version of the training manual, both programs were not properly designed to become "hits" in this type of television.

Because the criteria for success in corporate/institutional television are different than for other forms, these programs are produced differently. For example, they are *not* usually shot in idealized settings like those in prime-time sitcoms or afternoon soap operas. In general, programs that succeed in this type of television are found in settings that suggest specific areas of interest or study: a factory, a research laboratory, a corporate board room, a computer terminal, a business office, an agricultural processing plant. Also, the executives, doctors, managers, historians, and the like who are the "stars" of institutional programs may not look or sound like most prime-time actors.

Institutional programs are often designed to work with other media, such as computers, workbooks, audio cassettes, and three-dimensional models. This means production teams who work in corporate/institutional television should be prepared to produce supplementary materials. This was the case for a team hired to produce programs to introduce employees of an international corporation to a new set of procedures. They designed a handbook and a trainer's guide in eight different languages in addition to producing twelve, twenty-minute programs.

The institutional communicator usually works for organizations run by people who usually have not gained their position of prominence through their knowledge of television. They may know international business, school enrollment trends, hospital construction costs, or assembly-line production techniques; but most know little about how to use or evaluate television. So, in addition to the skills required to produce programs and supplementary materials, production teams must be prepared to teach others how to use media.

CASSETTE TELEVISION

Before the mid-1970s, feature films, classic television programs, and documentaries were seen in classrooms, theaters, museums, libraries, and on broadcast television. Rarely were they viewed on projectors or videotape machines in homes. Film projector and videotape playback units made before 1975 were expensive and, for most consumers, too complicated to operate. When inexpensive, easy-to-operate, 1/2 inch, videocassette recorders and playback units came on the market, a revolution in film and television distribution occurred. For the first time viewers could select *what* appeared on their television screens and *when* it appeared.

This type of television, which we call cassette television, provides new distribution opportunities for owners of existing films and classic television programs. Programs like *Brideshead Revisited*, *M.A.S.H*, *National Geographic Specials*, and *NOVA* are now being rented and sold through catalogs and stores along with feature films of every description, from classic silent movies to the *latest releases*.

In addition to creating new markets for owners of existing films and television programs, the arrival of inexpensive, easy-to-operate videocassette machines also resulted in new production opportunities. Such products as *Directors on Directing* and *Play With A Purpose* described earlier, can now be financed through revenues earned from the rental and purchase of these videocassettes. Other examples of programs that are produced solely for cassette television are "How-To" programs on subjects as varied as automobile repair and quilting; sports highlights of the NFL, NBA, and major college conferences; and educational/informational tapes for the medical, educational and insurance professions. There are even entertainment movies being produced just for videocassette distribution.

Popularity is certainly important in this type of television. The more copies purchased or rented of a video cassette, the more income earned and the better informed and entertained are viewers.

There are several special considerations for producing cassette television programs. First of all, these shows usually have small audiences of thousands or, sometimes, only hundreds. Teams producing for these relatively small and specialized audiences must approach their jobs quite differently than their colleagues in commercial or institutional/corporate television. In simple, bottom-line terms, they must keep their production costs down if they hope to make a profit.

TELEVISION PRODUCER:
Hank, Mike here. Did you speak with the publisher
about our idea?

AUTHOR
Yep, and he's willing to do all he can with distribution
and publicity once the tape is made. But he won't put
up any money. He was very clear about that.

TELEVISION PRODUCER
Pity there's nothing up front but I'm glad he wants in.
So, we need to find at least twenty grand. Got any
rich relatives?

AUTHOR
I hate to ask this but is twenty really enough?

TELEVISION PRODUCER
Yes, I think we can stay within that range *if*. There
are two if's: If we don't pay ourselves until we make
money on distribution. And if we keep production costs
down. Because we're going to distribute on cassette—and not going broadcast—we can shoot and
edit on three quarter or high eight. That will be much
cheaper and we really won't sacrifice anything.

AUTHOR
Fine. That's your department. I know nothing about
that stuff. So, to sum up, we can get the tape done
for twenty thousand dollars... which we don't have!

Serving small audiences and, at the same time, earning enough income to meet expenses and make a profit requires production teams to be more creatively involved in the financing of cassette television projects than in the other types of television. The producer and author in the phone conversation eventually produce their videotape. To do this they take out a loan of seven thousand dollars and find an investor to fund the remainder of the budget. The investor receives 25% of the net income(income after production and distribution expenses have been paid). If two thousand or more copies are sold annually (at $30.00 per tape), the author, producer and investor will begin to make a profit by the third year.

This scenario demonstrates one way to finance cassette programs for small, specialized audiences. Another is to work with sponsors who might provide funding in exchange for a credit at the beginning or end of a program. Drug and food manufacturers, for example, have sponsored programs on health and nutrition.

Another way of getting support is for production teams to co-produce with an institution that plans to buy their program or series. For example, a school district, hospital, museum, or television station might provide partial funding or might allow their facilities to be used in exchange for a copy of the product and recognition as sponsor or presenter. The series on television directors mentioned previously was produced in this way. A cable company provided facilities and materials worth fifteen thousand dollars in exchange for *first run* distribution rights of the series.

Closely related to the need for financing is the need to keep budgets low. Due to advances in the quality of less expensive, "non-broadcast" cameras and recording and editing equipment, skilled production teams can produce professional-looking products on relatively small budgets. For example, the producer in the earlier conversation plans to use "industrial quality" equipment instead of "broadcast. quality" equipment. He does this knowing that he will be able to create picture and sound quality that will do the job and, at the same time, keep production costs low enough so the program has a reasonable chance of being profitable.

Hits in cassette television, as with corporate/institutional television, do not necessarily look like hits on commercial television. Audiences who have paid to be entertained or informed in a specialized area need not be "hooked" to "stay tuned" in the same way as broadcast audiences. In fact, this type of viewer is apt to become impatient with programs that begin with highly produced introductions or contain slick production gimmicks. These viewers tend to be more concerned with a program's subject matter and presentation. For example, a series for viewers interested in learning about television production produced for cassette television might begin with a simple opening credit and then take the viewer behind the scenes and show lighting fixtures, dimmer boards, cables, mixing consoles and so on. A program on the same subject for a general audience might begin with a fast-paced montage with electronic graphics and excerpts from popular television programs.

Many cassette television series are designed to work with other media, especially books. Good examples of this are how-to tapes—how to cook, how to fix plumbing, how to pass the SAT's, etc. Production teams responsible for this kind of product need to be skilled in communicating with the written word as well as with television/film images and sounds.

SESAME ST...
A series of half hour educati...
pr...

THE MEETING O...
ASSOCIATI...
PUBLI...
An inedited va...
association' conferen...
Washington...

WILL'S STORY
A twenty minute program about the special relationship of a teenage boy and his grandmother. This tape demonstrates the important roles elder members of families and community can play in a young person's...

CHINA: CHANGE AND
CONTINUITY
A one-semester, interdisciplinary telecourse that explores aspects of the history, philosophy, religion, arts, language, literature and anthropology of China.

COLOR ADJUSTMENT:
BLACKS IN
PRIMETIME
A sixty minute, unprecedented documentary examining racial stereotyping in primetime television. The documentary provides a compelling case study of how network programming reflects divisive social issues while presenting them in the non-threatening formats of television entertainment.

THE MACNEIL/LEHRER
NEWSHOUR
...ally, hour long news program.

PUBLIC/EDUCATIONAL TELEVISION These are a few of the thousands of productions that fit into the next category of television, public/educational. Programs like these are distributed in a variety of ways. *The MacNeil/Lehrer Newshour* and *Sesame Street* are broadcast on public television. Telecourses like *China: Change and Continuity* are normally distributed on public television and on video cassettes. Cultural programs like *Color Adjustment* are distributed on public television and videocassette as well as on cable networks like A&E (Arts and Entertainment), Discovery, and BET (Black Entertainment Television). Programs such as the unedited proceedings of the meeting of the Association for Public Policy are seen on C-SPAN, a nonprofit network supported by the cable television industry. Educational programs like *Will's Story*, which is shown primarily to high school civics students, are distributed on videocassette.

Funds for these types of programs usually come from grants provided by a variety of organizations, some public, some private: the Office of Education, the National Endowment for the Humanities, the Corporation for Public Broadcasting (CPB), the Department of Transportation, the National Association of Cable Companies, the Ford Foundation, ITT, and Mobil Oil. These and other organizations are dedicated to providing programs with "culture," "diversity," "education," "enrichment," and "innovation."

Most people agree that viewers—especially young viewers—should be given the opportunity to see programs that are "educational," and "enriching." However, these words do not mean the same things to everyone. For example, a program about a small town symphony orchestra may impress one group as "cultural" and "innovative" while others describe it as "mundane" and "inappropriate for public television." Some people feel the unedited meetings of a Washington-based public policy association are an example of quality public/educational television. Others call the same programs boring or "elitist."

Other considerations particular to this type of television include: Should educational television for children have the "look" and pace of programs and commercials found on commercial television? Should funds be awarded for cultural programs for adults on subjects which only those with a college education can comprehend? Or should efforts and funds be spent on programs that have a broader appeal? Should public/educational television funds be used to import cultural programs from overseas, especially from Britain? Or should more funds be dedicated to programs about the American experience? Should the Corporation for Public Broadcasting and other public/educational funding sources support regional programs which help viewers learn more about their communities? Or should they use most of their funds for more expensive programs about subjects of national interest?

There are as many answers to these questions as there are critics, funding organizations, producers and distributors of public/educational television.

Another important consideration is how to measure the "success" of such programs. Sometimes getting good ratings is very important. One reason organizations like Exxon, ITT, and Mobil Oil provide the millions of dollars it takes to produce and distribute programs like *The MacNeil/Lehrer Newshour*, *National Geographic*, and *Masterpiece Theater* is the popularity of these programs with millions of upscale, public television viewers. In other words, it is good advertising. Popularity is also important to the individual public stations who pay fees to air these programs. If they are popular, the station is more apt to receive financial support from its viewers during fund raising campaigns. Ratings are also important to the Office of Education and the other organizations that fund such children's programs as *Sesame Street*, *Reading Rainbow*, and *Mr. Rogers*. Unless these programs are popular, viewed by millions of children, the millions of dollars spent on research, production and distribution cannot be justified and funding will be terminated.

Those who fund and distribute programs like *Color Adjustment* (a program about the stereotyping of blacks on prime-time television) are concerned with ratings and popularity; however, they also value critical acclaim and the public debate resulting from the programs they support. The same criteria is valued by those who fund and distribute the programs on the C-SPAN network. The number of viewers is not as important as making available to the American public in-depth programs about important national and international issues.

Some producers of educational programs have more precise measures of success. For example, an essential criteria used by organizations like the Annenberg/CPB (Corporation for Public Broadcasting) Fund, which supports university level telecourses, is the number of colleges or universities who adopt the telecourses. The same criteria is used when determining the success or failure of programs like *Will's Story*, the tape produced for high school students about the important roles the elderly can play in a young person's life. The total number of viewers is not as important as the number of schools that use the tape—which are normally distributed to schools free of charge.

Because there are so many different ways to measure the success of educational programs, each funding organization defines and evaluates proposals in its own way. This can affect the time and money it takes to raise funds. Some producers find it necessary to rewrite their proposals every time they approach a new funding organization.

Going through the time-consuming and often frustrating process of seeking support for educational/cultural programs is one of the most difficult tasks producers face in this type of television. It takes time to write proposals. Many different proposals must be written before one is accepted. Also many funding organizations prefer that a co-sponsor commit to a project before it does.

> I spoke with the people from the foundation. They like the proposal but would not commit funds until we hear if the National Endowment is going to support the series. And until I get the green light from the people at the National Endowment, CPB won't talk to me. Without CPB's support The Greenwood Foundation isn't interested either.
>
> —an independent producer

In summary, defining success for public/educational programs is not as easy as defining success in the other types of television. A production team whose programs earn high ratings on commercial television will be rehired to produce future programs. A team producing videocassette programs who sells enough cassettes to make a profit will be able to find backers for their next project. A team who trains, educates, or motivates the intended audiences of an institutional/corporate program in a cost-effective manner will likely be contracted to produce the institution's next project.

Whether a production team in public television continues to get funding for its projects depends on how well they have succeeded in educating or enriching the audiences. These are elusive goals which are difficult to quantify. While this can be frustrating, there also can be advantages. These goals mean different things to different people. So, when seeking new or continued funding, a production team that is having difficulty finding support for a program should not lose heart. If the idea is a good one, they should try new funding sources. With the diversity of interpretations of public/educational television's mission, there is bound to be an organization to support them.

Those makers of television programs who take the time to analyze the type of television for which they are producing and the ways their program or series will be judged, have laid the foundations on which successful programs are built.

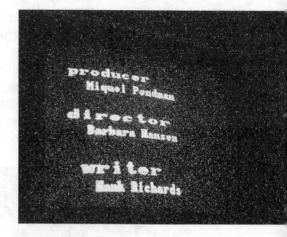

Chapter 3

The Production Team

Television programs are made by groups of people. Researching, planning, writing scripts, designing costumes, lighting scenes, building sets, recording pictures and sounds, editing and mixing sound, evaluating programs, supervising crews, keeping projects on budget and adhering to schedules is obviously not a one-person job.

Those who are successful in television production are specialists in all these areas. But they are also able to work as part of a group. Knowing how to write or research, or shoot beautiful images is not enough. One must also have the skills and temperament to work as a member of a team.

Production teams, like the productions themselves, come in many varieties. A team of twenty plans, researches, negotiates, writes, directs, edits and evaluates a dramatic series destined for national distribution. A team of three plans, researches, negotiates, writes, directs and edits a children's series for a local public television station. The former is housed in a modern office complex with secretaries, production assistants, computers, and sound and picture archives. The latter is headquartered in a small cubicle with a typewriter, audio cassette recorder and a 35-millimeter camera.

The size of production teams will vary depending on budgets and program objectives. But seldom are television programs made by one person. Production is a group activity.

PRODUCERS Producers are the leaders of production teams. Their primary job, like leaders in other fields, is to inspire others. They supervise, advise and, when necessary, cajole other team members to do their jobs. At the same time, producers must keep an eye on scripts, schedules and budgets making sure that programs get done at an acceptable cost and within agreed-upon deadlines.

In an ideal production situation, producers do not write scripts, design lighting or move cameras; rather, they oversee the work done by specialists in each area. However, in many local stations and cable companies the job of producer is combined with that of director, thus creating the role of producer/ director. In production centers at corporations and school districts, the jobs of producer and writer are usually combined into producer/writer positions. The same is true for many production companies that produce soap operas and sitcoms; the jobs of producer and head writer are often combined.

Writers are responsible for treatments, outlines, character sketches, and scripts. This work provides the structure, characters, narration and/or dialogue of a program.

WRITERS

The job of a television writer is not as simple to describe as, for example, the writer of a stage play. A play is assumed to be finished when a director, the crew and cast begin rehearsals. The stage director and stage actor may interpret the words and the action described in the play, but seldom do they change them. This is not the case in television. Most of the time, television scripts are starting points; not word-for-word, shot-by-shot descriptions of every detail of the finished program. In most instances, television scripts are written and rewritten by directors, actors and editors. Only after seeing how an actor performs or how the subject of a documentary looks and sounds on camera can a director and editor determine how much of the writer's script "works," and can be used.

For example, the script for a made-for-television movie includes the line "Get out of my way, old buzzards!" spoken by the film's evil protagonist to a group of elderly people. On the set, during rehearsal, the director decides that a threatening close-up of the evil character followed by a series of medium shots of the elderly, without any words spoken, is a much more effective way to "say" what the writer intended.

A documentary, an interview and other "real" events can, obviously, not be written beforehand. The best a writer can do is describe what *might* happen and what *might* be a useful structure. For example, a writer might describe the opening scene of a documentary as follows, "The sun rises over a flooded rice paddy as we hear the far away sound of chanting...." When the director and his crew actually go to shoot this documentary, they may not find the exact shot the writer described but they will endeavor to find an opening shot that has a similar impact. In fact, not until the documentary is edited will a final decision be made about which exact shot and sound track will open the documentary.

DIRECTORS The director's job is to select the cast or subjects, equipment, locations and crew that will convert the writer's vision into a television program. The type of program will determine what the director actually does. For example, the director of a commercial or a dramatic program has much more control over what happens than the director of a news program, documentary or an interview.

In general, the director of a program shot film style has more control over what eventually is seen and heard in a program than the director of a program shot in the television style. In the television style, the producer tends to make most of the production decisions: he or she is usually responsible for the final drafts of scripts, casting, set and lighting designs. Then, after these production decisions are made, the director takes over the program. In the film style, the director's involvement begins with the script and continues until the project is completed.

Designers are specialists who assist or work with directors. **DESIGNERS**
There are designers who plan and build sets, sound designers
who create sound tracks, and production designers who plan
and supervise the way light and cameras are used. There are
also costume, make-up, hair, special effects, and graphic designers. The type of designer needed for a production depends on
the content of the program as well as its budget.

Producers, writers, directors, and designers usually leave
technical functions to others. The production team's job is to
decide what is required; the technical crew takes care of running
the cameras, hanging lights, plugging in microphones, and mixing
sound tracks. Members of production teams must know what
they want from their equipment and crews and how to ask for it.
But knowing how to run or repair television equipment is usually
not the responsibility of a producer, writer, director or designer.

To some this description of television production as basically
nontechnical may be disappointing. We believe one reason many
are drawn to this field is their perception that it is an activity
which takes place behind cameras, in studios, and in editing
suites. The reality is that most of the work performed by most of
the people in television production takes place in front of word
processors, in rehearsal halls, and in offices where scripts, budgets and set designs (not to mention where to get a good cup of
coffee) are discussed.

In fact, the leaders of a production (producers, directors,
writers, and designers) must be careful not to spend too much
time around cameras, microphones, and videotape machines.

Television equipment has the power to seduce. In some ways it is too easy to make a picture with a television camera (point it into a lighted area) or a dramatic sound with an audio board (push a button) or an interesting transition with a video editor (pull a lever). Those who are seduced by the technology, however, tend to forget that an engaging television program must be well designed and well written as well as effectively shot and edited.

UNIT 2

UNIT 2

The Visual Language

The long, expensive and usually exciting process of making television programs ends on the television screen where moving images, music, narration, and sound effects become the news, a movie, a commercial, a situation comedy, an instructional program or any of the other types of programs found on that familiar box in our living rooms, offices and schools. Selection and control of these images and sounds is one way to describe the job of those who produce television programs.

As we select and organize words and sentences in an effort to communicate with you in this book, so the television production team selects and organizes the basic elements of its medium. These elements are combined into what we call the "visual language."

When I was beginning to learn Spanish, I formed my ideas in English and translated them to Spanish. Not only was this very tiresome but most of what I said sounded awkward in Spanish and, many times, was not understood by my Spanish friends. I remember my frustration when I failed to get a simple idea across such as "I like this dish," or "The store is just around the corner." And I also remember my great satisfaction when I learned how to structure my ideas in Spanish so that they were understood.

Those who communicate with television, like those who communicate with Spanish, use a unique language. They structure ideas in unique ways. The purpose of this unit is to describe this language and help you begin to use it effectively.

Chapter 4

The Frozen Frame

Let us begin our discussion of the visual language by looking at single frames from the *MacNeil/Lehrer Newshour*, the soap opera *Santa Barbara*, a documentary about aging in Soviet Georgia titled *A Toast To Sweet Old Age*, a program used as a selling device by a computer software company, and a commercial.

First, a frozen frame from the opening moments of *The MacNeil/Lehrer Newshour*. Mr. MacNeil is caught in mid-sentence as he looks down at his notes.

The production team responsible for this picture is saying, among other things, that Mr. MacNeil is a serious journalist and this program depends on words more than images or graphics to communicate. The lighting, shot composition, costume and background are designed to communicate this.

Mr. MacNeil's reference to his notes, his serious tone, his costume and background tell us that he is a television journalist who approaches his job differently than his colleagues in commercial television. First, the shot composition (medium close-up), angle (eye level), lighting (strong back or rim light, one side slightly brighter than the other, background slightly darker than the foreground) and focus (background slightly out of focus) follow conventional patterns used to present broadcast journalists on most news programs. But Mr. MacNeil's appearance and background tell us he does not completely fit into the conventional mold. His suit and tie are brown; his suit is squarely cut and slightly out of fashion. This is the costume of an academic or print journalist; it is not what fashion-conscious network anchors normally wear.

Also, the background patterns of the words "NEWS" and "HOUR" distinguish this news program from most others. Other news anchors are usually shown in front of banks of television monitors with technicians busy at work; backgrounds that tell the viewer to expect plenty of pictures and high-tech graphics. The MacNeil/Lehrer background produces a very different set of expectations. Here words, not images, dominate.

A computer software company uses a videotape to demonstrate its product. A frame from the program shows a woman buying a ticket from a young man using a computer in a modern ticket booth. Both subjects focus their full attention on the computer. It is bright and sunny outside and bright and evenly lit inside the booth. Both subjects are casually dressed in summer clothing. The scene is shot from a slightly low angle.

The team who produced this image is portraying a very complimentary image of the computer and its software. The computer, because of the dominant position it occupies and the angle at which it is shot, seems to be responsible for the ease with which this customer is being served. Without words, the production team is saying that modern, successful theaters like the one featured in this program are using the company's software program.

The following frames are from the soap opera *Santa Barbara* and the documentary, *A Toast to Sweet Old Age*. Take a good look at them. What is being said with lighting, backgrounds, angles, costumes, and the other elements of the visual language? You'll find the answer to this question at the end of this chapter.

The last item we'll look at is a commercial. Caught in this still frame is a happy five-year-old blond girl and her mother playfully sharing the task of loading a clothes dryer. The mother appears to be in her late twenties or early thirties. She is wearing a light blue blouse and blue skirt with touches of white in it; the child is wearing a white blouse with light blue shorts. The dryer is in the middle of a room with gingham wall paper and such decorative touches as unfinished wood and other "natural" materials. Behind the woman is an antique wooden chair and behind the child is an antique table. On the window sill are handmade baskets, a wind up clock, wooden bowls, and antique food containers. On top of the dryer and in the middle of the frame is the brightest item in the picture, a box of Downy SunRinse Dryer Sheets. It is bathed in yellow light. The woman is handing the child a single sheet which is also lit with yellow light. Behind the mother and child and the dryer is a window covered with old-fashioned wooden shutters. The same bright, yellow light used on the SunRinse Dryer Sheets seeps through the bottom portion of the shutters near the child.

The production team responsible for this image used the television language to say, among other things, that modern, affluent, caring homemakers use Downy SunRinse Dryer Sheets.

The five frozen frames just described provide dramatic examples of the visual language. Any one of them could be the basis of this section of the chapter in which we describe the specific elements of the visual language. Commercials, because of their short length and clear purpose, provide the strongest examples of how production teams use the visual language. For this reason the focus of our discussion of the elements of this language will be the *Downy SunRinse Dryer Sheet* commercial.

Setting

The production team who produced the Downy commercial created a modern laundry room with natural, wholesome decorations and furnishings (gingham wall paper, antique furniture, clock, bowls and vases). The sunlight seeping through the wooden shutters behind the dryer adds a special dimension to the scene. This laundry room is above ground in a very bright, open sunny place yet the woman keeps the shutters closed. She has the option of opening the shutters and letting in the sunlight but she keeps the room dark. Why? Later in the commercial we find the answer. The SunRinse Dryer Sheets are even better than the real thing. They exude all the freshness and cleanliness of real sunshine and can be used any time no matter what the weather or time of day. They are more dependable than real sunshine. Also, they are simple to use: even a child can add clothesline freshness to a load of laundry.

ELEMENTS OF THE VISUAL LANGUAGE

Lighting

Of all the elements of the visual language, lighting may have the most power. Simply turning off or adding one or two lights can significantly change the meaning of an image. The team who produced the Downy commercial created a lighting design with four bright spots: the box of Downy SunRinse Dryer Sheets, the sheet in the child's hands, the brightness seeping through the shutters, and the hair and faces of the mother and child. There is less light on the background (walls, dryer, antique baskets, bowls and clock) than on the foreground. This separates the woman and child from the background and makes the scene appear three dimensional. Unlike the real world, the television image contains only two dimensions. Lighting (along with focus) can be used to separate the foreground from the background and thus it helps create the illusion of depth, the illusion of the third dimension.

Props or Properties

A prop is an object one person can easily handle. The team selected and placed many important props in the setting: clock, baskets, bowls, food containers, and the box of Downy SunRinse Dryer Sheets. This selection of props tells the viewer a great deal about this woman and the kinds of products she buys. She obviously prefers products that are natural, "the real things," not artificial.

Casting

The person (or persons) selected to deliver the message of a commercial or program plays a crucial role in its success or failure. The production team selected for the role of the housewife a brunette in her late twenties with a winning smile. She has a simple, wholesome appearance. She does not have the features or figure of, for example, a fashion model. Compared to the fashion model, who must spend hours and hundreds of dollars on her looks, the woman in this commercial *appears* to be able to look presentable with little time, money, or effort. She seems to be the ideal wife and mother who is attractive and has the time and energy to effectively run a household.

The young girl cast as the daughter is a healthy looking blond with fair skin. Her healthy appearance demonstrates that this product is gentle to even the most sensitive skin.

Costume

The team selected a contemporary, loose-fitting outfit of white and skyblue cotton for the woman. Her clean, fresh-looking clothing, made of natural fibers, is a testimonial to the way Downy SunRinse Dryer Sheets work—making clothes look fresh, clean and "natural" (as if dried on a clothesline). Also, the color of the woman's clothing foreshadows the explosion of bright, blue sky and clouds that will fill the dark laundry room in four shots when the Downy SunRinse Dryer Sheet is placed in the dryer by the child.

The child wears a white blouse with blue shorts. They are also loose-fitting and appear to be made of natural fibers. Like the mother's clothing, they have a "clothesline" fresh, clean appearance. The color of the child's outfit also foreshadows the upcoming explosion of bright blue sky and fluffy white clouds.

Theater

Gestures, facial expressions, the movement of the eyes from screen left to screen right, the time it takes a character to cross a room...these are all elements which communicate. The mood or tone of a scene can change dramatically depending on how these subtle elements of theater are manipulated. The director of this commercial instructed the actress who plays the mother to act very matter-of-fact when she hands her daughter the sheet of SunRinse. The child takes the sheet and enthusiastically throws it into the dryer. These actions tell the viewer that (l) the product is so easy to use that even a child can use it and (2) both mother and child consider this activity a very important, maybe an essential, part of their day.

Composition

Picture composition involves other choices for the production team: which portion of the total scene to show the viewer and which elements of the scene to feature. In general, compositions are categorized as close-ups (CU), medium shots (MS), and long shots (LS). When photographing an individual, a close-up means showing just the head and shoulders, a medium shot includes the head and body, a long shot shows the entire body from head to toe.

There are modifications of these general categories of shot compositions. For example, the labels ECU or TCU are used for extreme close-up or a tight close-up. MCU means medium close-up and MLS designates medium long shot.

The production team who made the *Downy SunRinse Dryer Sheet* commercial decided to show the woman and child in a medium long shot allowing enough room within the picture for the gingham wall paper, the window with the light seeping through the shutters, the antiques, and the brightly lit box of SunRinse Dryer Sheets and the dryer.

This is an appropriate use of the television screen since it features only those elements that contribute to the message of this picture—that a SunRinse Dryer Sheet guarantees your clothes will be as fresh and fluffy as if dried in the outdoors. In a longer shot, the essential action of the sheet being handed to the child would not be adequately featured. In a closer shot, the frame would not contain all of the antique props or enough of the window and gingham wallpaper. This would lessen the impact of this commercial's message: that discerning homemakers who own objects that are hand-crafted and made of natural materials use this product.

Focus

The team chose to keep the woman, the child and the box of SunRinse Dryer Sheets in sharp focus while keeping the gingham wallpaper, the shutters over the window and the antique props slightly out of focus. This serves three purposes.

First, it separates the mother and child and the product in the foreground from the background. This emphasizes the most important elements of the shot. A commercial for an antique store might focus on the background instead of the foreground.

A second reason to separate foreground and background is to make the scene appear three dimensional. When foreground and background are not separated, a scene is flat and appears less realistic. Unlike the real world, the television image has only two dimensions. When foreground and background are separated through the proper use of focus and light, there is the illusion of depth. The third result of separating foreground and background with focus is to make the laundry room appear spacious, creating the illusion that there is considerable room behind the woman and the child.

Angle

In the *Downy SunRinse Dryer Sheets* commercial, the viewer looks up at the mother and child from a slightly lower angle. The production team chose this low angle to say that this woman and child are strong, smart, and in control. People we look up to seem to have control. Those we look down on seem vulnerable; seem to have little control. These illusions probably come from memories of childhood when we literally looked up to parents and other adults. Now that we are adults, we look down on small, vulnerable children. You can understand why low angle shots are often called "superior angle" and high angle shots are "inferior angle."

Color

It is certainly no surprise that color influences our reactions to what we see. Bright colors suggest happiness and joy. Dark colors are for somber moments. Red can be a hot, passionate color while blue is usually cool and soft. Color television and film offer the production team a rich palette to choose from. Decisions about which colors of the palette to use are crucial in all areas of picture design: lighting, setting, costumes, and graphics.

The two examples of the product (the box of SunRinse Sheets on the dryer and the sheet the woman hands the child) are presented in bright, golden light like that seen on very sunny days. The same type of light seeps through the lower portions of the shutters in front of the window near the child. The rest of the scene has a dull, brown tone to it that contrasts with these three points of golden light. The production team made these choices to indicate that this product is like the sun; it can make your child's clothing (and your child) clean and fresh.

Setting, lighting, props, casting, costumes, theater, composition, focus, angle, and color are some of the basic elements of the television language. But remember that we have been looking at a still, silent frame. Television is a medium that moves and makes sounds.

The two shots from the documentary about the elderly in Soviet Georgia contain a great deal of information. The theatrical way the man holds his head says something about boredom or impatience. The medals on the woman's coat indicate she was part of the government or the military. The indirect lighting, plants and open space in the background indicate that these two people live in a comfortable setting.

The closeup from the soap opera *Santa Barbara* also reveals much information. The woman's costume, makeup, and the way her hair is done indicate she is upper middle class. The setting with wooden relief on the door frames, plants and expensive wallpaper are additional messages about the social class of this woman. The lighting design with low light on the background and bright light on the woman's hair and shoulders creates an ominous tone. This is supported by the theater of the scene; she seems upset, angry.

Chapter 5

The Moving Image

What if we liberated the frozen frame from the *Downy SunRinse Dryer Sheets* commercial and allowed it to proceed?

MOTHER HANDS DAUGHTER A SUNRINSE DRYER SHEET.
ANNOUNCER (VO): Now when you…

MOTHER TURNS ON DRYER
…turn on your dryer…

SUNLIGHT SEEPS OUT OF DRYER DOOR

MUSIC/LYRICS: Turn on the sunshine

BACKGROUND BECOMES A BRIGHT BLUE SKY WITH FLUFFY
CLOUDS.
…turn on the freshness.

DRYER FADES OUT. THE BOX OF SUNRINSE DRYER SHEETS
AND CIRCULATING CLOTHES REMAIN IN THE OPEN SKY.

*ANNOUNCER (VO): Introducing SunRinse Downy Dryer
Sheets,*

CAMERA ZOOMS INTO CU CIRCULATING SHEETS.

So airy light, so sunny fresh

CLOTHES WAVING IN THE BREEZE IN FRONT OF BLUE SKY AND CLOUDS.
It's like hanging your wash in the sunshine

BOX OF DOWNY SUNRINSE DRYER SHEETS WITH SUN SHINING THROUGH THE WORD "NEW".
Music/lyrics: Turn on the sunshine…

WASH ON LINE WITH BRIGHT YELLOW SUN BEHIND

…turn on the freshness.

BOX OF SUNRINSE ON TOP OF DRYER, CAMERA WIDENS

SunRinse dryer sheets, new from Downy,

MEDIUM LONG SHOT OF SCENE IN LAUNDRY ROOM. (MOTHER AND DAUGHTER BOTH HAVE STRONG BACK LIGHT.)

ANNOUNCER (VO): The fabric softener that gives you fluffy softness too.

LAUNDRY ROOM WALLS DISAPPEAR. MOTHER, CHILD AND DRYER ARE IN FRONT OF CLOUDS AND BLUE SKY JOYFULLY HOLDING A BRIGHT YELLOW TOWEL FRESH FROM THE DRYER.
MUSIC/LYRICS: Turn on the sunshine…freshness.

BOX OF SUNSHINE DRYER SHEETS ALSO IN FRONT OF CLOUDS
AND BLUE SKY

ANNOUNCER (VO):   New SunRinse dryer sheets.

LOW ANGLE 2 SHOT OF MOTHER AND CHILD. THEY ARE IN
THE MIDDLE OF CLOUDS AND BLUE SKY. THE MOTHER HAS
WRAPPED THE CHILD IN THE BRIGHT, FLUFFY FRESHLY
DRIED TOWEL. A BREEZE BLOWS. THEY ARE BLISSFUL.

Music/lyrics: ...Come on in.

This message about *Downy SunRinse Dryer Sheets* becomes
even more interesting when it begins to move. We find out that
this mother and daughter share a fantastic journey when, thanks
to a *Downy SunRinse Dryer Sheet*, they and their laundry are
catapulted into open, blue sky. Over the final shot of mother and
daughter joyfully embracing a fluffy towel, we hear an invitation
to "Come on in," to the same kind of satisfaction this mother
and child are enjoying.

The production team used a number of other elements of
the television language to communicate this advertiser's message.
When we view more than one frame of this commercial, those
elements of the television language which relate to movement
become apparent.

CAMERA MOVEMENT

Television and film cameras are mounted on tripods, dollies,
cranes, jibs, steadycams, or the shoulders of camera operators.
There are two general categories of camera movement: 1) those
executed while the camera and the device on which it is mounted
(tripod, dolly, etc.)moves from one position to another and 2)
those executed when the device on which a camera is mounted
is stationary. First we will describe those moves executed while
the camera is moving.

Trucking
To truck left or truck right, the camera operator simply rolls or
walks with the camera mounted on a tripod, dolly, steadycam,

or his/her shoulder. One common use of this movement is to follow a subject or subjects from the side as in trucking alongside a couple walking through a park. Another common use of the trucking movement is to come upon the subject or subjects as if discovering them. For example, the camera trucks past trees and park benches before coming upon a couple walking toward it.

Dollying

To dolly in or dolly back, the operator moves the camera mounted on a tripod, dolly, crane, steadycam, or on his or her shoulder toward or away from the subject. Dollying in toward a stationary subject makes the subject appear to grow larger and usually more important. For example, in a courtroom drama, when the accused is sentenced, the camera dollies in to a close-up. Dollying back from a subject usually creates the opposite effect, making the subject seem less important. A dolly in to a subject can suggest that something is beginning, while a dolly away from a subject gives a sense of conclusion or ending.

Another application of dollying is to follow moving subjects. Dollying back as a subject or subjects move toward the camera gives the viewer the feeling that he or she is in the middle of the action. The same effect is usually created when the camera is dollyed in as a subject or subjects move away from the camera.

Pedestalling or Craning or Booming

This category of camera movement involves raising or lowering the camera during shooting. This can create dramatic effects. For example, a chase in which two police officers pursue a dangerous criminal is shot while the camera is craning up. At the climactic moment of the scene when the police draw their handguns, we see they are in the middle of a busy street, powerless, unable to use their weapons. A scene in which two lovers walk hand-in-hand toward the camera is enhanced by craning the camera down from a high, wide angle shot to an eye-level view of the happy couple. Without a camera change, the viewer is taken from a long, impersonal shot to an intimate, eye-level close-up.

Hand-held

When a camera movement is executed directly from an operator's shoulder or from a very flexible mount called a steadycam, it usually is a less solid, shakier movement than one executed from a tripod, dolly, crane or jib. This look is called hand-held or verite and many times adds authenticity or a sense of "reality" to a shot. An interview or even a dramatic scene usually seems more truthful, more like the news or a documentary, when shot in this way.

The following movements are executed when the device on which a camera is mounted is stationary.

Panning

To pan left or pan right, the operator simply turns the camera to the left or the right from a fixed position. Panning is analogous to turning your head to the left or the right to follow an action.

Tilting

To tilt up or down means the operator moves the camera on its vertical axis from a fixed position. Tilting mimics the way we "look something up or down."

Zooming

The illusion of moving closer to or away from the subject from a fixed position is accomplished by the zoom lens that makes an object appear smaller or larger.

There are no precise formulas to which a production team may refer when considering how or if to use any of these camera movements. A pan or tilt or zoom does not have a universal, immutable meaning. However, there are some general guidelines that can be useful.

The first and most important guideline is to use camera movement only when it is motivated by the script. A camera movement of any kind is a dramatic statement. With a pan, a tilt, or a truck, the production team is saying, "look here," or "follow me." If there is nothing of interest at the end of the pan, tilt, or truck, the viewer will not be as ready to "look" or "follow" the next move. The viewer could be disappointed if camera movement is not motivated by what is going to be seen or what is going to happen next.

The second guideline is a simple one. Be careful not to overuse the zoom. Zoom lenses are so easy to operate that production teams may be tempted to use them whenever a move to or away from a subject is required. A zoom in or out has quite a different quality or feeling than a dolly in or dolly out. Dollies approximate the way we see things while walking, running or driving toward or away from a subject. Zooming in or out is an illusion performed by the camera lens; the zoom lens magnifies or miniaturizes the subject, making it appear larger or smaller. Zooming in or zooming out has an artificial feel because it does not approximate any movement that we perform in "real life."

The third guideline is, when possible, select a camera movement on the basis of perspective. Many times a scene is presented through the viewpoint of a person in the scene. Knowing who this person is and what his/her state of mind is helps when selecting a camera move. For instance, in a western, a production team might show Main Street from the perspective of the town drunk by using stumbling trucks and unsteady dollies. When perspective shifts to the sober, fast-shooting sheriff, the team selects smooth dollies and pans. In an interview program, after the host asks a guest a penetrating question, the director calls for a slow zoom in to a close-up as the guest starts to respond. The zoom is from the perspective of the guest and represents the tension he or she feels. An on-the-spot news story shot with hand-held, jerky trucks and zooms seems more authentic than a story with smoother movements. The shakiness says, "this story comes to us from the perspective of an on-location journalist."

Not all shots or scenes are presented to the viewer from the perspective of a person in the scene. Sometimes the perspective is that of the director. The master shot, a wide shot of the whole scene, is normally shot from this perspective. The movement as well as angle and composition can tell us a great deal about the director's attitude toward the scene and how he or she expects us to perceive it. For example, the master shot of the haunted house in a horror film hints at the dangers that lurk inside. The shot begins high, looking down at the house then cranes down through the trees to a very low angle with the camera tilted to one side. The master shot of a class reunion in a light comedy is an eye-level dolly to a wide, open view of the happy event. The director is telling us that this is clearly not a threatening or dangerous place.

Other examples of programs presented from the perspective of the director are television news like the *MacNeil/Lehrer Newshour*. In the initial moments of the *MacNeil/Lehrer Newshour*, the program's director places Mr. MacNeil in the exact middle of the frame and in a slightly low angle; the camera slowly zooms in as he speaks. This is the director's way of saying that this person is important and that you, the viewer, should give him your full attention.

MOVEMENT INSIDE THE FRAME

This element of the medium's language is analogous to the movement of actors on the stage. In the theater we are not taken to the action with camera movement. The action happens in front of us in a clearly defined space.

This kind of theatrical movement can be performed inside the stationary camera shot, inside the frame. However, translation of an action from stage to screen requires some modification. Television and film cameras and editing devices select and magnify portions of an event for the viewer, while in the theater the audience gets one fixed and relatively distant view of the action on stage. When presenting an action on television or film screens, movement must be designed to fit into very limited space and action must be modified for the very close look it may receive. Two small steps by a character on screen are comparable to a brisk walk across a stage. A raised eyebrow on camera may have the same impact as a somersault in the theater.

Movement on stage is mostly from left to right or right to left. On screen a more effective movement within the television screen is from front to back and back to front. This is referred to as movement along the Z-axis.

There are a number of examples of effective movement inside the frame in the Downy Dryer Sheets commercial: the initial shot of the woman and child enthusiastically throwing the Downy Dryer Sheet into the wash; shots of bed sheets dramatically swaying in the wind and rays of sunlight bursting from the dryer.

Many automobile commercials feature sleek cars racing into the distance, away from the stationary camera. Dramatic gun battles are made even more frightening by the movement of a pistol barrel from the background toward the waiting, stationary camera.

Editing is the selection and ordering of recorded material—pictures and sounds—into scenes and the combining of scenes into programs. There is no more dramatic example of the production team's control over what is seen on the television screen than editing. Editing gives the team the power to create its own version of reality.

The editor of the Downy SunRinse Dryer Sheets commercial worked with two hours of visual material and two hours and fifteen minutes of sound material (music and narration). The editor then sifted through the pictures and sounds and selected thirteen images and two different sound elements which eventually became the Downy commercial.

The editor paid close attention to the way sound was ordered and mixed with the pictures. Sounds inevitably affect the impact and meaning of individual shots and scenes. For example, the shot of the mother and daughter embracing the fluffy towel in the final shot of the commercial is accompanied by a final upbeat segment of music and the words "Come on in." The music reinforces the positive contribution this product has made to the relationship of the mother and child, suggesting that this product does more than make clothes fluffy and clean-smelling. It also brings children and parents closer together. The phrase "Come on in" makes it clear that others, the viewers of the commercial, can enjoy similar familial bliss through purchase of Downy Dryer Sheets.

The discussion of editing which follows will first treat picture editing and then sound editing.

Picture Editing

Events or scenes that are televised "live" are as dependent on editing as programs shot and edited on film or videotape. For instance, something as seemingly straightforward as a "live" broadcast of a lecture to a group of students can be edited into a number of different versions. When, for example, the director of a televised classroom lecture selects shots of serious students taking notes after showing a close-up of the professor the viewer gets the impression that the professor has captured the attention of the students.

The opposite impression is created when the director selects shots of students fighting to keep their eyes open next to the same picture of the professor. In the actual lecture, there are both note takers and nodders. Through editing, the director determines which ones will represent the class.

Television programs are usually made up of more than one scene. The combining of scenes into large units is another phase of the editing process. We care who gets shot in the gun fight because we've learned in previous scenes about the hero's courage and honesty and the villain's cowardice and evil.

Another example of how scenes are combined into programs to convey meaning is found in the typical evening newscast. First we hear the national and international news, then the local news, and then the sports and weather last. If this program were edited differently, if the first scene were the weather instead of the national news, we would expect to hear about an impending blizzard or flood.

Once again, using the *Downy SunRinse Dryer Sheets* commercial, notice how the production team used editing to communicate its message.

Through editing the team clearly argues that adding a Downy SunRinse Dryer Sheet to a load of laundry will create two results: (1) clothes will be fluffier, fresher, and cleaner than laundry dried outdoors in the "real" sun and wind; (2) children who are members of families who use this product will love their mothers very much and be very happy. The commercial begins in a dark laundry room and ends, twelve shots later, with the transformation of the room into the sunny outdoors where carefree mother and child enjoy each other and their clean, fluffy laundry. What causes this miracle? The editing clearly demonstrates it is one Downy SunRinse Laundry Sheet.

1. MOTHER HANDS DAUGHTER A SHEET OF SUNRINSE DRYER SHEETS.

2. CU MOTHER'S FINGER PUSHING "ON" BUTTON.

3. MS OF DRYER; SUN LIGHT SEEPS OUT OF DRYER DOOR.

4. BACKGROUND CHANGES FROM LAUNDRY ROOM TO THE OUTDOORS.

5. DRYER FADES OUT. ONLY SUNRINSE DRYER SHEETS AND CIRCULATING CLOTHES REMAIN IN THE BLUE, OPEN SKY.

6. MS CLOTHES WAVING IN THE BREEZE IN THE MIDDLE OF BLUE SKY.

7. CU BOX OF DOWNY SUNRINSE FRESH DRYER SHEETS WITH SUN SHINING THROUGH THE WORD "NEW."

8. MS LAUNDRY ON LINE IN FRONT OF CLOUDS AND BLUE SKY.

9. MS OF BOX OF SUNRINSE DRYER SHEETS ON TOP OF DRYER, ZOOM BACK.

10. MLS OF SCENE IN LAUNDRY ROOM MOTHER AND DAUGH-TER BOTH HAVE STRONG BACK LIGHT.

11. THE WALLS OF THE LAUNDRY ROOM DISAPPEAR. MOTHER, CHILD AND DRYER ARE OUTSIDE IN FRONT OF CLOUDS AND BRIGHT, BLUE SKY. THEY CARESS A FLUFFY YELLOW TOWEL FRESH FROM THE DRYER.

12. CU OF BOX OF SUNRINSE DRYER SHEET IN FRONT OF THE SAME BLUE SKY

13. LOW ANGLE, MEDIUM 2 SHOT OF WOMAN AND CHILD IN THE MIDDLE OF THE BLUE SKY. THE MOTHER HAS WRAPPED THE CHILD IN THE BRIGHT, FLUFFY, FRESHLY DRIED TOWEL. A BREEZE BLOWS. THEY ARE BLISSFUL.

Transition

Closely related to the way a scene is edited are the transitional devices used to tie the different shots in a scene together. For example, there is a dramatic difference between fading to black, dissolving, or an instantaneous change called a take or a cut. Imagine how a simple interview like those seen on the evening news would change if the editor decided to use dissolves or fades to black or wipes between each shot instead of the conventional cut.

There are four general categories of transitions from which production team choose when moving from one shot to another.

1. **Take or Cut** An abrupt, instantaneous change from shot A to shot B.
2. **Dissolve** A gradual overlapping change from shot A to shot B until B eventually overtakes A. At the midpoint of a dissolve, shot B is superimposed over shot A.
3. **Fade** A gradual fading of shot A to black, then a gradual fading from black to shot B. The first half of this transition is a fade out and the second is a fade in. Most programs start with a fade in and end with a fade out.
4. **Wipes and Special Effects** These are catch-all terms for hundreds of dramatic optical and electronic transitions.

There are no textbook definitions or formulas to tell production teams which transitions to use and when. However, there are conventional uses for each type of transition which can help a team make appropriate selections.

The take or cut approximates the kinds of transitions we experience in the real world. For example, when sitting at the word processor, a man hears a noise. He looks up and sees a friend standing in front of him. Here's how this simple scene would be recreated on television.

```
SHOT #1: CU OF MAN SITTING AT WORD PROCESSOR.

CUT TO:
SHOT #2: MS OF THE SAME MAN. HE HEARS A NOISE AND
LOOKS UP.

CUT TO:
SHOT #3: MS OF A WOMAN.
```

In contrast to the realistic transition of the take, the dissolve approximates the way we dream. In general, the dissolve suggests movement into the past or future or to a different location.

```
SHOT #1: CU OF MAN SITTING AT WORD PROCESSOR.

DISSOLVE TO:
SHOT #2: MS OF THE SAME MAN. HE HEARS A NOISE AND
LOOKS UP.

DISSOLVE TO:
SHOT #3: MS OF A WOMAN.
```

In this version, the dissolve has two functions. The first is to indicate the passage of time. It suggests that a great deal of time has passed between Shot #1 and Shot #2. The second dissolve makes the friend's appearance a memory or a wish or an event happening in another office. Her appearance is not "real." She is not standing four feet in front of the man as she was in the first version of this scene where the cut was used.

A fade to black communicates a conclusion... "THE END."

A fade from black suggests a beginning. Therefore, a fade is a way of separating shots into distinct, unrelated scenes.

```
SHOT #1: CU OF MAN SITTING AT WORD PROCESSOR.
FADE TO BLACK.

FADE UP FROM BLACK TO:
SHOT #2: MS OF THE SAME MAN. HE HEARS A NOISE AND
LOOKS UP.
FADE TO BLACK.

FADE UP FROM BLACK TO:
SHOT #3: MS OF A WOMAN.
FADE TO BLACK.
```

Using fades instead of takes or dissolves has expanded this single scene into three scenes. The three shots are no longer directly related to one another. They are no longer a sequence of events happening at one time, but rather three separate events.

Transitional devices other than cuts or dissolves must be used with care. This is sometimes forgotten by directors and their assistants sitting in front of editing consoles where, with a simple push of a button or pull of a lever, an exciting transition can be created. Why not use a fancy horizontal wipe instead of a boring cut or dissolve? The answer, of course, is that using an inappropriate transition will confuse the viewer instead of help him or her understand the scene.

Let us return to the Downy commercial once more to see how the production team used transitions to support its message.

FADE FROM BLACK:
SHOT #1: MOTHER HANDS DAUGHTER A SHEET OF SUNRINSE.

CUT TO:
SHOT #2: CU MOTHER'S FINGER ON "ON" BUTTON.

CUT TO:
SHOT #3: MS SUN LIGHT BURSTING FROM DRYER.

DISSOLVE TO:
SHOT #4: MS DRYER IN FRONT OF CLOUDS AND BLUE SKY.

DISSOLVE TO:.
SHOT #5: CU OF DOWNY SUNRINSE SHEET FLOATING IN FRONT OF CLOUDS AND BLUE SKY.

DISSOLVE TO:
SHOT #6: MS OF CLOTHES BLOWING IN THE BREEZE ON CLOTHESLINE IN FRONT OF SAME CLOUDS AND BLUE SKY.

DISSOLVE TO:
SHOT #7: BOX OF DOWNY SUNRINSE DRYER SHEETS.

DISSOLVE TO:
SHOT #8: MS OF CLOTHES BLOWING IN THE BREEZE ON CLOTHESLINE.

DISSOLVE TO:
SHOT #9: MS OF PRODUCT ON TOP OF DRYER.

DISSOLVE TO:
SHOT #10: MOTHER AND DAUGHTER CARESSING A FLUFFY YELLOW TOWEL JUST OUT OF THE DRYER.

```
DISSOLVE TO:
SHOT #11: MOTHER AND DAUGHTER CONTINUING TO CARESS
THE TOWEL IN FRONT OF CLOUD AND BLUE SKY.

DISSOLVE TO:
SHOT #12: MS OF BOX OF DOWNY SUNRINSE DRYER SHEETS IN
FRONT OF CLOUDS AND BLUE SKY.

DISSOLVE TO:
SHOT #13: MS OF MOTHER AND DAUGHTER, THE DAUGHTER IS
WRAPPED IN THE YELLOW TOWEL. THEY ARE VERY HAPPY.
```

Sound Editing

The voice and music of the sound track, as well as the way these sounds are edited and mixed together, contribute as much to the meaning of this message about Downy SunRinse Dryer Sheets as the visual portion of the commercial.

In most instances, sound should be used for portrayal not for description. Hearing a narrator or an actor say "It was a very stormy night," over a scene of a stormy night, or hearing romantic violin music over a couple in a passionate embrace overstates the obvious. Overstatement usually disengages the viewer. Effective story tellers, television producers, and filmmakers engage their audiences by giving just enough information so that they can follow the story; but not so much that it becomes too predictable. Or, to put it another way, effective story tellers require their audience to participate, to fill in some of the pieces of the story.

In the Downy commercial, narration was used sparingly. However, the off-camera statements of the announcer contribute a great deal to the meaning of the commercial. His tone, as well as his words, make this contribution. Think of the many ways to say, "Come on in." Not all interpretations would serve the objective of the commercial.

The narration was recorded and mixed into the commercial long after the images were shot. This is common. Most production teams record sound and picture at separate times and in separate places. Some teams even use one set of actors for the visual portion of a scene and another set for the sound portion.

So, when the scene is produced, the audience sees one actor on screen moving his/her lips while hearing dialogue spoken by another. Music is another element of sound which is recorded separately and mixed into a program, film or commercial after production or after the visual portions of a scene are shot. For example, after all the visual portions of the Downy commercial were shot, a composer and musicians were hired, a recording studio was rented, and the theme music and lyrics were recorded. Weeks later, in a sound mixing studio, the sound and narration were mixed with the visual portion of the commercial.

Music can dramatically affect the impact of a shot or a scene. Tension, pace, and conflict are some of the results of music in programs or films. It certainly adds pace to the Downy commercial.

Sound effects and/or ambience (the sounds of a room or location) can also add a great deal to a scene. The sounds of sirens as a bank robber grabs an extra handful of hundred dollar bills; barely audible factory noise "under" an interview with the owner of a manufacturing company, wind blowing gently through the trees as a young couple goes for a walk on a spring evening; gun fire in the distance as soldiers march into battle are four of the hundreds of examples of how sound effects or ambient sound strengthens scenes.

SUMMARY We began this unit looking at single, frozen frames from the *Downy SunRinse Dryer Sheets* commercial, the *MacNeil/Lehrer Newshour*, the soap opera *Santa Barbara*, the documentary, *A Toast to Sweet Old Age*, and the program used as selling device for a computer software company, *Going to the Theater by Computer*.

We might have selected any one of these programs as the basis for our discussion of the visual language. However, the short, efficient commercial for Downy was a convenient way to point out how the production team used the visual language to "speak" to its audience. The production teams responsible for the other four programs used the visual language in much the same way.

For example, the team who produced the *MacNeil/Lehrer Newshour* selected a background, setting, costume, lighting design, and camera angle that indicates to the viewers a word-based, much more serious approach to the news than most television news programs.

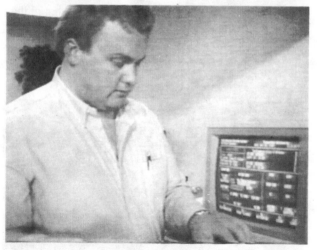

The team responsible for the computer software program used a strong background light on the wall behind an operator and a computer. This effect is a subtle spotlight on the star of this program, the computer software.

This dinner table scene at the home of the old woman in the documentary about the elderly shows her in medium shot; she is involved in conversation. The production team had many different shots of the woman from which to choose. There was a shot of her looking bored and uninvolved; another in which she pours a large glass of wine and drinks it without taking a breath. Replacing the shot of the woman in conversation with either of these would certainly have changed the meaning of the scene.

The flat lighting, wide depth of field (keeping background and foreground in focus) and melodramatic music selected by

the team responsible for *Santa Barbara* help create a two-dimensional world of make believe. This simpler-than-real-life world of the soap opera has no subtle gradations of focus, shadow, or mood. Everything we see and hear is either bright or dark, in focus or out, happy or sad.

This discussion of the visual language leads to the conclusion that there is no clear distinction between form and content in television. It is not enough to describe a television program in terms of plot or story. The content of a television program is contained in the way producers use lighting, editing, transitions, movement, sound, and the other elements of the visual language.

One of the more interesting parts of the production courses we teach happens during the viewing of students' work. It is our policy not to allow those who produced a program to speak until other members of the class have had an opportunity to give their reactions. Sometimes student producers become testy when their audience (the class) points out the interesting use of shaky camera, the humorous effect created when the host dropped his microphone, or the very dramatic setting created by the absence of background light.

"That wasn't important." "We didn't mean to say that." "You missed the point...didn't you hear what was said?" These are the cries of misunderstood student producers.

After tempers cool the student producers are usually able to see for themselves what happened. They did not pay enough attention to the way the audience receives information, intended or not, through the special language of television.

The Production Process

Almost all successful programs go through the same stages of production whether done single- or multi-camera. While this sequence is generally the same throughout the television and film industry, the words used to describe it vary from one production company or station to another, or from one part of the country to another. Some production teams use such terms as "pre-production," "production," and "post production" to label the different activities of making television programs. Others label these components "development," "writing," "editing," and "mixing."

We organize this process into three stages we call: commitment, design and, execution. These three words describe the full range of activities needed to produce a professional program.

There is a tendency for production teams, especially those just beginning to work in this discipline, to move too quickly through the first two stages. A common mistake made by first-time producers, directors, designers, and writers is to concentrate on cameras, casting, lighting, and editing before deciding exactly what it is they plan to produce. The reason for this may have something to do with how easy it is to operate a television camera, call an audition, hang a light, or make an edit.

The following three units describe a process that will help keep production teams on course.

UNIT 3

Commitment

The commitment stage begins when an idea for a program is conceived. It ends with the decision to produce or not produce a program. Too often this stage is given little attention and teams find themselves committed to ideas that are fatally flawed from the start. Studios and editing rooms around the world echo with the anguished cries of production teams who discovered too late that a program wasn't "working" or audiences weren't "getting it." Futile attempts might be made to resuscitate such disasters. "Hire another actor." "Go back and re-edit it." "Have the writer make it funnier." "It's too long." "It's too short." But it is usually too late for such a bandage approach. When programs fail, the flaw may not be the acting or the editing or the writing. These are only symptoms of failure at the earliest stage of the production process, the commitment stage.

Chapter 6

Proposals, Schedules, and Budgets

THE PROPOSAL Most television programs begin with a telephone call. A writer with an idea for an episode of a new prime-time situation comedy calls the show's producer. The general manager of a local television station calls a staff producer about a new program he thinks would help build larger audiences in the evening after the national news. The vice president of a large corporation phones the head of the media department and asks what can be done to improve the company's image after a major environmental disaster. An account executive at a large advertising agency asks one of the writers in the creative department to come up with an idea for an ad campaign for a new client. The assistant superintendent of schools asks the media coordinator about using television to improve career counseling. A Broadway producer calls an executive at a production company with an idea for a made-for-television movie. A college student calls a classmate to tell her, "I have this great idea for our next production assignment."

After the phone call, there is usually a "meeting." Hollywood is not the only place where the ability to "take" or "give" good meetings is valued. The Los Angeles based writer meets with the sitcom's producer to "pitch" his story before writing a treatment. In the New York ad agency, a writer meets with an account executive as the first step toward understanding the goals of the new advertising campaign. The corporate media director walks down the hall to meet with his boss. The head of the school district's media department brings his five staff members together for a brainstorming session. At the television station, the producer meets with one of the station's staff producers. The Broadway producer meets with the television producer over a cup of coffee at a fast food restaurant in the middle of Manhattan. The two students meet for pizza near campus.

The outcome of these phone calls and meetings is unpredictable. There may be a handshake followed by "Let's get back together" or "Keep in touch." Sometimes these interchanges mean just that. But, most of the time they mean, "This is as far as this program idea is going. Let's *not* keep in touch." In fact, most of these meetings do not result in a commitment. Many clients, sponsors, or funding agencies do not appreciate how expensive and time-consuming television production can be. And, sadly, most program ideas are not worth the time and money required to produce them.

Those few program ideas that do go on to production require the skills of a producer. Producers have the ultimate responsibility for guiding the program through the production process. And while clients, sponsors, bosses, and funding agencies usually know what they want, they may not know how to use the media to achieve their ends. In many instances, the producer's first job is clarifying or reworking the initial production idea.

Larry Fandango
Broadway Theatrical Enterprises, Inc.
2321 Broadway
New York, NY 10111

Dear Larry,

Yes, I am quite interested in participating in the project you mentioned at our meeting in New York. I believe it is the kind of movie in which USA, HBO or FOX might be interested. The positive press you got from your two stage hits this year gives us some real advantages when we present it to these networks.

While I am very positive about the project, the proposal is not where it has to be when we pitch it. What you're suggesting seems to be just a carbon copy of the stage play. It appears to be too stationary; events need to happen in more than the two locations. The story needs to be told in more visual terms; the characters are too dependent on words. I don't mean to imply that we compromise the essentials of the stage play. It is a very moving story and should stay more or less intact. But it was written for the stage and it must be adapted to the screen.

I propose we move ahead. A writer should be hired to do a treatment. If it's acceptable, have our lawyers draft a co-ownership contract. But before we offer it to USA, FOX, or anyone else we need to get a writer to rework it in some of the ways I mentioned above.

Let me know if this is satisfactory. I do hope it is. You have the beginnings of a quality film and we would like to be in on it.

Looking forward to your reply.

Sincerely,

Robert Sabor
IPW Productions

A second idea which we will follow through the commitment stage begins to take shape in the form of this memorandum.

MEMORANDUM

TO: Mr. Grabman, Director, Media Center
FROM: Grace Hall
SUBJECT: Career Guidance TV series.

Based on our conversation last Tuesday, our department proposes to produce 8 to 10 fifteen-minute
programs to supplement the district's career training
classes.

The objective of the series would be to motivate and
offer general information. It would not be to provide
"hard" information since this is done in the classroom
and with the assigned texts.

Each episode in the series would describe three or four
related careers. Then graduates from the district who
are successful in these careers will be interviewed or
shown in action on their jobs. This approach, I
believe, will not only explain the opportunities
available to our students, but will also demonstrate
how others with their background and education have
taken advantage of these opportunities. Let me know
if you like this approach. If you do, we will submit a
budget and schedule for your approval.

A third program idea becomes more concretes when the
producer at a large commercial television station meets with his
boss, the station's program manager.

PROGRAM DIRECTOR
What do you think? Can we pull off a slick, well produced weekly program about local events and celebrities?

PRODUCER
Sure, why not? We can do a great job but you know it will cost a lot more than we'll make on it.

PROGRAM DIRECTOR
*I know...if we break even for the first quarter I'll be satisfied. I see it as a chance to define ourselves as **the** local station in town, maybe it will bring back some of those loyal viewers we've lost. And if it's great, we might be able to get reasonable ratings and make some money.*

PRODUCER
Can I have a week to write you a proposal of the format as I see it?

PROGRAM DIRECTOR
That's fine...also give me a list of possible subjects. We need to know if there are enough people around here with the kind of panache this show needs. We're not going to get the numbers and the attention we need with PTA presidents and county softball champions.

The following week the producer submits a two-page memo to the program manager.

MEMORANDUM

TO: RALPH EDWARD
FROM: AL HAMMERALL
RE: LOCAL PROGRAM

The series will show off our community as a center of the arts, commerce, and education. To put it simply, it will show our viewers how much they have to be proud of. The bottom line goals are:
(1) Demonstrate that WORK-TV is the station in town dedicated to local issues.

(2) Produce a popular local program on which we, at least, break even.

(3) Hold viewers after the national news.

FORMAT: The focus of each week's program will be documentary, shot single camera totally on location featuring a local personality. These documentaries, of about fifteen minutes, will be introduced by Bill Strum, the anchor for the evening news. I see the opening to be something like the introduction used by **Front Line** on PBS, just long enough to connect the documentary to the series.

(continued)

page 2

Bill will be in a setting with a very local look to it. Maybe we borrow from Johnny Carson. But instead of L.A. in the background we see the skyline here in Landcaster. During commercial breaks and after the documentary, there will be studio segments in which Bill interviews the week's celebrity. When appropriate additional guests might be included in these segments. For example, if the week's celebrity is a local politician we may include in the final interview segment, the editor from the Journal or a political science professor from the college.

The way we frame each program is as important as the content. I suggest we build an opening sequence like a space landing—the first shot is of earth from space, each shot brings us closer to Landcaster and the valley, the final shot is WORK-TV. The program ends the way it begins, except in reverse, like a space launch. I've spoken to some local musicians we might commission to do something upbeat with the town's name in it. I'm getting samples next week.

I've also spoken to representatives from the university, chamber of commerce, the arts council, and our own news department. Each came up with ten solid people with panache. I am attaching a list. It indicates that there are enough interesting folks out there to sustain this type of format at a local level.

Let me know what you think.

Al

In institutional/corporate television (sometimes called industrial), producing and writing is often done by in-house media specialists called "slashes." They are producer/writers or sometimes even producer/writer/directors.

To understand how these people do their jobs, let's look at a scenario involving the "American Mammoth Gas Company," where the media staff includes three producer/writers, two secretaries, an engineer, and three staff members who run cameras and audio during production.

Last week, an explosion at one of the company's refineries in Texas killed two workers and created a toxic cloud which quickly spread over five counties. Residents in three nearby housing projects were evacuated and are now temporarily housed in a local school gymnasium.

The day after the explosion the Executive Vice President of Corporate Communications calls the senior producer/writer in Mammoth's media department to discuss the production of an in-house video tape about the tragedy.

PRODUCER/WRITER
I agree with you that TV might be a good way to tell our side of this story, but can you give me a better idea who we're making it for and what we expect it will do for us?

VICE PRESIDENT
I just feel television's the best way to go with this. We can show our version of what happened and what we're doing to take care of it. The CEO can speak directly to all our people out there and assure them we're responsible citizens.

PRODUCER/WRITER
So, the audience is...?

VICE PRESIDENT
The people in our regional offices. I don't want their sense of loyalty to the company to be tarnished by the press's view.

PRODUCER/WRITER
Anybody else?

VICE PRESIDENT
Our wholesalers and jobbers. We need to make them feel a part of the family too.

PRODUCER/WRITER
Those are two different audiences. When designing this thing, we'd be better off selecting one or the other. If we luck out and it works for both groups fine. But let's target either the wholesalers and jobbers or the regional office staff.

VICE PRESIDENT
That's a tough one. But, if I have to, I'll say the regional staff is more important but I would really like to hit both groups.

PRODUCER/WRITER
I'll do my best. But, again, I can't guarantee what works for one will work for the other.

Before writing a proposal for the V.P., the producer/director phones a free-lance videographer he worked with last year at the Texas refinery on another project. He instructs the videographer to shoot video of the disaster area and to interview at least ten people affected by the explosion.

PRODUCER/WRITER
I need three types of material. First, shots of the refinery and surrounding communities. Second, descriptions of the extent of the damage from anyone who is directly involved—residents, cops, our people at the refinery. And, third, positive testimonials from residents on how much the company has done to clean things up and get life back to normal. I need a cross section of residents...old, young, black, hispanic, women. On our side I need footage of middle management and workers. Got it?

FREE-LANCE VIDEOGRAPHER
I think so....I'll do my best.

PRODUCER/DIRECTOR
Call me tomorrow and let me know.

After the producer/director hangs up, he begins work on a memo for the Vice President.

TO: Norma Babcock, Executive Vice President, Corporate Communications
FROM: Cliff Kaplan, Producer/writer, Media Center
SUBJECT: Proposal for video on Hartsville explosion

The disaster yesterday at Hartsville presents us with an opportunity to take advantage of television's particular strengths: it is personal, it can take us to the scene, it shows instead of tells (which is always more compelling).

The video should be short, no more than ten minutes. It should take advantage of our ability to allow our national leadership to speak directly to the regions. It should address the charges which were made in this morning's press, that we have not acted quickly enough to aid the residents of the surrounding neighborhoods.

I propose this four-part approach:

PART ONE:

Stephanie Warren, Mammoth's CEO, from her office describes exactly what happened, gives details of accident, injuries, and damages.

APPROXIMATE TIME—2:00 MINUTES.

PART TWO:

Video from Hartsville with "on the scene" testimonials from residents and employees describing how much the company has done to help those who were affected and how much it has already done to clean up the environment. The CEO will voice-over portions of this sequence adding the amount of funds she has made available for aid to the community and describing in detail measures which our people took in the hours following the explosion.

APPROXIMATE TIME—3:30 MINUTES

PART THREE:

A state-of-the-company report to establish how this event will affect the fiscal soundness of Mammoth in the next two years. We need our people to understand that we have the inventories to meet demand, and that other refineries will have to go into overtime to make up for supply problems in some regions. I spoke with Margaret Jenkins in marketing and she promised me all the material I need to write a script by tomorrow evening. I suggest we use Richard Alberton, our national spokesperson, for this last segment.

APPROXIMATE TIME—5:30 MINUTES

PART FOUR:

A final statement by the CEO in which she reassures viewers that every effort will be made to make sure tragedies like this will never happen again.

APPROXIMATE TIME—2:00 MINUTES

The Vice President at Mammoth, the Broadway producer, the director of the media center at the school district, and the program director at the commercial station all tentatively accept what the producers have proposed. The producers move on to the next step in the commitment stage: establishing a production schedule.

PRODUCTION SCHEDULES

The period of time from commitment to completion of a television program is called "turn-around time." The turn-around time for every program will be different, depending on several factors. But, one factor which surprisingly does not bear on turn-around time is the length of a program. A twenty-second commercial can take as long to complete as a one-hour drama. Budget is also not a determinant of turn-around time. A sitcom with a budget of a hundred thousand dollars may have a turn-around time of one month while an instructional program budgeted at two thousand dollars may take five months to complete.

The major factors that *do* determine how long it takes to produce a program are 1) the amount of research, writing, and planning required before the production, 2) whether the program will be shot on location or in a studio, and 3) whether the program will be shot single or multi-camera.

Putting words, sketches, and designs on paper takes time. In addition, most treatments and scripts are usually written and rewritten many times before they are acceptable. Narration, dialogue, sets, lighting designs, and camera movements are better tested on paper before being put in front of casts, crews, and equipment.

> "The reason quality programs cost a lot of money has little to do with the cost of tape or studio time. These are expensive enough but the real costs come from all those hours trying out ideas and sound tracks or graphics, rejecting them and then going back to the drawing board. I have to pay a graphic artist, a secretary, and an editor whether I use their work or not."
>
> —an independent producer

The choice of whether to shoot a program on location or in a studio is another influence on turn-around time. Shooting on location is usually more expensive and time-consuming than shooting in a studio. When working on a city street, a convention hall, a sports arena, or in an apartment, it takes extra hours to transport and set up lights and equipment, and to organize crew and cast. Also, a delay caused by traffic, a flat tire, a rain storm, or misplaced cable can ruin a day's shooting on location. Such events will have little or no impact on a program produced in a studio. So, to protect against this, an extra day or two of "insurance" time is usually added to schedules and budgets of programs shot on location.

Following are the production schedules which attempt to predict the turn-around times of the four programs we are discussing.

PRODUCTION BUDGETS

Obviously, before a final commitment can be made by either client or producer, the program's costs must be agreed upon. Producing a budget, like producing a schedule, is part science and part guesswork.

A staff or in-house producer must approach budgets in a slightly different manner than a producer hired on a free-lance or per-project basis. The in-house producer usually works with a staff, has an office, and production facilities maintained by the organization for which he or she works. This means that the in-house producer's budget may include expenses that are part of the fixed overhead of his or her organization. Even though studio, cameras, and secretaries are paid for out of general, fixed overhead, they should be included in a budget.

> *The only way to avoid a false sense of security when working with salaried staff and in-house facilities is to make a precise budget and schedule and stick to it. Pretend a missed deadline or unplanned hour in the studio costs real money not the paper kind. If you don't work this way, you'll be surprised how you end up at the end of the year having spent thousands on projects that were only worth hundreds, something that makes the bosses very unhappy.*
>
> —*an in-house producer*

Individual items in a budget can be categorized as either fixed or negotiable (sometimes referred to as "below" and "above-the-line"). These distinctions are especially relevant when dealing with unions and guilds. Some fixed expenses are those which have been set by union contracts. Technicians' hourly salaries and contributions to a union's pension fund are examples. Other fixed expenses are those which are published in *rate cards*. The hourly rental of a television studio or an editing suite are examples of rate card items.

Items in a budget which cannot be determined by their fixed or published rate can be negotiated. Such negotiated items can range from talent fees to the costs of securing copyright releases.

The specific items of a budget for one production will be different from those of another. Some of the variables that influence the size of a budget are: the number and types of staff and cast required, the amount of time needed in studios or at an editing console, and whether or not the program is produced under the jurisdiction of a union. Also, whether a program is intended for a large, national audience or a small, local one will influence costs. Programs for large, national audiences tend to require the services of highly paid producers, writers, directors, and designers as well as the use of expensive camera, graphic, and editing equipment.

There are many production costs which have little to do with cast or cameras. Secretaries and phone companies must be paid. Contributions may have to be made to a union pension fund. Insurance often must be provided, both medical and liability. If the production team, cast, and crew have to travel to distant locations, their transportation, housing, and meals will have to be budgeted. The cost of breakfasts and dinners must be anticipated with the same seriousness as the cost of videotape.

While the following budgets for the four different programs differ, all four producers arrive at their budgets the same way. All of them list anticipated expenses (called line items) in those categories common to all television programs. Then, after totaling their figures, each adds 10 percent to cover inevitable, unpredictable expenses or contingencies.

To more clearly indicate the different ways all four programs would spend money, we present this comparative line budget.

I. PERSONNEL	BERGEN	GETTING AHEAD	IN THE VALLEY	MAMMOTH OIL
A. Production Team:				
Producer	45000	900	2500	3500
Assistant Producer	15000		1200	1200
Writer	15000	800	1500	1000
Director	55000	850	2000	2300
Set Designer/Art Director	25000		2000	
Lighting Designer	25000		900	
Graphic Artist	25000	150	500	500
Sound /Music Designer	25000		500	
Casting	10000			
B. Support Staff				
Secretarial	15000	100	500	900
Bookkeeping	4500		1200	
Legal	25000		1000	
Transportation	9500		250	
C. Technical Crew				
First Camera	40000	700	9000	3500
Second Camera	25000		2000	
First Sound	40000	550	3000	1500
Second Sound	25000		1000	
Editor	36000	600	3000	600
Assistant Editor	15000			
Sound FX/ Loop Editor	30000			
Production Assistants	14000	200	500	500

D. Talent

	Bergen	Getting Ahead	In The Valley	Mammoth Oil
Leads	125000	750	2000	1500
Extras	40000		500	
Agencies	15000			

II. FACILITIES

	Bergen	Getting Ahead	In The Valley	Mammoth Oil
A. Studio and Facilities	45000	800	1000	2500
B. Location Equipment	55000		990	1500
C. Administrative Offices	15000	200	2000	950

III. MATERIALS

	Bergen	Getting Ahead	In The Valley	Mammoth Oil
A. Film Stock	40300			
B. Film Processing & Sound Transfer	58100			
C. Tape Stock	5500	125	250	450
D. Sets	78000	145	1900	1000
E. Costumes	32000			
F. Props	1600	25	100	
G. Tape to Film Transfer	5000			
H. Miscellaneous (Office, Graphics,etc.)	3100	50	250	500

IV. ANCILLARY EXPENSES

	Bergen	Getting Ahead	In The Valley	Mammoth Oil
A. Transportation	10000	65	100	1100
B. Food & Lodging	15000	100	250	850
C. Insurance	18000		400	400
D. Rights & Legal Fees	11000		100	400
E. Security	7000			500
F. Pension Fund	4500			
G. Promotion	17000		2500	

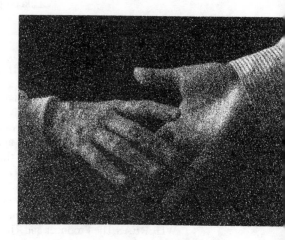

Chapter 7

Contracts

The last step in the commitment stage is the creation of a program contract. Some contracts take the form of legal documents that carefully specify each item of the commitment between producer and client. The term contract can also be used informally: agreements made over lunch and sealed with a handshake. Whatever form it takes, the contract describes the program or series the producer agrees to provide within a specified amount of time and money.

There may be more than one contract submitted to a client. If a proposal is found to be too expensive or time-consuming, or if the program described is not exactly what the client had in mind, the producer may modify the document. The commitment stage is a time for negotiations and even in this last step, give and take is quite normal.

The contract for *Bergen*, the made-for-television movie, is a fifteen-page document prepared by an attorney.

MEMORANDUM OF AGREEMENT

AGREEMENT made this 15th day of December, between the Independent Production Workshop (hereafter known as IPW), a Pennsylvania Corporation having its principal place of business at 233 Avenue of the Americas, New York, New York (herein "The Executive Producer") and BROADWAY PRODUC-TIONS of 155 Palm St., Boston, MA., (herein "The Producer") in connection with a television program tentatively entitled "BERGEN" (herein "The Work").

WHEREAS The Producer and The Executive Producer have discussed and agreed upon the terms pursuant to which The Executive Producer shall provide financing for The Work in such a manner as described below, paragraph 19.c.

WHEREAS The Executive Producer and The Producer wish to confirm their agreement in writing.

NOW, THEREFORE, in consideration of mutual covenants set forth below, the parties agree as follows:

Following this page of the contract are several pages that detail the legal arrangement between the executive producer and the production company regarding budget and turn-around time.

The contract for *Getting Ahead* is prepared by the in-house producer of the proposed series. In essence it is an expanded version of the initial memo from the producer to the assistant school superintendent, plus a production schedule and budget.

TO: PJM, Assistant to District School Superintendent
FROM: RWW, Producer, Media Department
SUBJECT: Proposal for Getting Ahead, an eight-part TV series.

On the basis of our conversation last week, our department is prepared to produce eight fifteen-minute programs to supplement the district's career-training program.

The tapes would cover the following eight broad job categories: Manufacturing, Service, Transportation, Education, Computers, Medicine, Law, Communications.

The purpose of the series (working title "Getting Ahead") is 1) to introduce students to a wide range of careers and 2) to show examples of some of our graduates who have "gotten ahead." This approach will supplement material covered in the classrooms, counseling sessions, and textbooks. The resulting tapes will be distributed on videotape. Students will be able to view them in counseling offices around the district or in their homes.

The series' budget and schedule are shown below. The budget is based on the assumption that we do all shooting on district property and that your staff handles the routine typing, duplication, etc. The schedule is also based on the assumption that we get approval within two weeks.

If we don't begin this month, the schedule will be complicated by staff vacations and we won't be able to complete the series by the end of the school year.

	HEDULE
	search. Writing of series
	a general description of
	le for approval by
	ent's office.
	d pre-production work on
	o and five. (We are
	the scripting of these two
	fore beginning the other six.
	episodes, are, in a sense,
	will be evaluated and
	tested before we begin the other six.)
Feb 13-20	Production and editing of episodes two and five.
Feb 20-25	Testing and evaluation of episodes two and five.
Mar 1-5	Re-editing or reshooting of two or five as needed.
Mar 9-27	Scripting of episodes one, three, four, six, seven, eight.
Mar 31-April 13	Production and editing of six episodes.
Apr 15-May 1	Testing and evaluation of total series.
May 1-30	Reshooting and re-editing as needed.
Jun 1-25	Duplication and distribution of series to schools.

The proposals for *In the Valley* and the program for the Mammoth Corporation are also prepared by the producers in charge of these projects.

FORMAT:
In the Valley is designed for either Wednesday or Thursdays at seven PM after the national newscast. Each episode contains a documentary of a local, well known celebrity. Before, during commercial breaks, and after the documentary, there will be studio segments in which Bill Strum, host of the series, introduces and interviews the week's celebrity. When appropriate, additional guests might be included in these segments. For example, if the week's celebrity is a local politician we may include in the final interview segment, the editor from the Journal or a political science professor from the college.

The way we frame each program is as important as the content. The opening sequence will be like a space landing—the first shot is of earth from space, each shot brings us closer to Landcaster and the valley. The final shot is WORK-TV. The program ends the way it begins, except in reverse, like a space launch.

PRODUCTION SCHEDULE:
One month to organize the production team, test the format,

MAMMOTH OIL

TO: Norma Babcock, E.V.P. Corp. Com.
FROM: Cliff Kaplan, Senior Producer, Media Center
RE: Video for Inter-company Network on Tragedy in Hartsville

I've looked over everyone's comments on the proposal I circulated yesterday. Based on these suggestions, I've made the following changes.

First, I agree with Linda that we should open with the CEO on site. If we begin with the CEO in her conference room she appears too remote. This proposal assumes we will shoot both her scenes at the refinery in Longberg, New Jersey for its proximity and refinery views.

Second, I have given more emphasis to the Hartsville plant by adding an on-camera statement from Frank Bush, director of tech services there, and by increasing the amount of footage about the tragedy and what happened immediately afterwards.

REVISED STRUCTURE:

PART ONE: ACTUALITY FROM NIGHT OF EXPLOSION (TIME: 1:00-1:30)

This will be a highly produced segment which will quickly establish what happened at Hartsville and show as dynamically as possible how Mammoth responded. I will use footage from the local television station plus material I had shot there. My intention is to feature action views of employees and staff working with people in the community. The Mammoth logo on our trucks and uniforms will help make this statement. This opening montage ends with a soft wipe to the title: RESPONSE! ON TIME!

PART TWO: CEO IN FRONT OF REFINERY (TIME: 2:00-3:00)

1. Gives detailed explanation of what happened and how company worked with authorities in the community to restore order and help those who were injured.

2. Promises support to employees who need it.

3. Recounts company's impressive safety record of fifteen years without a major accident.

PART THREE: AFTER THE EXPLOSION (TIME: 3:00-3:30)

1. Footage of explosion, injured being cared for and clean up after the explosion (scenes narrated by the CEO.)

2. Statement by Frank Bush, Director Technical Services, Hartsville.

PART FOUR: PUBLIC STANCE AND REROUTING (TIME: 5:00)

1. Alberton states Mammoth is strong enough to withstand this tragedy. However, we will need to make some accommodations.

2. Need to dip into our inventory.

3. Need to route 20 percent of product from Denver, Helena and Casper refineries to southwest storage in Phoenix.

4. Need to assure all wholesalers that Mammoth is committed to maintaining our supply at committed levels.

PART FIVE: COMMITMENTS TO IMPROVE SAFETY STANDARDS (TIME: 1:00)

CEO in interior shot at Longberry refinery giving final message. After initial sentence we fade to sequence of shots of Mammoth personnel and members of the community working together to clean up damaged buildings and streets.

1. Mammoth is a good citizen.

2. We will do everything possible to recompense the people of Hartsville and assure them that nothing like this will ever happen again.

The commitment stage concludes when clients, bosses, or funding sources accept or reject contracts. If a contract is accepted, producers are committed to move their production ideas into the next stages of the process: the design and execution.

The contracts for *Bergen, In The Valley* and the Mammoth Corporation Video, *Response On Time* are approved. *Getting Ahead*, the series on career development for the school district, is initially approved but the approval comes too late in the year for the production team to complete the series on the date scheduled for use. The project, therefore, cannot be produced.

UNIT 4

UNIT 4

Design

No two programs are designed exactly alike. But every program goes through some version of the design stage. A made-for-television movie takes more than a year to script, rehearse, plan lighting, sets, and costumes. On the other extreme, out of necessity, a segment for the evening news is designed in a thirty-second strategy conference between producer, reporter, and videographer.

Whether news or drama, in a studio or on location, there are few opportunities to analyze or weigh alternatives when filming or recording begins. Therefore, successful production teams make as many decisions as possible before shooting.

Those who do not take full advantage of the design stage usually experience television's special brand of anarchy. Television crews, cast, and even equipment have a tendency to go their separate ways when not given strong leadership, and the results can be disastrous!

In the last two chapters we followed four ideas for television programs through the commitment stage. Three of the four, *In the Valley*, *Bergen*, and *Response, On Time* received commitments and move into the initial stages of design.

Chapter 8

Treatments & Scripts

Once commitments are made to program ideas, production teams are formed. At WORK-TV this happens when the production manager authorizes the producer to hire a writer on a free-lance basis and assigns a staff director, set and lighting designers, and graphic artist to the series. At IPW Productions the producer assigned to *Bergen* also hires a writer and begins the process of hiring a director and production staff. At Mammoth Oil, the producer/writer is given a partial go ahead to begin forming his production team. However, before his boss, the Vice President of Corporate Communications, gives her full approval, she wants to meet and discuss the script outlined in the proposal.

(THE PHONE RINGS AT THE MEDIA CENTER AT MAMMOTH. THE PRODUCER/WRITER PICKS IT UP.)

VICE PRESIDENT
Cliff, Norma here. I have some questions about the plans for the video. Let's meet over lunch tomorrow. I wish it could be sooner but that's my first free moment. We haven't had much time since this thing broke.

PRODUCER/WRITER
Lunch tomorrow is fine. But I need to move quickly on some things, even before we meet. Can I hire a free-lance director and begin spending money on graphics and music?

VICE PRESIDENT
What kind of numbers are we talking about?

PRODUCER/WRITER
The director will cost us three to four grand. I don't expect to spend more than two on the graphics and music.

VICE PRESIDENT
I don't know where I'm going to find that kind of money. But, we're on a tight deadline, go ahead...we'll work it out.

PRODUCER/WRITER
Great! Thanks......I'll see ya' tomorrow at... Where do we meet?

VICE PRESIDENT
The executive dinning room, twelve fifteen.

At WORK-TV the producer, writer and director assigned to *In the Valley* have their first production meeting.

PRODUCER
Barb, I want you to talk with the people at the newspaper and the arts council and come up with three or four prospects for the first show. Write up a paragraph or two on each.

WRITER
How detailed do you want those?

PRODUCER
No more than a typed page. Include things that make the prospect outstanding...different..and whether there are any interesting production angles. Is he or she any good on camera? Also, it would be useful to know whether there's any existing film or tape on the people you select.

DIRECTOR
I can begin working on the opening and closing sequences.

PRODUCER
Ok, bring in something for our next meeting. I'm going to start talking with Mike and Gwen about the sets, titles and bumpers. I'll ask them for a few rough sketches next time we get together.

WRITER
Which will be...?

PRODUCER
Wednesday at three.

At the conference room at IPW Productions, over coffee and bagels, the television producer assigned to *Bergen*, the Broadway producer who brought the stage play to IPW, and the writer hired to adapt the play to television meet for the first time.

WRITER
I gotta' tell you, I am really pleased to be on this project. Bergen is a great a play!

TELEVISION PRODUCER
Yep. But it's no film script. At least not yet. I want you to restructure it. It has to move out of the two rooms. It depends too much on words.

BROADWAY PRODUCER
I hope you're not going to turn this serious drama into Miami Vice.

TELEVISION PRODUCER
Of course not. If we wanted Miami Vice we'd do Miami Vice. I am as committed as you to this thing. I don't want to compromise the intelligence of the stage play in any way. But, to tell a story...any story...on television the rules are different.

BROADWAY PRODUCER
Different than?

WRITER
Different than the stage. Here plot development needs movement, montage, music, action.

BROADWAY PRODUCER
Sounds like Miami Vice.

WRITER
It also sounds like a lot of other things. Great movies, for example.

TELEVISION PRODUCER
Time out! Time out! Let's look at the script instead of arguing about what television and film are. You guys sound like second year film students!

> WRITER
> Sorry. All I was saying is that we have to translate the script to television.
> We can't just put it, as is, on the screen.
>
> BROADWAY PRODUCER
> Apology accepted. This is all very new to me.
>
> TELEVISION PRODUCER
> Let's stop here and give Fred ten days or so to work up a treatment. We'll
> continue this then, when we have something in hand.

At WORK-TV the writer for *In The Valley* begins to look for guests for the first episode. In the morning she speaks with the president of the Chamber of Commerce and the public relations director at the University. She spends the afternoon reading local newspapers and magazines at the county library. The next morning, she views three films and a stack of videotapes that have segments featuring the people she is considering for the first program. Late in the afternoon she sits down at her word processor and writes the following descriptions of possible subjects for the first program in the series.

#1 THE MAYOR

An obvious choice for episode one of Valley is a program featuring the mayor. She is a colorful, dynamic character who is no stranger to the camera or the television studio. Her political career certainly is local. She began as a part-time party organizer while at the university and worked her way up through the ranks.

She's committed to the city and the region and there are plenty of "war stories" about how she's fought the bureaucrats in Washington and the state capitol to support this claim. I found tons of material about her at the library, at the *Daily News*, at the university, and here at the station. There's footage of her doing everything from debating her opponents to singing in her church choir. There are many reasons why she would be a good choice. However, there is one problem with beginning the series with her. She is up for election in less than two months and will probably use the occasion to tell the viewers that her administration has done everything right.

#2 RONALD FAIRFIELD, JOURNALIST

Another good candidate for episode one is the feature columnist at the *News*. He is a man who grew up in the Midwest and, in the tradition of Hemingway, followed the troops to the front. After a career in "the big time" (London, Paris, the U.N.) he settled here. While not a hometown boy, he is someone who knows and is committed to the community. His books clearly reflect the lifestyle of his adopted region.

There are numerous articles about and by him but not a lot of visual material. His office, however, is filled with memorabilia. Some of this could be used. Actually, even if there were a great deal of film or videotape to supplement an interview with him, I would suggest using it sparingly. He is one of those "talking heads" with something to say.

Even if we didn't decide to use him as the featured guest on the first episode, we might want to keep him in mind for a regular spot on the show. He could perhaps deliver one of his columns, which are usually of a humorous, light nature; just right for our time slot.

#3 THE COACH OF THE CHIEFS

Another colorful figure who would make an interesting subject for the first program is Franklin Roberts, coach of the Chiefs. Roberts has lived here most of his life. In fact, the only time he lived outside the county was during the war and when he played for the Red Sox.

Not only does Roberts distinguish himself as the long-time coach of our triple-A baseball team, but he has also participated in local politics. And even though never victorious, he has run two of the more exciting political campaigns in the city's history. He was the candidate for city council president twice.

The angle of a program on the coach has to be baseball. He lives and breathes it. He is a colorful figure but he may be too narrow for our regular audience. If you aren't a baseball fan (which I am not), you have trouble understanding him. On the other hand, we all loved Casey Stengel and nobody understood him.

#4 THE MAESTRO

Giorgio Rozando is an outsider who brings to the community an international reputation. Under Rozando, the Opera Company has become a focus of community interest and attention. After seasons in which one couldn't give a ticket away, opera has become the thing to do.

Rozando's press office has boxes of pictures, films, and tapes of him singing for and sipping with kings and presidents. Like the coach, there is only one angle here: opera. Also, while he has an apartment in town, he does not have much to do with the community. Still, he is an international star and without doubt, the most colorful of the four choices. His apartment, family, and car (a red, 1955 Mercedes convertible) seem right out of a Fellini film.

If we don't decide to use him for the first episode, he would certainly be a candidate for something in the future.

At Mammoth Oil, the producer/writer meets with his production team. He has hired, on a free-lance basis, a director he used a year ago on a training program the company produced to teach workers new safety procedures. Another member of the media department who is strong in audio design will be the assistant director for the project. A graphic artist from the company's publications department will work on the design of titles, credits, and any supporting graphs or tables which might be needed.

PRODUCER/WRITER
The footage I had shot in Hartsville just arrived by air freight. There seems to be good stuff on the fire and clean up as well as plenty of testimonials. Kate, take a look at it and begin to put together a rough cut.

DIRECTOR
Ok. Do I use the proposal as an outline of what your looking for?

PRODUCER/WRITER
Yep, I have a luncheon meeting tomorrow with the V.P. I can't write the script until we meet. So work from the proposal.

GRAPHIC ARTIST
Do you need anything from me?

PRODUCER/WRITER
Yes. I need you to sketch out ideas for opening credits. They have to be special. We need that slick, newsy look...graphics moving over the company's fire trucks rushing to the scene...you know what I mean.

GRAPHIC ARTIST
I'll see what I can do. When do we get back together?

PRODUCER/WRITER
Tomorrow at two.

Treatments are used in fiction as well as documentaries. In fiction they are very useful first steps in the writing process. Writers usually submit treatments to producers and only after they are approved do writers prepare word-for-word, action-by-action scripts. Most documentaries are not written into scripts and the treatment is, therefore, the only document from which a production team works.

> *Treatments are a game we who make documentaries play with ourselves. Of course, we cannot predict exactly what will happen when we interview someone or when we shoot a scene. We have to stay loose and respond to whatever happens that is exciting and worthwhile. On the other hand, if we don't have something in mind when we go out to interview or shoot a scene then we will not be in a position to get anything interesting or worthwhile.*
>
> *—a documentary producer*

The writer hired by IPW Productions to adapt *Bergen* to television sits hunched over the keyboard of his computer. The deadline for the script is tomorrow. As he writes, he will refer to the copy of the treatment he wrote several weeks ago which both the producer and executive producer approved.

BERGEN TREATMENT   PAGE 22

Bergen picks Robin up at her house and they drive to the bowling alley together. There's the usual tension of close friends who haven't seen one another for a long time. Robin makes casual conversation with compliments about Bergen's car. Though she sounds sarcastic, it's clear she's impressed. "Leather seats, eh? Plastic not good enough for the big business executive?"

Inside, the bowling alley is almost deserted. Bergen has to shout "anybody home?" to get set up with an alley. While they put on their shoes and look for bowling balls, Robin tries to break the news about her relationship with Ramoz. "You remember Ramoz, don't you?"

"Remember him? People used to mistake us for brothers."

So far he is quite pleased with most of his adaptation. He feels it is true to the stage play while, at the same time, contains the action needed to "work" on television. Just last night he rewrote a scene from the play which took place in the Munoz living room when Bergen is threatened by his sister's ex-boyfriend. He moved the scene to a bowling alley which gives it local color and more of a sense of Bergen's isolation from his roots.

Another example of the kinds of changes he has made is reflected in the opening scene. In the original play, the protagonist, Bergen, walks up to the front door of his parent's home and is greeted by his elderly father who has not seen him for three years. The door opens and his father, seeing his son in a business suit, says, "Bergen....you look good.. like a regular member of the country club." Here is how the writer adapted the scene for television.

1. VIEW THROUGH WINDSHIELD OF MOVING CAR. LATE AFTERNOON.
Willie Nelson is heard through the roar of traffic. The view through the windshield is very confusing because there are many exit signs from which to choose, coming upon the driver very quickly.

TITLE OVER WINDSHIELD.
The title fades and we cut to ECU of Bergen as he tries to decide which exit to take. This is unfamiliar territory. He may have decided too late.

2. LS OF CAR RACING TO GET IN FRONT OF TRUCK SO HE CAN MAKE HIS EXIT.
Music continues until loud roar of trailer's horn drowns it out.

3. MCU OF BERGEN.
He is slightly shaken but pleased with his victory and celebrates by turning up the music.

4. LS FROM MOVING CAR OF FACTORY WITH PICKET LINE IN FRONT.
Hold as camera picks up individual strikers and dollies past...then stops.

5. CU OF BERGEN.
He is uncomfortable, turns.

6. MLS OF BERGEN'S PARENTS OPENING FRONT DOOR GREETING HIM.
Their appearances and dress are similar to the strikers. Bergen is dressed in suit and tie.

                    MR. MUNOZ:
Bergen....you look good! Like one a' 'dem guys at the country club.

In the play, after the father's statement, there are four pages of dialogue. In the adaptation, the scene ends with a close-up of Bergen's reaction to his father's statement.

At the Mammoth executive dinning room, over lunch, the Vice President and producer/writer meet to discuss the proposal. Both have copies of the document in front of them.

VICE PRESIDENT
As I told you yesterday, there are a few things I'd like to see changed. First, the title, "Response, On Time" is just too flashy for this kind of program. Come up with something more,...more corporate. You know what I mean.

PRODUCER/WRITER
Yes. I think I do... We'll come up with something. What else?

VICE PRESIDENT
We need to go into more detail on the rerouting issue. That's very complicated and needs more than a minute or two.

PRODUCER/WRITER
OK. But remember this is a general response. We can follow up the tape with print.

VICE PRESIDENT
I realize that but I still want some detail on how rerouting will effect work schedules and our expansion plans.

PRODUCER/WRITER
OK...I'll write that in. Who's my source person on this?

VICE PRESIDENT
Marv in our office. Then there's segments three and four....with, what's his name?

PRODUCER/WRITER
Alberton?

> **VICE PRESIDENT**
> Yes, Alberton. I don't think he should be used in those final, key segments. One of our people should be on camera...like Margaret or Chuck in Marketing.
>
> **PRODUCER/WRITER**
> I really disagree here. He's a professional communicator, that's what we need. And, he's our spokesperson. People, our people as well as the general audience, connect him with the company.
>
> **VICE PRESIDENT**
> But he doesn't know anything about our plans....
>
> **PRODUCER/WRITER**
> Everything will be scripted. We'll pass everything he says past you.

The luncheon meeting goes on for another forty-five minutes. Most of the time is spent discussing the pros and cons of using a professional announcer/actor in segments three and four instead of a Mammoth executive. The producer/writer convinces the Vice President that the actor is not thought of as an outsider by the company's employees and that he has the skills to get the message of the tape across to its viewers. However, to keep the Vice President happy, the producer/writer promises to shoot a back up version of the segments using a marketing Vice President. As they part, the producer/writer promises to have a draft of the script on the Vice President's desk in a day.

At IPW Productions, the writer hired to adapt *Bergen*, the Broad-way producer, and the television producer from IPW discuss the writer's script. In general, the television producer likes what he sees, but the Broadway producer wonders if the writer has taken too many liberties.

BROADWAY PRODUCER
The problem, my problem with the scene is....I'm afraid the father-son conflict will be buried behind this tractor trailer chase you start with.

TELEVISION PRODUCER
I disagree...I think it works. A strong, engaging opening. It'll work.

WRITER .
But he may have a point. It could be too strong...it all depends how it's shot.

TELEVISION PRODUCER
And edited. But that's what television is about. It's a nice touch. We need it.

BROADWAY PRODUCER
I'm not convinced. I think that first dialogue with the father is crucial.

TELEVISION PRODUCER
Trust us.

BROADWAY PRODUCER
Do I have a choice?

At WORK-TV, the writer and producer get together for a short meeting to discuss the person to be featured in the first episode of *In The Valley*.

PRODUCER
Both the coach and journalist are great. The only question is, who's going to be on the first program. Barb, I'd like you to prepare two treatments: one for the coach and one for the journalist. We'll make the decision on who goes first at our next meeting.

To prepare for the next production meeting, the writer reviews her notes and begins to write two treatments: detailed descriptions of what she imagines the finished documentaries on the coach and the journalist will look and sound like. Here are portions of the treatments the writer of *In the Valley* prepared for the producer.

RONALD FAIRFIELD, JOURNALIST
Sequence I: 1-1/2 Minutes.
  Ambience of early morning coffee shop.
  Close up of coffee being poured into "take out" cup, donut drops into a bag, wide shot of Eddie of EDDIE AND ELLEN'S on fifth street. Row of customers buried behind their copies of the News. One or two peak out. MLS of Fairfield as he acknowledges these greetings. Fairfield takes his bag, pays the bill and exits. We follow him walking the rest of the two blocks to his office at the News. In voice-over, we hear Fairfield say:
  THAT HE HAS BEGUN HIS MORNINGS HERE AT EDDIE'S AND ELLEN'S FOR THE LAST FIFTEEN YEARS. HE COMPARES LANDCASTER TO THE FAMOUS CITIES IN WHICH HE LIVED WHEN HE WAS A CORRESPONDENT.

Sequence II: 1 Minute.
  Photomation using material from his office and his scrapbook showing Fairfield shaking hands with prime ministers, popes and kings as well as enjoying the tourist attractions of the two capitals.
  NARRATION OUTLINING HIS CAREER.

Sequence III: 2 Minutes.
  Interview with Fairfield in his office in front of his bookcase.HE IS ASKED ABOUT THE TIME HE SPENT A WEEKEND WITH THE ROYAL FAMILY AND THE TIME HE VISITED WITH THE POPE.

Sequence IV: 1-1 1/2 Minutes.
  "Man on the street" interviews with people around the city. They are asked if they read Fairfield's column. Those who say yes are asked to recall a favorite excerpt or two.
  END THE SEGMENT WITH FAIRFIELD READING A PARAGRAPH ABOUT WHICH HE IS ESPECIALLY PLEASED.

FRANKLIN ROBERTS, COACH
Sequence I: 1-1/2 Minutes.
  Montage of close-ups of faces of fans at MacArthur stadium.
  PLAY-BY-PLAY OF BILLY BONS, VOICE OF THE CHIEFS.
  "IT`S THE TOP OF THE NINTH...TWO MEN ON.....ONE OUT..."
  Cut to close-up of the Chiefs catcher giving a sign to his pitcher.
  "THE PITCH..."
  MS the coach in the dugout at the stadium chewing tobacco and spitting at a regular five second intervals. He gives a sign to the catcher, scratches his head, takes off his cap, and spits again.
  "AND....ROGERS STRIKES HIM OUT...."

End sequence with MCU of coach. A slight smile of satisfaction lights up his face as he watches his pitcher strike out the batter.

Sequence II: 2 Minutes.
Shots of the coach in the club house congratulating his ballplayers on their victory as we hear him in voice over. The sequence ends with a close-up of Rogers, the pitcher.
HE TALKS ABOUT THE KIND OF DREAMS PLAYERS HAVE IN THE MINOR LEAGUES. HE COMPARES THE OUTLOOK AND DREAMS OF HIS YOUNG PLAYERS WHO HAVE NEVER BEEN TO THE MAJORS AND THE OLDER, VETERANS WHO HAVE BEEN THERE.
Cut to Franklin's office in the club house. His walls are covered with photos of ballplayers and trophies. He is framed so the trophies are directly behind him but out of the depth of field.
HE TALKS ABOUT HIS DREAMS. DOES HE DREAM ABOUT BEING CALLED UP TO THE MAJORS? DOES HE DREAM ABOUT THE CHIEFS WINNING ANOTHER AAA PENNANT? DOES HE DREAM ABOUT GETTING BACK INTO POLITICS AND GETTING ELECTED TO OFFICE?

Sequence III: 2 Minutes.
Stock footage and newspaper photos of Franklin's two runs for elected office.
NARRATION EXPLAINS THAT HE HAS RUN FOR CITY COUNCIL TWICE. WHILE HE LOST BOTH TIMES HE HAS BEEN PRAISED BY THE PRESS AND ELECTED OFFICIALS FROM BOTH PARTIES FOR HIS INNOVATIVE IDEAS.
Sequence ends with excerpt from his consolation speech from the last election in which he promises he will not give up the fight for a new youth center.

Sequence IV: 2 minutes.
Black and white photo of Mickey Mantle. Then dissolve to MS of Mantle in his Manhattan office.
MANTLE TALKS ABOUT HOW MUCH HE LEARNED FROM FRANKLIN WHEN HE PLAYED FOR HIM IN THE MINOR LEAGUES.
Black and white photo of Hector Rodriguez.

The writer of these treatments and her producer know that the documentaries which will eventually be produced will probably not cover exactly what is outlined in these treatments. However, to repeat what was said earlier, the treatments are very useful guides when a team begins shooting and interviewing.

After reading the two treatments, the producer of *In The Valley* calls the writer to tell her he has decided to feature the coach in the first program of the series. "I find the coach the more colorful character," he tells her. He also tells her to complete the script of the first program as soon as possible so the director, set designer, lighting designer, and their staffs can take a look at it.

She completes the script a week later.

IN THE VALLEY — EPISODE I — COACH ROBERTS.

VIDEO:	AUDIO:
FADE UP TO: OPENING TITLE SEQUENCE (:50)	MUSIC: UP AND UNDER.
	ANNOUNCER: (VO)
	In the Valley, a program featuring the events and people who make the news in Landcaster.
INSERT: FOOTAGE OF ROBERTS ON THE PLAYING FIELD.	This evening we meet Franklin Roberts. For fourteen years the coach of the triple-A Chiefs, and twice candidate for city council president.
LS SET WITH STRUM AND GUEST.	He's here with us in the studio when we come back.
COMMERCIAL BREAK (:90).	MUSIC OUT.
MS STRUM ON SET.	
	STRUM:
	Today we begin an ex- periment. We're going to try something that most everyone in television thinks cannot be done. We are going to produce a full blown, early-

evening program about local issues and events. We think our city deserves this kind of attention. And, if you agree, we're in business. If not, then its back to **Entertainment Tonight** and the rest of the programs that are really not about Landcaster and really don't help you know your city. We hope that **In the Valley** gets you more involved in your community and more informed about how many interesting things are going on in Landcaster. Now, for instance, when's the last time you went to MacArthur Stadium?

DISSOLVE TO DOCUMENTARY, SEGMENTS I AND II, (10:00).

COMMERCIAL BREAK, (2:00).

CU STRUM.

STRUM:

We pick up our story on the steps of the capital, the night before the election. It was a very eventful evening, as you will see.

DISSOLVE TO DOCUMENTARY, SEGMENTS III AND IV, (9:00).

COMMERCIAL BREAK,
(2:00).

MS STRUM.   STRUM:
                                    Let's get back to the
                                    game. The pennant's on
                                    the line. Mitchell is on
                                    the mound. It's the top
                                    of the ninth.

DOCUMENTARY SEGMENTS V
AND VI, (6:30).

DISSOLVE TO M2S STRUM   STRUM:
AND COACH.
                                    Before we talk to the
                                    coach about that last
                                    game, here is another
                                    feature of **In the Valley**,
                                    a calendar of the impor-
                                    tant events of the week.

(THE CHAMBER AND ARTS   (THE CHAMBER AND ARTS
COUNCIL WILL SUPPLY THE   COUNCIL WILL SUPPLY THE
COPY AND PHOTOS HERE.   COPY HERE.)
(3:30)

M2S OF STRUM AND COACH.   STRUM:

                                    (Three minute interview
                                    based on the Coach's
                                    thoughts about local
                                    politics and his team's
                                    chances of capturing the
                                    pennant for the second
                                    year in a row. Here are
                                    questions that should
                                    keep the conversation
                                    lively.
                                        -What is the status
                                    of the new youth center?

	-Should the city accept the state's man-date that a low level nuclear waste site be placed in the Valley Creek area?
SHOTS AS SEEN FOR INTERVIEW.	-What was it like growing up in Landcaster fifty years ago?
	-What are the chances of the Chiefs' rookie stars, Smith and Jordon, making it to the majors?
	-Are we going to win the pennant this year?
CU STRUM.	STRUM: We thank Coach Roberts and wish you and the Chiefs all the best this year. That's it for us today. We hope you've enjoyed our first program. See you next week....**In the Valley**.
DISSOLVE TO CLOSING SEQUENCE, (:30).	MUSIC UP.
KEY CREDITS.	
FADE TO BLACK.	MUSIC OUT.

It's 10:00 a.m. at Mammoth. The producer/writer receives a phone call from the Vice President approving the script. Minutes after hanging up, the producer/writer asks his secretary to call all members of the production team to a meeting that afternoon.

At the meeting, he distributes copies of the script and, with the director, begins making crew assignments, reserving studio time, scheduling travel, and all the other arrangements necessary to complete the design stage and move the program toward completion.

To: Norma Babcock, E.V.P. Corporate Comm.
From: Cliff Kaplan, Producer Media Department
RE: Final Draft of Script for Video on Hartsville
Explosion, **The Company Responds**.

Please read the attached draft of the script and let me
know your reactions as soon as possible.

Thanks.

THE COMPANY RESPONDS (draft—2/22)

OPENING GRAPHICS KEYED OVER FOOTAGE OF COMPANY TRUCKS
PUTTING OUT FIRE AT THE HARTSVILLE REFINERY.

NARRATOR (VO):

On the evening of March 31, fire broke out at a
secondary, low grade storage facility at the Mammoth
Hartsville, Texas refinery. The fire quickly spread,
severely damaging storage, transport and refining
sectors of the plant.

FOUR-FIVE TESTIMONIALS FROM MAMMOTH EMPLOYEES, PEOPLE
WHO LIVE NEAR THE REFINERY, THE HARTSVILLE POLICE AND
FIRE CHIEF.

FLASHING LIGHTS OF AN AMBULANCE, DISSOLVE TO LS OF
REFINERY.

NARRATOR (VO):

Minutes after the alarm sounded, the company's fire
unit was on the scene.

FOOTAGE OF FAMILIES BEING EVACUATED FROM NEIGHBORING
AREAS.

NARRATOR (VO):

Local authorities were informed of the need to evacuate nearby residences.

SCENES IN THE LOCAL HOSPITAL SHOWING MEDICAL CARE BEING GIVEN THE INJURED.

NARRATOR (VO):

Mammoth medical personnel began coordinating their efforts with local hospitals.

DISSOLVE TO CEO IN FRONT OF LONGBERY REFINERY. PAN TO HER FROM TANKS.

CEO:

Those images from the Hartsville explosion are ones I hope we will never see again. The deaths of Mammoth employees Tom Bradley and Connie Wigham and the two Hartsville firemen, Bruce Long and Adam Goldberg, are tragic losses which I deeply regret. Let me point out that this was an accident, in every sense of the word. I intend to find out why a fully insulated filler cap would collapse without warning and cause such devastation. Just two hours before the explosion, that cap passed a routine inspection. I share with you pride in Mammoth's unblemished safety record and I want to make sure this is the first and last time that record is compromised.

MONTAGE OF SHOTS OF THE DAY AFTER THE ACCIDENT—NO NARRATION, MUSIC BED. MAMMOTH PERSONNEL WORKING WITH HARTSVILLE FIRE PERSONNEL, REFINERY ADMINISTRATIVE OFFICES USED AS FIRST AID STATIONS, MAMMOTH EXECUTIVES WORKING WITH LOCAL LEADERS AT CITY HALL.

ESTABLISHING SHOT OF THE ADMINISTRATIVE WING OF THE HARTSVILLE REFINERY THEN TO SHOT OF OFFICE OF FRANK BUSH, DIRECTOR OF TECHNICAL SERVICES IN HARTSVILLE,

AND TO FRANK SPEAKING DIRECTLY TO CAMERA.

BUSH:

In the last forty-eight hours, I have witnessed men and women from this plant risking their lives to help others and minimize losses. Some of our people have not slept for three days. Thanks to this kind of effort we're on our way back. That applies to the refinery and to those who work and live in this community.

RICHARD ALBERTON IN FRONT OF MAP OF MAMMOTH SUPPLY LINES. (WE WILL ALSO DO A VERSION OF THIS SEGMENT WITH MARGARET JENKINS, V.P. MARKETING.)

ALBERTON:

The rebuilding that Frank speaks about will affect the whole company...and our activities in a number of areas—public relations, marketing and routing. In the public relations area, all wholesalers will be receiving these materials.

EXAMPLES OF THE POSTERS AND INFORMATION PACKETS.

ALBERTON:

Please do all you can to make sure they are displayed and read. Also we will be running this television spot in most regions.

SHOW TWO VERSIONS OF THE AD.

ALBERTON:

For the next four months, twenty percent additional production will be routed from plants in Denver, Helena, and Casper for storage in Phoenix.

SHOW MAP AS HE POINTS TO IT AND SHOWS ROUTE LINES.

ALBERTON:

You'll receive a complete breakdown on these changes in the next issue of <u>Report</u>. In the meantime, if you have any questions, call Paul Mueller at the home office, extension 9909.

REPEAT OPENING SHOWING EXPLOSION AND COMPANY FIRE TRUCKS RESPONDING THEN TO CEO IN MONITORING CONTROL CENTER IN LONGBERY REFINERY.

CEO:

The events of the last days and the negative publicity that we received means many of your customers...the wholesalers in the system... will have serious concerns about our ability to meet commitments. You should reassure them that they will not be left short.

REPEAT SEGMENT SHOTS SHOW CLEAN UP.

CEO (VO):

We were there in Hartsville meeting our responsibilities. With your support and hard work we will be there throughout the nation supplying product to those who depend on Mammoth...continuing to prove that this company is concerned with more than just increasing profit margins. We are dedicated to serving the public and leading our industry.

CLOSING TITLE SUPERED OVER FROZEN FINAL SHOT OF MONTAGE. THEME MUSIC UP AND OUT OVER MAMMOTH LOGO.

—END—

At IPW Productions a messenger carries a thick envelope marked "BERGEN" into the production offices and hands it to a secretary. Knowing the producer is anxiously awaiting a script, the secretary rushes it into the producer's office who immediately opens it and begins reading.

1. VIEW THROUGH WINDSHIELD OF MOVING CAR. LATE AFTER-
NOON.
   We hear the roar of traffic then Willie Nelson, from the cassette player in car. The view through the windshield is very confusing because there are so many exit signs from which to choose and they are coming upon the driver very quickly.

TITLE OVER WINDSHIELD
The title fades and we cut to ECU of Bergen as he tries to decide which exit to take. This is unfamiliar territory. He may have decided too late.

2. LS OF CAR RACING TO GET IN FRONT OF TRUCK SO HE CAN MAKE HIS EXIT.
Music continues until loud roar of trailer's horn drowns it out.

3. MCU OF BERGEN.
He is shaken but pleased with his victory and celebrates by turning up the music.

4. LS FROM MOVING CAR OF FACTORY WITH PICKET LINE IN FRONT.
Hold as camera picks up individual strikers and dollies past. Then stops.

5. CU OF BERGEN.
He is uncomfortable, turns.

6. MLS OF BERGEN'S PARENTS OPENING FRONT DOOR GREETING HIM. Their appearances and dress are similar to the strikers. Bergen is dressed in suit and tie.

MR. MUNOZ:

Bergen....you look good! Like one of those guys down at the country club.

7. KITCHEN, SAME DAY.
CU of elderly woman, Bergen's mother, Gladys Munoz, drying her hands, quickly brushing her hair out of her face. She smiles but there is a hint of sadness in her expression. She leaves the room then returns to check and turn off the oven.

8. ENTRANCE HALL
MS of Bergen as he sees his mother. He hesitates for a beat then embraces her.
CU of Mrs. Munoz. Her eyes brighten as she returns Bergen's affectionate hug.

9. KITCHEN, LATER. DIRTY DISHES PILED IN THE SINK.
MS BERGEN AND PARENTS DRINK COFFEE AFTER SUPPER.

BERGEN:

The old turkey...he knew what he was doing, I guess.

MR. MUNOZ:
What are the new people like?

BERGEN:

They're businessmen, Pop. They maximize profits so they'll get raises and be able to send their kids to college.

MR. MUNOZ:
And become like them.

BERGEN:

Naw, they're into the next round. Their kids study art and social work.

MRS. MUNOZ:

(As she offers more coffee to the men.) How long do you think it will take?

```
          Bergen declines. His father does not.

                           BERGEN:
                    Depends on...the union...

          Mr. Munoz gets up in anger.
```

After the producer finishes the script, he looks out the window to gather his thoughts. Five minutes later, he turns to his desk and writes a note:

> *Give this a read. I think it works. Let me know by the end of the week if you agree.*
>
> *—Al*

He then calls his secretary and tells her to send copies of the script and his note to his executive producer at IPW Productions and to the Broadway producer who owns the stage play. A week later, he receives approval to move the project to the next stage when he will hire a director. This director's first task will be to begin the process of casting, designing costumes, and arranging sets, lighting, sound, and graphics.

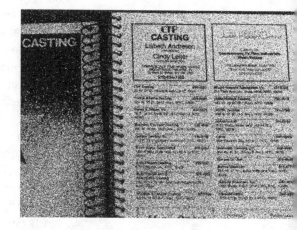

Chapter 9

Casting

When the writers have done their jobs and scripts and treatments are completed, the other members of the production team begin doing their jobs.

For example, the program director at WORK-TV assigns a videographer and sound person from the news department to work with the Producer of the series on the documentary on Coach Franklin Roberts. He also assigns a staff director, graphic artist, and set and lighting designers to the show. The producer, videographer, and sound person meet and discuss the treatment and agree on a tentative shooting schedule. The schedule cannot be finalized until Bill Strum, the host of the program and Coach Roberts, his family, and team, are contacted.

The producer/writer of *The Company Responds* views sequences of the explosion in Hartsville which the director edited together from the material shot at the scene of the explosion. The producer/writer compliments the director on how well paced and professional the sequences look. However, "they are much too long and they do not contain enough shots of Mammoth equipment and personnel," he tells her. The director plans to begin reediting the next day. The producer/writer next turns his attention to the shooting schedule for the other sequences in the program and asks his assistant to check on the availability of the key personalities featured in the videotape: the CEO, Alberton, and Frank Bush.

The producer of *Bergen*, after receiving final script approval from the Broadway producer and his bosses at IPW Productions, hires a director, a production designer, a director of photography, a costume designer, and a casting director. An editor, a make-up artist, lighting designer, music composer, and other specialists will be added to the production team later in the process after locations and cast have been selected.

Before their first meeting, the director of *Bergen* sends her casting director a copy of the script and brief descriptions of each of the characters in the film. These character sketches are very useful when the casting director contacts casting agencies and the agent of a "name" actor she thinks is right for the lead.

BERGEN MUNOZ: A man in his early thirties who returns to his hometown as a representative of the new owners of the major manufacturing company in town. He has an M.B.A. from Rutgers and is well trained in the hard nosed, anti-union business tactics of modern, international corporations. He is the oldest of three brothers. His two younger brothers are factory workers like his parents. One lives in California, the other in Michigan.

Bergen was married but is divorced. There were no children. He has not been home for two years because he could not face the constant union-management arguments he and his parents got into when he was home. He has some sympathy for the union of which his parents and brothers are members but he is management and is very loyal to his corporation.

GLADYS MUNOZ: Mother of Bergen, late fifties. She is second generation German, church going, and dedicated to her family and her union. While raising her three boys she worked at the local factory part time. When the boys left home she joined her husband as a full-time employee and active union member. Her church and her union are the two most important things in her life.

The talent agencies go through their files and contact several actors who would be right for the film's four major and ten minor roles. The talent agencies then send these names, with resumes and photographs, to the film's casting director who, working with the director, selects thirty actors to be auditioned. Next, the casting director rents a small studio, hires a two-person crew, and begins scheduling auditions.

When producing dramatizations of any sort, it is obviously very important that the right actors and actresses be cast. No matter how well written a dramatic script, it will fail if the actors are not believable. And, being a believable actor on screen is quite different than being believable "live" or on stage. For this reason the director videotapes the auditions and bases her decisions on how the actors appear and sound on camera.

Even though each actor is given a copy of the script before the audition, the director will not pay too much attention to how they recite dialogue. What she is most concerned about is how naturally an actor fits into the role for which he or she is auditioning. This, more than how well a piece of dialogue is delivered after a first reading, will determine whom she casts.

During the auditions, the director sits next to a television monitor in the back of the studio. Ten feet away, actors perform in front of a camera.

ASSISTANT DIRECTOR
Quiet. Quiet please!

DIRECTOR
(To the camera operator.) Tighten up to a medium shot. (To the actress.) You are on the phone. (To an assistant.) Give her the phone. (Assistant hands phone to actress.)

ASSISTANT DIRECTOR
Roll tape.

DIRECTOR
You are on the phone speaking to your husband about the fight you two had last night. That's page 25, scene 2. Begin with the script and then ad lib for a little bit.

(The actress does as she is asked.)

DIRECTOR
Good. Now hang up and walk to the window to see if your son has returned home yet.

(She does.)

(Signals for another actress to come forward as he speaks to the actress finishing the audition.) Nice job. We'll make our decision by the end of the week and we'll let your agency know by Monday. Thanks.

After two days of auditions, the director casts most of the characters. Also, she hears from the agent of the "name" performer interested in the lead. He wants the part. All that is left is to cast a few "extras." The casting director calls three more agencies. They assure her that they will find the people she needs within a week. They are true to their word. Ten days after auditions began, all the roles are cast and contracts are negotiated and signed.

The producer of *In The Valley* is also concerned with casting. The day after he receives the final draft of the script from the writer, he contacts Bill Strum, the anchor of the evening news, to make sure he is available to host the show. He also meets with the coach and his family and gives them a brief rundown on what to expect during the week the crew will follow them around shooting and interviewing for the documentary. The producer also has his assistant select three members of the Chiefs baseball team who are colorful and "good" on camera. These three will be interviewed for the documentary and asked to describe the coach's style, tactics, strategies, and so on.

The producer/writer of *The Company Responds* also "casts" his programs. Sometimes producers and directors of institutional programs forget that casting is as important to their success as it is to the success of programs on broadcast television. The cast of *The Company Responds* includes Stephanie Warren, CEO of Mammoth; Richard Alberton, professional actor; and Frank Bush, Director of Technical Services at the Hartsville Refinery.

Chapter 10

Sets & Lighting

All three of the production teams we are following must be concerned with production design or the "look" of their programs. However, only the team producing *Bergen* includes persons with the titles "Production Designer" and "Director of Photography." Production design and photography of *In the Valley* will be handled by the director and videographer of the documentary segment and the director, set, and lighting designers of the studio segment. There are various contributors to the design and photography of *The Company Responds*; the free-lance videographer who shot the footage the night of the explosion, the director and videographer of the location segments, and the director, set and lighting designers of the studio segment.

LOOKING THROUGH THE CAMERA

Television, like other media, offers us only suggestions of the real world. Our imaginations fill in the rest. Notice how little information you need from the television screen to create entire rooms and landscapes. One tree and a bench suggest a park; you fill in the lawns, trees, paths, lakes, and so on. An out-of-focus bank of monitors with two or three shadowy characters moving in and out of the background suggests a busy news-room. One or two tables, a few patrons, and the noise of several different conversations are enough to create Abe's Diner or Le Gourmet. In these examples, the viewer's imagination fills in all but that very small portion of the set which is captured in the camera's lens. Ironically, some of the most effective television settings are assemblages of incomplete details. Some of the least effective, least dramatic sets show too much and therefore limit the viewer's opportunity to use his or her imagination.

These principles apply to scenes shot in front of sets in studios as well as news and documentary scenes shot in front of real settings on location. Often set and lighting design means selecting an appropriate real background and creatively using available light.

The first step toward using lights, backgrounds, and sets effectively is recognizing that the camera "sees" very differently than the human eye. For instance, the television camera renders a much more narrow view of the world than what we normally see. Because of this, a set or real background must be directly behind a subject or it will not be picked up by the camera lens. As obvious as this may sound, it is interesting how frequently inexperienced designers make the mistake of looking at sets with their own eyes and not through the camera lens. It is only when one sees what the camera sees that he or she can judge if the subject and the set are framed correctly.

Another characteristic of television that affects how sets and lighting are designed or how backgrounds are selected is the relatively low quality of the television image. The television screen is a rough mosaic of crisscrossing lines. Even the highest quality television image contains significantly much less information than what we see with our eyes. Detail can be lost in this insubstantial television picture. For this reason, television lighting and set design must be executed in bold strokes. Subtle gradations of light and form which are visible to the eye may not be rendered by the television camera.

Another important consideration is that the camera only sees in two dimensions: horizontal and vertical. However, the illusion of the third dimension,depth, can be achieved by keeping the background out of focus.

In many instances, the camera lens will show only a portion of what it "sees" in focus. This area of focus is called the *depth of field*. One way to narrow the depth of field and thereby keep the foreground out of focus is to shoot in low light. When there is relatively little light, the lens aperture or iris must be "open" or set to a low f-stop. F-stops are the measurements used on a camera lens to indicate the relative size of the opening of the lens aperture.

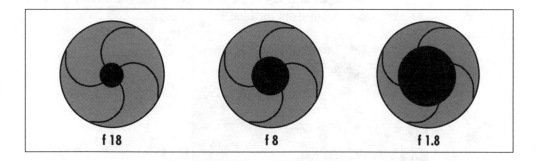

f 18   f 8   f 1.8

Most lenses have f-stop settings of l.8, 2.8, 4, 5.6, 8, 11, 16, and 22. The lower numbers represent wide or open apertures and the higher numbers represent closed or narrow ones. When shooting a scene with a film camera, cinematographers use a light meter to 1) measure the amount of light on the scene and 2) determine which f-stop is appropriate.

Most lenses on video cameras have a built in light meter that sets f-stops automatically. Most lenses also have a "manual" switch which allows the videographer to take the lens off automatic. Professional videographers normally use the automatic iris like a light meter before shooting a scene. Then, when the scene is about to be shot, the videographer switches the lens to manual. This technique allows the videographer to set the lens aperature or f-stop for specific lighting designs. For example, when a videographer is preparing to record a medium shot of a brightly lit woman in front of a dark background, he zooms the lens into a close-up of the face when the lens is set to auto iris. After the lens automatically selects the appropriate f-stop for the woman's face, the videographer switches the lens to manual and zooms it out to the medium shot he plans to record.

A narrow depth of field can also be created by shooting a scene with a long lens. The length of camera lenses are measured in millimeters. Lenses of 10-45 MM are described as *short* lenses, 50-75 MM are called *normal* and lenses over 100 MM are called *long* A zoom lens usually contains all three categories. For example, some zoom lenses contain lengths of 10-100 MM, others 12-120 MM and others 20-200 MM. When a 20-200 MM lens is "zoomed in", it is shooting with a *short* lens; when it is "zoomed out" it is shooting with a *long* lens. So, the depth of field can be narrowed by using a zoom lens in the "zoomed out" position.

Another contributor to depth of field is separating backgrounds and foregrounds. The further away a subject is from the background, the better the chance that he or she will be out of the depth of field. Another way to separate background and foreground is to use less light on the background than the foreground.

A further example of how the camera "sees" very differently than the human eye is the camera's tolerance for dramatic extremes of dark and light within one scene. A very bright or "hot spot" on someone's forehead is not usually distracting to the eye; it may be to the camera. It is usually not unpleasant to look directly at a person in bright, full sunlight. Many cameras are not able to produce a balanced picture in such conditions because the gap between the darker portion of the scene (the person) and the bright sunlight is too great. As a general rule, when shooting with a video camera, the gap between lighting extremes in a scene should not be more than 2 f-stops.

Another difference between the human eye and the camera is the way each sees a scene that contains both artificial (tungsten or neon) light and daylight. The television and film camera "sees" or renders daylight one way and artificial light in another. The human eye working with the brain automatically adjusts for these differences; the camera is not as sophisticated.

If a camera is adjusted for artificial, tungsten light, and daylight is the source of illumination in the scene, it will appear abnormally blue. If a camera is adjusted for daylight and tungsten or artificial light illuminates the scene, it will appear abnormally orange. Normally a scene contains either daylight or tungsten and not a mixture of the two. However, when the two types of lights are mixed, the color temperature of a tungsten light can be converted to daylight with a blue gel. Daylight may be converted to the color temperature of artificial or tungsten light with an orange gel.

SET DESIGN

Most television studio walls are covered with a *cyclorama*. The cyclorama, or cyc, is a neutral surface of white, black, or blue. The most common types of cyc are curtains hung from studio ceilings on tracks. Weights can be attached to the bottom of these curtains so that they hang straight and smooth, presenting a flat, wrinkle-free surface.

Cycs provide an Alice-in-Wonderland background with no beginning and no end. They become a blank canvas on which set and lighting designers can create whatever is needed. A box

of toys, a ball, a hanging Batman poster and pastel light reflected off the cyc transform it into a child's room; a desk, a rug, and splashes of light suggest an office.

When constructing a realistic set in a studio, walls should be high enough (a minimum sixteen feet) to allow for long and low angle shots. Also, in most instances, walls need not be nailed together; they can be connected with braces or clamps. This

allows for last minute changes and the option to open or remove a wall for special situations. For example, there may be a need to place a camera or a light where a fireplace or door used to be. Also braces and clamps make it easier to break down the sets and store them.

Following are the set designs and resulting sets for the studio portions of *In the Valley* and *The Company Responds*.

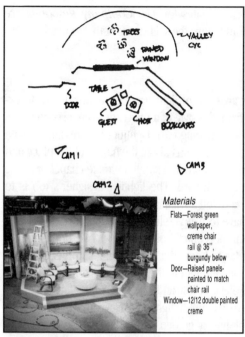

Materials

Flats—Forest green
wallpaper,
creme chair
rail @ 36",
burgundy below
Door—Raised panels-
painted to match
chair rail
Window—12/12 double painted
creme

Set design & resulting set for *In the Valley.*

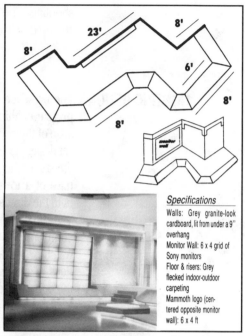

Specifications

Walls: Grey granite-look
cardboard, lit from under a 9"
overhang
Monitor Wall: 6 x 4 grid of
Sony monitors
Floor & risers: Grey
flecked indoor-outdoor
carpeting
Mammoth logo (cen-
tered opposite monitor
wall): 6 x 4 ft

Set design & resulting set for *The Company Responds.*

Many programs that are shot single camera are produced on location. When this occurs, the person in charge of sets selects the appropriate street corner, or office, or restaurant for a scene and makes the necessary arrangements to secure the location on scheduled shooting days. The designer also makes sure there is adequate power for lights, parking for trucks and cars, and anything else that might influence the way a scene is shot (light from open windows, size of doors, existence of freight elevator, noise from nearby factories or highways, and so on).

The directors of *In The Valley* and *The Company Responds* would like to be as prepared for their location shooting as the director of *Bergen*, but their production schedules and the size of their staffs make it impossible for this to happen. Only some of the sites for the documentary portion of *In The Valley* are visited by the videographer and the director before shooting. The location sites for *The Company Responds* are surveyed only hours before the scenes are actually shot.

LIGHTING DESIGN

The presence or absence of light provides opportunities to express everything from the style of a program to the psychological state of the program's protagonist. Lighting, in combination with set design, gives us suggestions about the nature of the place and the size of the space. Are we in a small, intimate chapel or in the nave of a towering cathedral. The lighting designer's job is to help the director take full advantage of these opportunities.

We do not have to watch television to appreciate how light contributes to our perception of the world. We don't need a watch or a calendar to know if it's noon on a summer's day, or dusk in autumn, or midnight in the dead of winter. At midday in the summer, the light is full and flat. There are few shadows. Backgrounds have as much light as foregrounds. At dusk in autumn, the light has a golden hue and falls off to shadow gradually. At midnight in winter, the moon or street lamp creates islands of light and shadow with abrupt, fast fall off to darkness.

Most television lighting designs are modeled after what we find in the real world. The families we see in situation comedies are bathed in the light of carefree, sunny, summer afternoons; brightly lit offices, or kitchens. The mystery series is lit with dim columns of illumination that cut into the darkness like the light found on moonlit mountain roads or alleyways at midnight. A romantic scene has flickering light like that created by candles or reflections from a calm country stream in late afternoon. We know a character is sitting in a car at night because his chin and neck glow in reflected light from the dashboard.

Lighting Equipment

Before we discuss the basic principles of lighting design, we will first look at the instruments which are the designer's tools. There are basically two categories of light fixtures from which designers make their selections. One category includes those fixtures that project light directly onto the subject. The second category includes those fixtures that produce indirect, diffuse light.

Direct light is more intense and easier to control than diffuse light. The shadows thrown by direct lighting instruments are sharply defined while the border between diffuse light and shadow is more gradual. Direct light falls off to shadow abruptly. Diffuse light falls off gradually to shadow.

Scrim (above left)
Spun glass (above center)
Gels (above right)

To soften light from either a direct or diffuse lighting source, a screen material called a scr*im* can be placed in front of a light. Another way of softening light is by placing sheets of *spun glass* or specially made plastic in front of a light fixture. To change the color of the light, colored gels mounted in frames can be placed in front of lighting instruments.

A fresnel

The most common type of studio light fixture that produces direct light is the *fresnel*. Fresnels are also used on location for dramatic programs and commercials, but usually not for documentaries or news.

The fresnel is relatively portable and easy to handle, A lense mounted in front of the light bulb (filiment) makes it possible to produce both direct light and diffuse light. This flexibility is

Smaller, direct lights

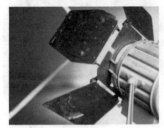

Barndoors and a flag

possible because the light's bulb (filament) can be moved closer to the lens to produce a "spotted" or direct light, or further from the lens to produce softer or more "flooded," diffuse light.

There are a variety of portable light fixtures used on location which produce direct, controllable light. These fixtures are lightweight and designed to be broken down into small, easy-to-carry units. While not as precise as the fresnel, they provide a variety of light intensities. These smaller, direct light fixtures have names such as *spots*, *moles*, *omnis*, *kickers*, and *inky-dinkies*.

The light from direct lighting instruments like fresnels or spots can be limited or more precisely controlled with devices called *barndoors* and *flags*. Barndoors have flexible flaps and fit on the front of light fixtures. They are used to restrict or block portions of the light's throw. Flags are pieces of black cloth or metal also used to restrict or block portions of light but they are not mounted directly on the lighting instrument.

Scoop (above)
broad/pan (above center)
and strips (above right)

Some common types of diffuse lighting instruments are *scoops*, *broads* (or pans), and *strips*. These lighting instruments produce flat, even light that can be used to create a bright, shadowless look. Because diffuse light is almost impossible to control, scoops, pans, and broads are normally not used for dramatic lighting designs with shadows and background areas that are darker than the foreground. Fixtures like the fresnel, which produces direct light that can be controlled, are preferred in these situations.

There are a variety of portable light fixtures which produce diffuse light. However, many experienced lighting designers prefer to create diffuse lighting designs on location by "bouncing" the light produced by direct lighting instruments off white cards, umbrellas, or walls and ceilings.

In most cases, the surface off which light is "bounced" should be white. If, for example, walls and ceilings are blue or green the "bounced" light will also be blue or green.

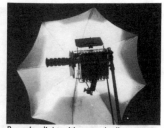
Bouncing light with an umbrella.

Light fixtures are central to any lighting system. However, a system needs more than fresnels, scoops, and broads to operate. There must also be a way to position lights at appropriate angles and heights. In the television studio, this is accomplished with a ceiling grid where lights are hung above the studio floor, out of the view of the cameras. On location and in special situations in the studio, fixtures are placed on light stands or poles. Also, lights can be hung from wall moldings, doors, or furniture by clips called *gaffer's clips*.

In addition to being hung at an appropriate angle and height, a light fixture needs to be connected to a power source. In television studios this is normally done with a system of cables and a *dimmer board*. A dimmer board is a device that varies the intensity of individual lights or groups of lights.

On location, especially in news programs and documentaries, there is usually neither the time nor opportunity to plug lights into a dimmer system. In such environments, lights are usually plugged directly into the nearest power source.

A Dimmer Board

A Basic Model of Design

A designer needs more than these tools to create effective and believable lighting. In television and film, the hardware of lighting is employed according to a basic model of how light signifies mood and atmosphere in the real world. We call this model *four point lighting*. Understanding the concept of four point lighting is the key to creatively using light in a studio or on location. Four point lighting is a way of describing the options available to the person in charge of lighting.

When lighting a three dimensional object, there are four points at which light may be directed: 1) the front left, 2) front right, 3) top back and 4) background. The two front lights are called *key* and *fill lights*.

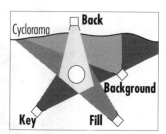

The key is the stronger of the two lights. It is called the key light because it usually indicates the direction and quality of the *primary* light source in a scene, whether it be the sun (at a high angle and bright orange) or a fireplace (at a low angle and reddish). The fill light is used to soften or completely eliminate the shadows created by the key light.

The back light serves as a rim or hair light. It casts light which outlines the hair and shoulders of subjects and helps to separate them from the background.

The light which illuminates the background is called, appropriately, the background light. This light provides clues about place and space. The background light at low intensity revealing a shelf of leather bound books tells us we are in the office of a lawyer or scholar. A bright background of rock star posters tells us we're in a teenager's bedroom.

A lighting designer may choose not to use all four points in the lighting scheme. If a subject is meant to be dramatically lit only on one side of the face, there is little or no need for fill light. If a silhouette effect is desired, all front light (key and fill) would be eliminated. Understanding that the absence of light can be as powerful as its presence is essential to an intelligent use of the four point lighting scheme.

Ideally, four-point lighting is implemented with light fixtures that limit the flow of light so that each of the four points are separate. When a designer has this kind of control, he/she can literally paint with light.

Four-point lighting principles are used in the controlled setting of the studio as well as on location where there is usually much less control. For example, in an office a subject is placed in front of a window so that the front of his face and his background is illuminated by daylight coming through a window. His hair is lighted by a spot with a blue gel in front of it.

The principles of four-point lighting also apply to scenes with more than one subject. However, if a scene has a large cast, each person in the scene will not have his or her own set of four point lighting. One light can serve more than one function. In the diagram to the right, notice how one backlight or one key light is used for three and four subjects. Also, note how many of the key lights serve two functions. Light #3, for example, is a key light for two subjects and a backlight for two other subjects.

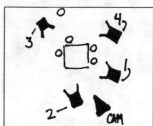

There is a difference in the way four-point lighting principles are employed in programs shot television style compared to those shot film style. Film style allows a more precise application of four-point lighting design because each shot is handled separately. Lights can be adjusted each time the camera or talent's position changes.

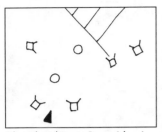
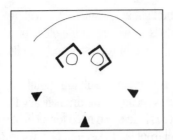

Film-style Lighting in *Bergen* (above) and Television-style Blocking in *In the Valley* (right)

Shooting television style requires a more general approach because the same lighting must be used for more than one camera or talent position.

Notice, above, how many camera positions the lighting designs for the studio portion of *In The Valley* must cover. On the other hand, the scene from *Bergen* in the bowling alley will be produced one shot at a time and the lighting for this scene can be changed every time the camera is moved.

Coach Interview using bounced light (above) and *Bergen* "lit" with white card (above right).

In the interview with the coach in his office, above left, the videographer and his assistant used bounced light and one direct back light to light the scene.

In this scene from *Bergen*, above right, the lighting designer did not need to use any artificial light. He simply bounced existing day light off a white card in the direction of the actor to create their lighting design.

Light is a powerful communicator when manipulated purposively. It gives indications about the mood and atmosphere of a scene. It can create a sense of space: the inside of a cathedral, the cramped confines of a jail cell. It provides clues about how an audience should respond to a scene: bright, evenly lit scenes suggest comedy and lightheartedness while dark, shadowy ones suggest a more serious or even ominous mood. Light can penetrate the human mind and soul and reflect whatever psychological or spiritual state it finds there. Remember the gloomy interiors inhabited by the characters in *Psycho*. Remember the radiant sunshine theme throughout the *Downy Sunrinse Dryer Sheets* commercial.

TCR 07:03:47:16

Chapter 11

Sound

The elements of the sound tracks of the three programs we are following are collected throughout the production process. But the final, "mixed" tracks are not completed until the last stages of production.

For example, most of the sounds of the explosion at the refinery at Hartsville, the sirens of fire engines rushing to the scene, and the comments of rescue workers that are part of the final sound track of *The Company Responds* are recorded at different times and places than the pictures that these sounds accompany. In fact, during most of the editing process the director/editor works with the sounds and pictures separately. First she edits a silent picture; then she organizes all the elements of the sound track on separate reels of audio tape. After the producer/writer approves her editing plans, she mixes the sound elements together and adds them to the picture.

The sound tracks of three scenes of the documentary on Coach Roberts for *In The Valley* feature play-by-play descriptions of the game. They also contain comments by the coach and two of his players, music and narration. All of these sound elements are recorded after the footage of the game is shot. They are mixed together into the finished sound track during editing.

MIXING   *Sync* sound or *synchronous* sound is a term used to describe the sounds recorded at the same time a program's pictures are recorded. The sync elements of the sound track of *Bergen*, the words spoken by the actors on camera, are edited along with the picture. However, sound effects, music and voice-overs are recorded long after the shooting and editing of the picture are completed. Then, the director, working closely with his sound designers, an editor, and a music composer, decides how the elements of the different parts of the sound track are mixed together into one balanced, composite track.

This activity is normally done in a sound studio where the edited picture with sync sound is played on a videotape recorder which is interlocked with a multi-track audio recorder. When two machines are interlocked, they start at the same time and run at exactly the same speed. Interlocking is done with *SMPTE* time code, an eight digit numbering system which is electronically coded on video and audio tape. This code indicates hours, minutes, seconds, and frames (thirty frames of video per second). An instrument called a *time code synchronizer reader* on both the videotape recorder and the multi-track audio recorder "reads" the two identical time codes and, thereby, keeps the two machines interlocked or in sync.

To produce a mixed sound track, the sound engineer (under the supervision of the producer, director or sound designer) records the different elements of a program's sound track onto the multi-track recorder. Each element of sound (sync sound of each speaker, music, sound effects, ambience, roomtone, etc.) is recorded onto a separate audio track at the *precise* position where the sound will eventually be heard in the program.

For example, when a sound effect of a car is called for at SMPTE time code 01:11:05:01 (1 hour, 11 minutes, 5 seconds, and 1 frame), the sound engineer rolls the multi track audio recorder to this point and records the sound effect on one track of the multi-track recorder. The same is done for every other element of the sound track.

After all the elements of the track are recorded onto the multi-track recorder, they are played back through a sound mixing console and mixed and balanced into a composite sound track.

Most television sound tracks are created long after scenes are shot and edited. Some exceptions are sporting events, news and quiz shows, and interview/discussion programs which are produced "live" or "live-on-tape." The sound for such programs is recorded and mixed at the same time as the rest of the program.

Like the sound tracks of single camera programs, sound tracks of multi camera programs are kept separate until the program is produced. The sound engineer, working with the director, prepares music, sound effects, and narration on reel-to-reel audio tape, cartridge or compact disc. He or she also selects the appropriate microphones for the "live" or "live-on-tape" portions of the program. Then, during the production, again under the supervision of the director, the sound engineer blends all the elements of the sound track together.

There are no simple formulas to determine how many elements of music, voice, sound effects, roomtone, or ambience a sound track should contain at any one moment. There are times when one element is all that is required, or even when silence is most appropriate. There are other instances when a very dense sound track, filled with as many as twenty different elements of sound, is appropriate.

The sound tracks of both *In The Valley* and *The Company Responds*, will contain four elements—ambience, two voice tracks and a music track. The sound track for *Bergen* will have ten voice tracks, two ambient tracks, three music tracks and three sound effects tracks for a total of eighteen elements.

MICROPHONES   A key step in the creation of a sound track for both single and multi camera is selecting appropriate microphones. This is usually done by the sound engineer based on the general recommendations of the producer and/or director and/or sound designer.

> *PRODUCER*
> *For sequence seven we'll need a highly directional shotgun and a bidirectional on a stand, plus something that can handle the higher frequencies. His kid plays this flute-like instrument that sounds like a castrated clarinet.*
>
> *SOUND ENGINEER*
> *How do you plan to use the bi-directional? On or off camera?*
>
> *PRODUCER*
> *On camera.*
>
> *SOUND ENGINEER*
> *Will we be moving around on this shoot?*
>
> *PRODUCER*
> *Yes. We're shooting at four locations in less than two hours, most of them outside. And wind may be a problem. It can get very blustery there.*

Producers, directors, and designers must have a basic understanding of microphone design to make recommendations to sound engineers or to select microphones themselves. The producer of *In The Valley* certainly does. His recommendations reflect his knowledge of the essential features of most microphones: pickup pattern, use, frequency response, and durability. Let's break down and analyze the above conversation as it applies to these features.

Pickup Patterns

PRODUCER
**For sequence seven we'll need a highly direc-
tional shotgun and a bidirectional on a stand**, plus
something that can handle the higher frequencies. His kid plays this
flute-like instrument that sounds like a castrated clarinet.

SOUND ENGINEER
How do you plan to use the bi-directional? On or off camera?

PRODUCER
On camera.

SOUND ENGINEER
Will we be moving around on this shoot?

PRODUCER
Yes. We're shooting at four locations in less than two hours, most
of them outside. And wind may be a problem. It can get very
blustery there.

The sensitivity of a microphone is related to its pickup pattern or
the area in which the instrument is most sensitive to sound. The
sounds that are within a microphone's pickup pattern are said
to be "on mic" while those sounds outside a microphone's
pickup pattern are described as "off mic." Some microphones
are designed to capture sound within the full 360 degrees that
surround them. Others are designed to pick up only the sounds

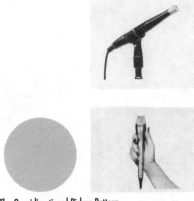

The Omnidirectional Pickup Pattern
The Bruel & Kjaer 4004 (top) and Shure SM 63 (bottom) are two commonly used omnidirectional microphones.

The Bidirectional Pickup Pattern
The Coles 4038 (top) and Neumann U 89i (bottom) are two commonly used bidirectional microphones.

that exist within specific parts of those 360 degrees.

Microphones that pick up sound within the full 360 degrees are called *omnidirectional*. For obvious reasons, *bidirectional* microphones are the type used for duets and interviews.

The narrower the pickup pattern, the more directional the microphone. *Unidirectional* pickup patterns are sensitive in only one direction. Because the majority of unidirectional microphone response patterns are shaped like a heart, unidirectional

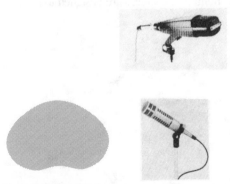

The Cardioid Pickup Pattern
The Sennheiser 421 and the Electro-Voice RE-20 are two commonly used cardioid microphones.

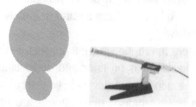

The Supercardioid Pickup Pattern
The Sennheiser 416 is a commonly used supercardioid microphone.

The Hypercardioid Pickup Pattern
The Neumann KMR 82i is a commonly used hypercardioid microphone.

microphones are usually called *cardioid microphones*.

Hyper or supercardioid microphones have more narrow and more directional pickup patterns then cardioid microphones.

Most microphones are designed with one pickup pattern, however some microphone are designed to perform with more than one pattern.

Microphone Use

PRODUCER
For sequence seven we'll need a highly directional shotgun and a bidirectional on a stand, plus something that can handle the higher frequencies. His kid plays this flute-like instrument that sounds like a castrated clarinet.

SOUND ENGINEER
**How do you plan to use the bi-directional?
On or off camera?**

PRODUCER
On camera.
SOUND ENGINEER
Will we be moving around on this shoot?

PRODUCER
Yes. We're shooting at four locations in less than two hours, most of them outside. And wind may be a problem. It can get very blustery there.

A second way to distinguish among microphones is by their use. For instance, some microphones are designed to be used on-

camera. Others are meant to be hidden or off-camera. Some microphones are designed to be hung from a stand or a mount; others are designed to be held.

Examples of on-camera microphones are those seen in the hands of journalists on location, or on floor and desk stands during studio talk shows, and in front of singers in concerts.

The most common type of hidden microphones are tiny instruments that can be disguised as pins or tie-tacs or concealed under scarves and neckties.

Hidden microphones are often "wireless"; that is, their signal is transmitted to the audio console by a tiny FM radio transmitter. Wireless microphones have the obvious advantage of freeing the talent from the constraints of an audio cable.

Off-camera microphones are positioned out of camera view, usually on a boom stand or a boom pole. Microphones held at camera level and pointed directly at the speaker in the same way a gun is pointed at a target are called *shotgun* microphones.

The PZM is another type of off-camera microphone. PZMs are attached to flat surfaces like tables, walls and floors and transmit the sound which resonates from the surface on which they are attached.

Frequency Response

A third way of describing a microphone concerns its frequency response. For example, some microphones respond well to the frequency range of the human voice and do not respond as well to frequencies out of this range. Others pick up the higher or "brighter" frequencies of, for example, a clarinet and do not respond well to those that produce "darker" or basser tones.

Some microphones are designed with additional elements to filter or cut out specific types of sounds. For example, *pop* or *blast filters* protect from sound distortion, overload, or explosive pops. Wind screens which fit over microphones are commonly used to filter blowing sounds caused by wind or breathing.

Bass roll-off filters are also important accessories which neutralize unwanted bass tones or distortions from placing a microphone too close to a sound source.

Durability

The fourth way of describing microphones is by their durability. This quality is especially important when shooting on location. A microphone may have the appropriate pickup pattern, be designed for the right on- or off-camera use, and have just the right tone quality for the scene to which it is assigned, but if it breaks in transit, it is of no use. Some microphones are too sensitive to movement and change in temperature to be used outside a studio.

A microphone's durability is directly related to the way it is constructed. The essential element of a microphone is its *diaphragm*. When attacked by a sound wave, the diaphragm vibrates. These vibrations are converted to electrical current which is carried through cables or transmitted by radio to an audio console. From there, they are distributed to video or audiotape and eventually to television sets where electricity is reconverted back to sound waves.

How a microphone's diaphragm is constructed will determine its durability. For instance, a *ribbon microphone* is a type of instrument with a thin, metal ribbon for a diaphragm. This type of diaphragm produces a very pleasing, mellow sound but is very sensitive and can break easily. They, therefore are more commonly used in studios than on location.

Condenser microphone design consists of two parallel metal plates, one moves and one is stationary. The movable plate is connected to the diaphragm. An electronic charge is generated between the two plates. When the diaphragm moves, the electronic change varies and, thereby, translates the movement of the diaphragm to electrical energy which can be amplified for broadcast or stored on audio or videotape. This type of microphone generally produces very high quality sound and is commonly used in studios. However, most are too sensitive for location work.

Dynamic microphones (or moving coil microphones) have diaphragms made of metal coils. For most purposes, the dynamic microphone is the more durable instrument and is, therefore, the most commonly used for location shooting—especially documentary production where equipment's durability is often put to a test.

For the studio portion of *In The Valley*, the director requests unidirectional microphones on stands to be used on-camera plus an off-camera boom mic. The sound for the majority of the documentary scenes will be recorded with a shotgun fitted with a wind screen.

The director of *The Company Responds* asks his sound engineer for a unidirectional microphone with wind screen on a boom for the on-camera presentations of the CEO and a tie-tac for the scene of the technical director at Hartsville. He will use a unidirectional microphone also on a boom but without wind screen for the studio segment of the program.

The director of *Bergen* requests two unidirectional microphones on booms and three radio tie-tacs for the actors. He also tells the sound engineer how important it is to get "clean" ambience. To make sure this happens, the sound engineer plans to use a PZM type microphone to pick up ambience and roomtone.

MICROPHONE PLACEMENT AND AMBIENT SOUND

Microphone placement can affect the way we perceive sound in the same way that camera angle and composition affect how we perceive a picture. A microphone placed near a speaker provides an intimate sound quality comparable to the feeling produced by a close-up. The feeling of a long shot is enhanced by placing a microphone some distance from the speaker.

When the microphone is away from the speaker, the ambience or background noise can be heard more clearly than when the microphone is close. Ambient sound can be used to advantage. The sounds of rushing waves on a stormy beach or the rumble of traffic on a crowded street corner or the chirping birds outside a kitchen window can do as much as set, props, and lights to create a sense of place.

Ambient sound can also add authenticity or believability to what is seen. An interview in front of a factory will seem much more authentic if the noise of the factory is mixed into the sound track. A scene of a criminal breaking into a car on a city street will be more interesting if the sound of police sirens are part of the sound track. If the sirens are loud, it will suggest help is on the way. If barely audible, the suggestion will be that the criminal will not be caught in the act. Adding such atmosphere is often referred to as "sweetening" the sound track.

Ambient sound or roomtone (the tones or sounds of location settings) should always be collected immediately before or after a scene is shot. This extra ambient sound is usually added to the sound track during editing or mixing. The addition of a consistent, uninterrupted additional track of ambience or roomtone will "bury" the sound changes that may be heard every time there is an edit within a scene. For example, in a scene shot in a factory, the background noise changes every time there is a shot change. This calls attention to the way the scene is edited and makes the scene seem jumpy and poorly edited. When an uninterrupted track of ambient sound of the factory is added, the scene appears to flow more smoothly.

Sound effects collections are another source of ambience sound. They can be especially useful for production teams who shoot in a studio or on a sound stage where there is no ambient sound. During mixing, after scenes are shot and edited, the sound effects of traffic or chirping birds can be added to sound tracks.

Another way to collecting ambient sound is through *folley*

sound stages where visual portions of a program are shown on a screen in a sound studio while performers create ambient sounds. For example, the ambient sounds of a fight scene in a restaurant are added after a scene is shot and edited. Two folley artist watch the scene in a sound studio. They are surrounded by pots and pans. When an actor on screen is thrown across the room, hitting his head on a row of pots that fall to the floor, the folley artist in the sound studio hits the wall with two pots then drops them to the ground creating dramatic ambient sounds in sync with the action on screen.

The purpose of a sound track is to help communicate the content of the script. Ideally this is done by complimenting, not duplicating what the program's pictures show. When a scene in *The Company Responds* shows houses on fire near the refinery, it is unnessary for a narrator to say, "The explosion at the refinery started these fires." The viewer can figure this out. On the other hand, it is appropriate for a narrator to tell the viewer the extent of the damage and if there were any injuries. This is information the pictures do not convey.

Music, like narration, can be too obvious and not allow the viewer to figure things out for him/herself. In a scene in *Bergen*, the protagonist and his high school girlfriend meet for the first time in nine years at a local bar. When they meet, they look deep into one another's eyes showing they are still very much in love. After reading the scene the sound designer suggests using romantic music with the scene.

No, never. We're not going for laughs here.

SOUND DESIGNER
Then what do you suggest?

DIRECTOR
I think the sounds of a game on the television set in the bar would work well. It contrasts nicely with the scene and adds energy and pace.

The sound tracks for *In the Valley* and *The Company Responds* do not contain such dramatic contrasts. For example, the music track for *In The Valley* is a bright jazz number which works very well with the upbeat opening and closing sequences. The music in *The Company Responds* is borrowed from the company's commercials. It seems to be a good choice because it has a modern, "hi-tech" quality. Also, it connects the videotape to Mammoth's national advertising campaign.

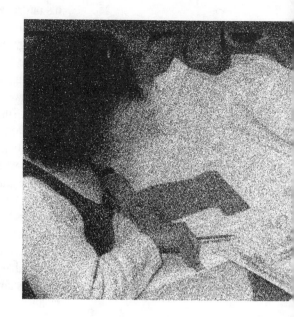

Chapter 12

Costumes

Costumes are important to television productions because clothing which will be worn for a program should satisfy some basic character and technical requirements. It's obvious that what someone wears should be suitable for the context and personality of the character they represent. Formal attire affirms formal relationships and settings; informal dress suggests a casual mood and atmosphere. What a character wears can give clues about social class and economic status. Older persons usually are dressed differently than younger. For example, when Dan Rather took over the anchor spot from Walter Chronkite, CBS spent considerable time and money to determine the style and color of his on-camera costume. Without just the right sweater or tie, it was felt the younger, more aggressive Rather might not appeal to the program's older, more conservative target audience.

The technical requirements of costumes for television are not quite so obvious. Highly reflective materials in clothing and flashy jewelry can sometimes cause problems with contrast within a scene. They can create distracting "hot spots" or a "blooming," washed out look of the area immediately surrounding the offending object.

So, when possible, costumes worn for television should be carefully planned or designed. However, only the director of *Bergen* has a costume designer on her staff. The other two directors have to take care of this important production element themselves.

The director of *In The Valley*, for example, meets with a fashionable downtown clothier who provides a casual, open shirt costume for the news anchor who will host the show. The clothier does this in exchange for a credit at the end of the program. He also knows that once the program becomes a regular series, he will have the opportunity to show off a new outfit each week.

The producer/writer of *The Company Responds* is also concerned with costume design. He writes a memo to the CEO's office describing what the CEO should wear for the taping next week.

TO: Barbara Jones, Office of the CEO
From: Cliff Kaplan, Media Center

Here are our suggestions for the CEO's dress for the videotaping sessions next week.

For the shoot outside the refinery Longberry she should wear a raincoat with a scarf with red and blue stripes.

For the final scene inside the refinery she should be in a tan or brown suit, off white blouse with a simple necklace which is not highly polished and does not reflect too much light.

Please have her bring these outfits in the day before the shoot so we can make sure they look good on camera.

Thanks.

In addition to this memo, the producer/writer calls Frank Bush in Hartsville and Robert Alberton's agent in Los Angeles. He asks Bush to wear a light brown jacket, blue shirt and solid colored tie for his taping session. Bush has the coat and shirt but all of his ties are patterned. The producer/writer tells him not to worry. "We'll bring the tie." Richard Alberton's agent in Los Angeles is told that Alberton should wear a conservative blue suit, white shirt and solid maroon tie to his videotaping session.

At their first meeting, the director of *Bergen* and the costume designer she has hired discuss the "look" of the clothing for the film's main characters.

> DIRECTOR
> I want the son to wear those baggy corporate suits with button down collars and wing tip shoes while his father wears work boots and plaid, wool shirts. His mother is a cross between the two. She is fashion conscious to a degree. She might wear a colorful scarf or sweater with work jeans and work boots.

Ten days later the costume designer brings the following
sketches to her meeting with the director.

Chapter 13

Graphics

The opening and closing sequences of all three programs (*In The Valley*, *Bergen*, and *The Company Responds*) use electronic graphics for titles and credits. The words of the titles move around the screen, change colors and even shape. At the end of *Bergen* the credits are designed to appear to roll from the bottom of the screen to the top while those for *In the Valley* appear to pop out of doors and windows of stylized drawings of local landmarks. There are no credits at the end of *The Company Responds*; only the Mammoth Company logo which is an animated representation of a drop of oil rising through the ground and transforming into a large "M" in bright neon red against a cloudless sky.

The equipment used to produce all of this graphic magic can cost hundreds of thousands of dollars. But graphics for television can also be produced with relatively inexpensive personal computers and "off the shelf" software, provided the final computer images can be integrated into the video image. Those who use this equipment must be skilled in both graphic design and computer technology.

Some producers choose to purchase the services of "out of house" production companies that specialize in graphics rather than invest in systems and personnel to do the work themselves. This is the case at the media center at Mammoth Corporation where *The Company Responds* is being produced. The animated company logo which appears at the end of all its videos was designed and produced by a graphics company for Mammoth three years ago. On the other hand, WORK-TV, where *In The Valley* is being made, has the equipment and technicians to produce complicated, animated graphics themselves.

In order to demonstrate to either an "out of house" graphics company or to an "in house" technician what they want, producers, directors, and graphic artists sketch out their designs in storyboard form long before they are produced and incorporated in the program. The storyboard for *In The Valley* is prepared by the staff graphic artist at WORK-TV. He sketches these after reading the script, and discussing the general look of

the program with the producer, directors, and set designer. They all agree that the concept of approaching Landcaster from outer space is the desired effect of the opening sequence and leaving Landcaster for space the theme of the closing sequence.

The graphics needed within *The Company Responds* are designed to look like those seen on a network news program. The producer believes this approach will help reinforce some of the statistical information cited in the program, as well as communicate the seriousness of the program. The storyboards for these sequences are not as complete as those for *In the Valley*. They are sketched by the program's assistant director who, obviously, does not have the same skills as the graphic artist at WORK-TV. But the ideas and designs they represent will quickly be made to look very professional when entered into the "TV Paint" software program which the producer/writer has on the computer in his office.

While the sketches for the *In The Valley* sequences contain more details than the story board for *The Company Responds*, both sets of storyboards do their jobs. They provide an idea of what is envisioned.However, they do not give a sense of what can be done with color and three dimensional rendering. Throughout production, there are many conversations between those who designed the graphics and those who produced them. Some of these discussions take place over the phone and some in front of video monitors containing examples of how the graphics might be produced.

The resulting graphic sequences for the two programs certainly look like the original storyboards. However, they also contain some new elements which were discovered during the production process.

The graphics for *Bergen* are discussed in much more general terms in the early stages in the production process than those for *In The Valley* and *The Company Responds*. The director of *Bergen* knows she wants to begin with opening credits over Bergen driving down the freeway with the music of Willie Nelson in the background and she hires a graphic designer to produce sketches of how this might be done. The designer offers three versions of how this opening sequence might look.

These storyboards will help the director and the director of photography to plan how the opening sequence will be shot. However, the director will not make a final decision about the precise design of the graphics until the opening scene is edited. She approaches the closing graphics the same way. She will not decide on a design until the movie is completed. However, she considers superimposing the closing credits over the headlines and newspaper photo announcing the union has purchased the factory in Bergen's hometown. The director requests her graphic designer to sketch this out so she can get an idea of the feasibility of this design.

In most production environments there are essentially two ways to produce graphics: by hand and with computers. By far the most common technology today is the computer. But a graphic artist can draw or paint imaginative and eye-catching designs that are more distinctive than those done on a computer. No matter what the technology, however, the same principles apply when designing and producing graphics.

The first design principle concerns the amount of information that actually reaches a viewer's television screen after the picture is processed through the camera and the transmitting or recording/playback equipment. Only about two-thirds of the total television image reaches the viewer because the size of the picture picked up by the camera is larger than what the viewer eventually sees. The portion of image that is reproduced on the screen is said to be within the "essential" or "safe" area. Material that falls outside this area will not be seen by the viewer. The graphic artist therefore must plan to have everything appear within this essential area of the frame.

PRINCIPLES OF DESIGN

The second principle is that the graphic artist must work with the fixed proportions of the television frame. The television screen is a rectangle with measurements in a 3:4 ratio; three units high by four units wide. This is the *aspect ratio* of television. The smallest portable television screen and the largest video projector screen have this same fixed scale of 3:4. This means designs must conform to this ratio or risk awkward reproduction on the video screen. Tall, slender designs will not fit into the television box any better than squat, stretched-out designs.

The third and most important principle is that television and film graphics usually do not stand alone. In most cases, graphics "work with" sound tracks, movement, foreground, and background. This means the viewer has a great deal more information to comprehend than just a graphic. So, when designing graphics, especially graphics with written words, designers must be careful not to overload the viewer with so much information that he/she cannot digest what is being communicated. A good rule of thumb is that there should be no more than three lines per frame, and only three words per line.

In most cases, television and film graphics are not finished by the graphic designer. In multi camera, television style production it is the director who decides where and how the graphic will be used; in single camera, film style production it is the editor, working with the director, who decides.

Graphics designs are begun by graphic artists in front of computer screens, drafting tables, and 35mm still cameras; they are completed by directors in control rooms and editors in editing suites.

UNIT 5

UNIT 5

Execution

The final stage in the production process is when all the pieces are put together. This is a time of action. General discussions about script, casting, costumes, sets, lighting, and sound are usually over at this stage and most of the production team's time and energies are dedicated to fulfilling decisions made earlier.

The team producing *In The Valley* begins the execution stage ready to shoot and edit the documentary on the coach. The team is also well prepared to produce the live, studio portion of the program.

The team responsible for *The Company Responds* enters the execution stage prepared to photograph the CEO at the Longberry refinery, the technical director in Hartsville and Richard Alberton on the studio set. When these segments are completed, they will be combined with the edited scene of footage shot the night of the explosion.

The *Bergen* production team enters the execution stage with a production book containing detailed plans to shoot at twelve different locations in fifteen days. Then, after the material is shot, their schedule allows for a month of editing and sound mixing.

Chapter 14

The Company Responds

It is ten P.M. on a Monday evening. In the media center on the fourteenth floor of Mammoth Corporate Headquarters in midtown Manhattan, the producer/writer and director of *The Company Responds* sit in the center's conference room eating Chinese take-out. As they finish the last bites of their dinners they discuss their production schedule for the next week.

PRODUCTION SCHEDULE
THE COMPANY RESPONDS
WEEK OF 4/3

4/5 Set construction
     Call CEO's office to confirm arrangements for 4/6
     Alberton flies to NYC (USAir, 443) 4:00 p.m.
     Production meeting via phone with Hugh Clark in Dallas
     about Bush sequences in Hartsville.
4/6 8:00 a.m.—   Travel to Longberry, NJ
     10:30 a.m.— Shoot CEO Sequences
     12:30 p.m.— Return to New York
     2:00 p.m.—   Shoot Alberton Sequences: Astoria, Queens
     4:30 p.m.—   Shoot Bush sequences in Hartsville
4/7 8:00 a.m.—   Off-line (rough cut) session
     2:30 p.m.—   Executive management screening
     5:00 p.m.—   Audio edit/mix
4/8 8:00 a.m.—   On-line edit
     4:00 p.m.—   Duplication (25 copies)
     6:00 p.m.—   Distribution first 25—Overnight Priority
                  Ov/Nt Duplication (120 copies)
4/9 9:00 a.m.—   Distribution of remaining 120 copies—next business
                  day delivery.
     Noon—   Follow-up strategy meeting/post mortem 11th floor
                  conference room. Lunch served.

PRODUCER/WRITER
I think the best way to handle things is for you to take care of the shoot Wednesday in Longberry. I'll stay here and take care of loose ends. Then we'll meet in Astoria for the studio segment with Alberton.

DIRECTOR
I don't mind doing Longberry but will the CEO be upset? She's never worked with me.

PRODUCER/WRITER
In many ways it will be easier for you to handle her… you're an outsider. She won't try to push you around.

The producer/writer is referring to the last two stages of the three-stage editing process: on-line editing and sound mixing. The first stage is off-line editing.

EDITING

Off-line Editing

Off-line is normally done on relatively inexpensive and easy to operate editing equipment which performs simple, straight cut sound and picture edits.

On this type of straight cut editing equipment there is one videotape machine that plays back and one machine that records. Edits are made by selecting a section of videotape on the playback machine and recording it onto a videotape on the record machine. Many straight cut editing consoles have audio equipment like cassette, reel-to-reel tape decks, and CD's connected to them. This allows the editor to add sound from sources other than the videotape on the playback machine.

Off-line editing is normally performed on duplicates of camera originals or first generation tapes. These duplicates usually have burned-in SMPTE time code, meaning that the eight-digit number which indicates hour, minutes, seconds, and frames is superimposed on the picture, making it easy to read during editing and viewing of rough cuts.

There are two categories of edits: assembly and insert. To understand the differences between the two, one needs to know that the signal recorded on a videotape contains as many as six separate types of electronic information: a control track, an image, as many as four channels of audio, and SMPTE time code.

An assembly edit is one in which all elements of a videotape are transferred or edited from one videotape to another—from the playback machine to the record machine. An insert edit is one in which there is the option to edit a selection of the contents of a videotape into another. An editor may choose to use the picture and all the sound tracks of a videotape or may choose to use just the picture and only one of the sound tracks. In other instances, the editor may use all the sound tracks and not the picture. For example, in the opening montage of The Company Responds the editor combines shots of the explosion at the Hartsville refinery from one tape with the voices of rescue workers from another tape with an insert edit. Later, the editor uses a shot of the Hartsville fire chief speaking, then replaces the shot of the fire chief with fire engines arriving at the site of the explosion. This kind of editing cannot be done with assembly editing because sound and picture cannot be separated.

Assembly editing is used for very simple editing and for copying or dubbing sections of programs. Because it gives the editor much more flexibility, most editing is done in the insert mode.

Before a tape will accept an insert edit, it must have a control track. A control track serves the same function as sprocket holes in film. The control track contains electronic pulses that keep the videotape stable and running at a constant speed. An assembly edit includes the control track; an insert edit does not.

Blacking a tape is the normal process of "laying down" a control track. Before editing, an editor records or lays down black onto the record tape—the tape onto which the program will be edited.

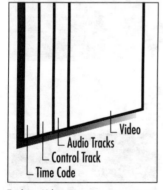

Tracks on Videotape

In most instances, sound and picture quality are not important when off-line editing. What is important is that the editor and other members of the production team see and hear the edited tape well enough to determine if the order and length of shots and sounds are appropriate. For example, at the executive management screening scheduled for 4/7, a rough cut will be shown to upper management to get their approval of the project before on-line editing begins. At the meeting, the Executive Vice President and a representative from the CEO's office will view grainy video images with dropout, burned in SMPTE time code and an imperfect sound track. Because these executives have viewed rough cuts before, they know that the final product will not have any of these problems. They ignore the grain, dropout, burned in time code, and muffled sound track and concentrate on how well the program tells the company's point of view of the Hartsville tragedy.

On-Line Editing

By contrast, on-line editing is when the quality of picture, sound, and transitions are the primary concerns. This is the time when the finished product is produced, not a time of experimentation or testing. On-line editing leads to finished products meant to be viewed by audiences who would be distracted by poor technical quality.

Ideally, on-line editing is performed with A-B editing systems which allow the editor to do more than insert and assembly edit.

On-line, A-B systems usually contain equipment which makes it possible to key graphics into a program, perform special effects transitions, dissolve from one shot or sound to another, and to change color and contrast. On-line editing suites also usually include equipment which allows the editor to control sound quality and do limited sound mixing.

To prepare for on-line editing, editors produce edit decision lists which are based on the decisions made during off-line editing. Each sound and picture edit is precisely listed on paper or typed into a computer.

Time Code	Edit No.	Description
02:04	8	Kristie stabs
10:50	9	Zack squeals
13:43	10	Vaughn runs up
20:21	11	CU John bleeds
34:37	12	Logan jumping

Some editing systems are operated manually. That is, the editor makes each edit. Others are computer controlled. After the "in" and "out" points of each edit are typed into a computer, edits are made automatically.

Sound Mixing

Sound mixing is the third and last step in the editing process. Complicated sound mixes are usually performed in sound houses, specialized production houses where separate sound elements are balanced, equalized, and mixed together into a composite sound track. However, simple sound mixes with three or four elements can be created in on-line editing suites. After the picture portion of a program is edited, sound tracks can be mixed in with audio insert edits. For example, in the opening scene of The Company Responds, after the visual portion of the scene are edited, the audio editor inserts a mixed track containing ambient sounds and the voice of the CEO.

Editing can be a very creative activity. The work of the editor is certainly as important as that of the videographer and the sound person. And sometimes the editor plays a more important role than the other production team members. There are many examples of scenes that can convey very different impressions depending on how the editor does his or her job. A good example of this is a scene of the night of the fire and explosion at Hartsville.

#1 LS refinery bursting into flames
#2 CU worker A looking up in shock
#3 CU of worker B running for cover
#4 MS wooden frame house with sand box and tricycle in front yard, faces of worried children in window seen in background.
#5 MS worker B with fire behind him making phone call.
#6 MLS Mammoth fire trucks rush onto the screen
#7 MLS of children
#8 CU fire being extinguished

This sequence gives the impression that the courage and dedication of Mammoth workers kept families safe in the community near the refinery. If, for example, the director/editor had not included shots #4 and #7 a very different impression might have been created. The viewer would not have been reminded how children living in the nearby community were threatened by the explosion.

EXECUTION: THE COMPANY RESPONDS

It is nine A.M., two days before the final product is scheduled to be duplicated and sent out to all the regional offices, the producer/writer sits in front of a television monitor in the midtown offices of Graphic Productions Inc., the company producing the thirty-second opening graphic sequences for The Company Responds. Next to the producer/writer is one of the three owners of the company, who worked on the graphics every day last week. She is trying to hide her frustration. She thought she was done yesterday when she sent a copy of the opening and closing graphic sequences to the producer/writer at Mammoth. She was very surprised when he called this morning to say the graphics were unacceptable and that he was on his way to her office to explain in-person what he wants.

> *PRODUCER/WRITER*
> *We're close but it's too slow for the foreground. And it doesn't look enough like the opening of a national news program. What if you begin with a map of the U.S. under the Mammoth logo.*
>
> *GRAPHIC PRODUCTIONS CO-OWNER*
> *That's easy enough to do. (SHE TURNS TO HER COMPUTER AND MOMENTS LATER, THE SCREEN FILLS WITH A MAP OF THE U.S.) How's this?*
>
> *PRODUCER/WRITER*
> *That's sort of what I'm looking for . . . but not quite.*

Thirty miles away the director sits in the front seat of a mini-van as it speeds down the New Jersey Turnpike toward Longberry, New Jersey. The driver is a production assistant who is part of the four-person crew hired for the day by Mammoth. The other three members of the team, the videographer, the sound person, and Q-TV or teleprompter operator, are in the back seat. Behind them is their equipment. The van exits and follows the signs to the refinery. As they approach the front offices of the sprawling complex, they notice a stretch limousine.

> *DIRECTOR*
> *I hope that's not the CEO. She's not supposed to be here for another hour.*

Back in Manhattan, at 11:00 A.M., the producer/writer leaves Graphic Productions Inc. with a videotape containing new opening and closing graphics. He is very pleased. When he gets back to his office he finds a message from the free-lance videographer

hired to shoot Frank Bush in Texas. The message reads:
"URGENT. CALL IMMEDIATELY."

VIDEOGRAPHER
To be blunt, Bush is a disaster on camera. He can't read the teleprompter, he can't remember his lines and he can't ad lib. Got any suggestions?

PRODUCER/WRITER
This is Bush's first time on camera. He thinks his career is riding on how well he performs. Also, you may be rushing him. Not giving him the time he needs.

VIDEOGRAPHER
No way... I couldn't be more patient.

PRODUCER/WRITER
Relax. I'll talk to him... then get back to you in twenty minutes.

VIDEOGRAPHER
This is not my specialty. Can't you be here?.

PRODUCER/WRITER
No. Too much going on here. I'll get back to you in twenty minutes.

VIDEOGRAPHER
I should charge you double for this.

At the Longberry refinery, the director meets with the CEO and her assistant.

DIRECTOR
Ms. Warren, nice to see you this morning. I hope you're not expecting us to be ready for you until 10:30. That's the scheduled time and it will take us at least an hour to set up.

> *CEO*
> *We're here early for a meeting.*
>
> *ASSISTANT*
> *Ms. Warren will be available at 10:15, we'll need to move the videotaping up a few minutes. She has to be back in Manhattan earlier than expected. Where do you want us to be at 10:15?*
>
> *DIRECTOR*
> *Ah, we'll get to you. Where will you be?*
>
> *ASSISTANT*
> *In the plant manager's office.*

The director counts to ten, takes a deep breath, and wonders where to place the CEO's scene in the short time she and her crew have to set up. As she considers her options, a young man approaches and introduces himself, "I'm from the manager's office. What do you need?"

> *DIRECTOR*
> *A miracle. . . . I need a place with a good view of heavy refining equipment Ideally, inside. That will keep the noise down.*

The young man from the plant manager's office takes the director and the crew to two sites: a room just inside the main entrance and an executive office on the second floor. Both are available and both have views of heavy equipment and are quiet. Without hesitation, the director chooses the room near the main entrance. Its ceilings are two feet higher than the other room, has one window and is dark. The office upstairs has two wall-sized windows, is very bright, and has a low ceiling.

The higher ceilings and limited light in the room will make it much easier for the director and her crew to get the kind of lighting they need. The bright daylight coming into the room through the two wall-sized windows upstairs would have to be covered before a controlled lighting design could be created. In the downstairs room, because there are high ceilings, a back light can be clipped to the ceiling on the frames holding the acoustical tiles. This back light will separate the CEO from the background. In the smaller room upstairs this could not be done because the ceilings are too low. In the larger room light fixtures can be placed far enough away from the CEO so that the distance will diffuse some of their intensity and, thereby, lessen the number of unpleasant hot spots on the subject and her background. The different color temperatures of the tungsten light coming from the light fixtures and the daylight coming from the window can be dealt with very easily by placing an orange gel over the one window in the larger room. Changing the color temperature of the daylight in the smaller room upstairs would be more difficult.

Having decided how to light the room, the director and crew set up their cameras, lights, microphone, and a teleprompter before the CEO is scheduled to appear. The director and the videographer have a quick meeting to discuss how to light the scene and where to place the camera. She is especially concerned that the camera be placed so the heavy equipment in the background is clearly seen.

DIRECTOR
What about beginning on the smoke here and you can then pan into a medium shot.

VIDEOGRAPHER
It could work. But I think you'd be better off with her walking into frame and then dollying in from over there near the door. You know like those new Ford ads.

DIRECTOR
I see what you mean. I think that will work as long as you begin with the smoke in the background. That's very strong and will cut nicely with what comes before.

While the director and the videographer make their final plans, the sound person sets up a shotgun microphone and lavaliere microphones. She will be prepared to use either one, depending on what the director decides. The teleprompter operator quickly sets up his gear and makes sure it is working. He inserts a computer disk containing the CEO's script and runs it through at the speed he expects the director will want.

It is l0:05, ten minutes until everything has to be set up and tested. The production assistant is outside taping the orange gel to the outside of the window.

The sound person has a pair of headsets on and is speaking into the lavaliere microphone, the one the director has decided to use. The teleprompter operator's gear is next to the camera, ready to go into action at the push of a button. The CEO's first sentence is on top of the screen.

The videographer points his camera at a PA who is "standing in" for the CEO. Then the director turns her attention to a small television monitor and a waveform monitor. The television set is useful because it contains a color image of what the camera photographs; the camera's view finder has only a black and white picture. The waveform monitor contains a graphic display of the electronic signal which helps the videographer determine if there is adequate light, if the iris is adjusted properly, and if there are any hot spots. For example, he notices a "spike" which represents a hot spot on the waveform monitor right where the CEO will stand. He tells the production assistant to "flag" the key light, which solves the problem.

The director notes that it's just about time to send for the CEO. But before she does, she asks the crew if they are ready to begin taping.

VIDEOGRAPHER
As soon as I record a quick test.

AUDIO PERSON
Mic's working. All we have to do is pin it on her.

TELEPROMPTER
I ran the script down. I'm ready.

DIRECTOR
Then, Bobby, run down to the manager's office and tell her ladyship we are ready for her.

At l0:20, the CEO is in front of the camera and reads from the teleprompter.

CEO
"Those images from the Hartsville explosion are ones I hope we will never see again. The deaths of Mammoth employees Tom Bradley and Connie Wigham and the two Hartsville firemen, Bruce Long and Adam Goldberg, are tragic losses which I deeply regret...."

DIRECTOR
That's very good. You look very natural. But try speaking to the lens as if you are talking to just one person, not a group.

CEO
It would be easier, if that thing...

DIRECTOR
The teleprompter?

CEO
That thing was closer.

DIRECTOR
No problem.

The CEO reads the script from beginning to end but still does not project in the way the director suggested.

> **DIRECTOR**
> *Ah, that's better! But, Ms. Warren, can we try something? Imagine that you are meeting with one employee who saw the news last night. He's convinced that another fire could break out where he works. He's been told we have very sloppy safety standards.*
>
> **CEO**
> *I'm not an actress.*
>
> **DIRECTOR**
> *I know. All I want is that you talk to one employee who is scared about losing his job and getting seriously injured.*

At 11:30, after the tenth take, the director sighs deeply and shouts, "That's it...check the tape." The videographer plays back the last take and looks at it on the monitor and through the waveform monitor. At the same time the audio person listens to the sound through his headsets. Both indicate it is fine.

> **DIRECTOR**
> *Thank you, Ms. Warren...we're done. Sorry to have kept you longer than planned but I think it was worth it. Your final take is very strong.*

"It takes more than I thought," the CEO says with a slight smile before moving on to her next meeting. After she leaves, the director turns to her crew.

> **DIRECTOR**
> *Nice job! We're just about done but, before we have lunch, make sure you record five minutes or so of room tone here and another five outside and let's get a couple of pick-up shots just to play it safe.*

The room tone the director refers to is the ambiance or sound of the room where the scene was shot and the general sounds of the refinery. These will be added to the pictures during editing. The CEO's performance will appear much more authentic with the hum of the machinery from the refinery in the background. The "pick up" shots the director refers to are shots of storage tanks, intricate piping, and the Mammoth and the American flags waving in the wind together. These might be used to introduce the scene or to intercut throughout the CEO's scene.

Back in New York, the producer/writer hangs up the phone after a long conversations with Frank Bush, the director of technical services in Hartsville who is reluctant to appear on camera. The producer/writer assures Bush that the scene will not be used unless he looks and sounds credible. "If there is any chance you will appear less than competent, we'll cut your scene," he promises.

After hanging up with Bush, he calls the videographer in Texas hired to photograph Bush, and tells him to return to the refinery and Bush's office. He also suggests ways he can change Bush's attitude toward being videotaped.

PRODUCER/WRITER
Unpack the camera and microphones in the van and carry them through the building. Let everyone in his office see all the gear that is going into his office. That ought to push up his stock and make him feel important. Let him deliver his lines from the script. It will take longer to get a good take, but he told me he was not comfortable with the teleprompter.

VIDEOGRAPHER
I'll do what I can.

These phone conversations cut into the time the producer/writer has to get to the studios in Astoria. He, the director, and Richard Alberton are scheduled for a rehearsal at 2:00 PM and a taping of the Alberton scene at 3:30. Luckily, traffic is light this afternoon, so he makes the ten-mile drive in fifteen minutes.

The producer/writer and the director arrive at the studio at just about the same time. Richard Alberton and his agent are not there, which worries them. They only have two hours to shoot the scene and the studio has been booked by another client in the evening so it is impossible to reschedule if they are "no-shows."

The Astoria studios are set up for both multi and single-camera production. Each studio has a control room for live or live-on-tape production. In addition, the Astoria studios are used as sound stages. This is how the director will use the studio assigned to her. She will not direct the scene from the control room but will stay in the studio standing next to the camera while Alberton delivers his lines—if he shows up.

Earlier in the week the producer/writer called the Astoria studios and reserved two hours of studio time and all facilities and personnel needed for the Alberton scene. These requests were written into facility request forms and crew assignment sheets and forwarded to the production supervisor assigned to the project.

It is 1:50. The set in studio B is in place. The lighting designer is setting lights in accordance with the light plot used for the Mammoth television spots, which are shot on this set. Two production assistants assist him, one is high in the lighting grid, the other is at the lighting panel.

ASTORIA STUDIOS	
Request for Facilities	
Client: Mammoth Oil **Date:**	
Reservation Code: half day	

STUDIO		LIGHTING #
Television		
☒ A		☒ 3
☐ B		☒ 12
Film / Sound		☒ 2
☐ 1		☐

> LIGHTING DESIGNER (To the PA at the Lighting Panel)
> Put the fresnel in forty-three on its own dimmer.

The PA follows all the designer's instructions then fills out a light board plot which indicates what lights are connected to which dimmers. This document is very useful when the lighting designer needs to fade up or down any part of the lighting design. For example, when the designer decides that the light on the set needs to be darker, he shouts out "fade down the background lights" and the PA, using the light board plot and seeing that all background lights are connected to dimmer number four, goes to the dimmer board and fades it down.

FUNCTION	DIMME
Alberton Fill (for Camera 3)	3
Cam 1 Background	4
Cam 2 Background	4
Cam 3 Background	4
Backlight for LS	5

> **LIGHTING DESIGNER**
> Would someone stand on the set so we can check lighting. *(A PRODUCTION ASSISTANT STANDS IN THE MIDDLE OF THE SET.) (TO ANOTHER PRODUCTION ASSISTANT ON THE LIGHTING GRID.)* Flood it a little, scrim it, close the top barn door.

It is 2:00 P.M. The production supervisor notices the producer/writer and director as they walk into the studio.

> **PRODUCTION SUPERVISOR**
> I'm Sam Nassar, we spoke on the phone last week.
>
> **PRODUCER/WRITER**
> Nice to meet you. I'm Cliff Kaplan from Mammoth and this is Cat DeAngelis, our director.
>
> **DIRECTOR**
> How much more time do you need to set up and get the crew in?
>
> **PRODUCTION SUPERVISOR**
> We should be all ready to go in another fifteen minutes.
>
> **PRODUCER/WRITER**
> Our talent is flying in this morning and should be here any minute—we hope. Which way is the green room? Where can we...

Before the producer/writer can finish his sentence, a production assistant interrupts and tells them that Richard Alberton has arrived and is waiting for them in the green room. They hurry off to meet with him and begin rehearsing.

PRODUCER/WRITER
Richard, we want you to play this a little more low key than the way you present yourself in the television spots. This tape goes just to Mammoth employees and customers. So, think of your scene as a chance to speak to old friends.

DIRECTOR
Do you have any questions about the script and your movements?

ALBERTON
No, I don't, but let me read though it and you tell me if I sound Ok. "The rebuilding that Frank speaks about will affect the whole company and our activities in a number of areas—public relations, marketing and routing. In the public relations area...all wholesalers will be receiving these materials."

DIRECTOR
Ah, the delivery's not right yet. It's still a little too much on the commercial side. Can you soften it even more? Let's change the opening to you sitting on the edge of the desk. From the top please.

ALBERTON
"The rebuilding that Frank speaks about will affect the whole company...and our activities in a number of areas....."

It is 2:20 P.M. The producer/writer, director, and Alberton are about to move to studio B. But before they leave the green room, the director asks Alberton to show her the neckties he brought with him and she selects one. In the studio, the director asks Alberton to stand in the middle of the set so the camera person can frame him in close-up. The close-up appears on a television monitor in the studio and serves as a mirror for the make up artist as he combs Alberton's hair and powders his forehead. The monitor's image also helps the director and lighting designer decide if Alberton and his suit and tie are appropriate for the scene. The suit and tie pass the test; the lighting designer decides the backlight on Alberton needs to be faded up.

Once everyone is satisfied with how Alberton looks, camera and talent blocking begins.

DIRECTOR
OK, Richard I want you to walk from the edge of the set toward the camera as you deliver your lines and I want the camera to dolly from screen right to the left as he walks, ending up on a medium close up.

CAMERA OPERATOR
Got it. Ready when you are.

DIRECTOR
Ready in ten...

FLOOR MANAGER
...Ten, nine...

ALBERTON
(HE BEGINS WALKING TOWARD THE CAMERA AS HE SPEAKS.) "The rebuilding that Frank speaks about will affect the whole company... and our activities in a number of areas..."

The director wisely uses movement which best suits the small television screen. In most instances, it is more effective to have talent move from background to foreground and visa-versa instead of from left to right or right to left. Another way of describing this is by saying television movement should be executed with the Z-axis.

The dollying movement of the camera as Alberton moves forward is another way the director enriches this scene with movement. It creates a fluid movement suggesting the viewer and Alberton come upon one another. Also, it forces the viewer to pay attention to the impressive lighting and set pieces in the background suggesting Mammoth has the resources to withstand any financial problems created by the Hartsville explosion.

After Alberton walks through his entrance, the director asks the boom operator to bring the boom onto the studio floor so he, too, can rehearse.

> **DIRECTOR**
> *Let's try a run through with lines. Audio, let me know if Richard's level's are Ok. Floor manager, get me into a rehearsal please.*
>
> **FLOOR MANAGER**
> *Stand-by, in twenty seconds... this is a rehearsal... ten, nine, eight, seven, six...*
>
> **ALBERTON**
> *The rebuilding that Frank speaks about will affect the whole company...and our activities in a number of areas..."*

During the rehearsal, the producer/writer notices there is a shadow on Alberton's face created by the boom. He quietly tells the director who immediately speaks with the boom operator.

> **DIRECTOR**
> *Please reposition the boom to the right... out of the key light.*

A reflection of the producer/writer's professionalism is the way he handles this problem. Instead of speaking directly to the boom operator, he allows the director to take care of the problem. If he had done otherwise, it might appear to the crew that the producer did not have full confidence in the director.

After the third run through, the boom shadow disappears and the camera movement works perfectly with Alberton's walk. However Alberton's presentation is flawed because he is still too stiff and formal. Here is an instance when the producer intervenes directly. He feels it is important that Alberton know that he is not pleased with the performance.

> **PRODUCER/WRITER**
> *Richard, please warm up your delivery. Remember what the director said, the viewers of this tape think of you as one of them, an old friend.*

Seven takes later, and ten minutes after the two hours scheduled for the shoot, the director and producer/writer are satisfied.

DIRECTOR
That last take is right on the money. Floor manager make sure engineering has it recorded.

FLOOR MANAGER
I just got word it's fine. . . no problems.

PRODUCER/WRITER
Ok let's get the close-ups of the posters and the long shot of the set then we can strike. We're only ten minutes behind schedule. Thank you Richard, it was great working with you.

Early the next morning, the producer/writer pops his head into the editing suite where the director is preparing to finish the rough cut which is scheduled to be shown at noon to the CEO, and the Executive Vice President.

PRODUCER/WRITER
Cat, I had a thought last night. I want you to add three or four of those very dramatic shots of the flames destroying homes near the refinery to the opening and closing montages. Any problem doing that?

DIRECTOR
I can do it easily enough, but why?

PRODUCER/WRITER
For now I am going to say, because I am the boss.

The director finishes the rough cut with the additional shots of burning homes in three hours. At 11:50, she and the producer/writer are in the elevator on their way to the executive conference room on the thirtieth floor.

They are both nervous about the meeting. If the executives do not approve the rough cut they will not be able to do the on-line editing scheduled at a post production house that afternoon. And if the on-line editing is not completed by 8:00 P.M. then it will be impossible to make duplications for overnight express delivery later tonight. Unless the tapes go out tonight, they will not be on the desks of the twenty-five regional executives who are expecting them tomorrow morning.

The director breaks the silence.

> DIRECTOR
> Don't you think we overdid it with all those shots of burning buildings? It makes it look like all of Texas burned that night. I know they are going to ask us to change that.
>
> PRODUCER/WRITER
> I hope you're right.
>
> DIRECTOR
> Then why did you ask me to put it in?
>
> PRODUCER/WRITER
> They need something to tell us to do. We're making it easy for them. And even easier for us.

This elevator arrives on the thirtieth floor. "This is not the first time you've done this," the director remarks as they exit and walk toward the conference room.

They are the first to arrive, which gives them a chance to put the videotape with the rough cut into a playback unit at the front of the room. The executives enter and take their places. The producer/writer asks if they are ready. They nod.

The director touches the play button and the electronic graphics keyed over long shots of the Hartsville refinery the night of the explosion appear on the screen followed by the Mammoth theme music and narration.

ANNOUNCER
"On the evening of March thirty-first, fire broke out at a secondary, low grade storage facility at the Mammoth Hartsville, Texas refinery. The fire quickly spread, severely damaging storage, transport and refining facilities of the plant."

Fifteen minutes later the tape concludes with the voice of the CEO and images of Mammoth employees working to control the fire. The final shot is a frozen frame of a Mammoth employee holding a young child.

CEO
"We were there in Hartsville meeting our responsibilities. With your support and hard work we will be there throughout the nation supplying product to those who depend on us, continuing to prove that this company is concerned with more than just increasing profit margins. We are dedicated to serving the public and leading our industry."

EXECUTIVE VICE PRESIDENT
That's very strong S.W., very strong.

CEO
I think it does the job. In general it's very effective but those early shots of the fire. You'll have to make some changes there.

EXECUTIVE VICE PRESIDENT
I had the exact same thought. They don't represent what happened.

PRODUCER/WRITER
Oh, you didn't like that? Well, we'll look at our footage. I think we can take care of that. If we do, is it approved? We need to move quickly to get it out tonight.

CEO
Yes, with those changes. You captured what we want to get out to the regions very well.

Afterward, the director finishes the edit decision list and sound run-down sheets. To do this she refers to the tape logs and the time code on the rough cut.

TAPE LOG					PAGE #: 3	OF TOTAL: 15	
TITLE: The Company Responds				LOGGED BY: Durrins			
SHOOTING DATE: 8/4				DIRECTOR:			
TAPE #	SHOT #	TIME START	TIME END	AUDIO	DESCRIPTION		STATUS
3	1-5	01:00:30:00	01:04:20:00	Sirens And Police Giving Directions	MLS + LS shots of fires on BANDEDOI sheet		+
3	6	01:04:30:00	01:06:25:00	Interview with Chief Sanchez	MS of chief hand held - Good MATERIAL in BACKGROUND		+
3	7-12	01:06:35:00	01:09:40:00	Police on radio	Low light shots of police & radio & squad car		SOME GOOD STUFF -

The tape logs help her locate sound elements. From the time code on the rough cut a precise list of the length and order of pictures is created. Obviously, the list does not include the extra shots of burning buildings that were added for the screening at noon. The transitions that will be used in the final cut are also written into the edit decision list. However, the director will have the opportunity to try them out and make final decisions during on-line editing.

After the edit decision list and run-down sheets are completed, the director rushes to the post production house where, working with a technician/editor, she matches the sound and picture edits described in the rundown sheets and edit decision lists. Six hours later, a finished product is produced with "clean" audio and video and a variety of dramatic transitions including dissolves and wipes.

As the last edit is being made, the director calls the producer/writer to ask him to come to the production house to view the finished product. He arrives while the final sound is being mixed. The Mammoth logo fills the screen and the music swells before fading out. "May we see it from the beginning," the director asks the technician/editor. He rewinds the tape and plays it from the beginning. After the Mammoth logo fills the screen and the music swells before fading out for a second time, the producer/writer shakes the director's hand and sighs deeply.

The following morning, in Mammoth offices around the country, the regional directors of refineries and distribution centers sit down with their staff and watch, *The Company Responds.*

Two weeks later, after all 145 tapes have been viewed in Mammoth offices around the country, the media center's research department sends out a questionnaire related to the program.

I. After watching this program, state to what extent you agree or disagree with the following statements:

	STRONGLY AGREE	AGREE	NOT SURE	DISAGREE	STRONGLY DISAGREE
a. The company acted responsibly during and after the trouble at Hartsville.	☐	☐	☐	☐	☐
b. The company is in financial trouble.	☐	☐	☐	☐	☐
c. The company's image has suffered because of the Hartsville explosions.	☐	☐	☐	☐	☐
d. The company is caring toward its employees and customers.	☐	☐	☐	☐	☐

II. Do you expect the events at Hartsville will have an impact on your job?

☐ Yes ☐ No

If yes, what impact?

☐ Increased reponsibilities

☐ Less work

☐ Relocation

Of the 98 managers who respond, 80 percent found the tape very valuable. One respondent took the time to add a short paragraph.

> For the first time in the five years I've been in charge of distribution here in Wakefield, I feel the home office understands how important it is that we are included in the communications loop.
>
> The video gave my staff confidence to believe that everything possible was being done to alleviate the problems caused by the tragedy in Hartsville and all the negative publicity that followed. You made my job much easier. Thanks.
>
> Joan Carpenter
> Distribution Manager, Wakefield, Alabama

Chapter 15

In The Valley

DOCUMENTARY SEGMENT It is four P.M. The producer of *In The Valley*, and a videographer and sound person from the News Department at WORK-TV are driving down the freeway toward MacArthur Stadium. Today they begin shooting interviews and game footage for the documentary on the coach.

PRODUCER
I want to begin in the coach's office. His room is on the dark side, so we have to bounce a light off the ceiling and use a back light. And I want to use a tripod.

SOUND PERSON
How do you want to mic him?

PRODUCER
We'll go with the shotgun. If nothing else, this first session should get him used to us and the gear.

VIDEOGRAPHER
How much tape do you figure I need before the game?

PRODUCER
An hour ought to do it. We'll speak to him in his office for a half hour or so, then follow him around the locker room or wherever he goes before the game. We'll do all this hand-held with one or two lights . Also, I may speak to some of the players so be prepared to cover me if I jump in and start asking questions.

VIDEOGRAPHER
Ok...but I'll need at least fifteen minutes to set up before the game.

After parking and unloading their van in front of the Chiefs' locker room, they are met by a security officer who tells them they cannot enter the locker room without a pass. The producer explains that the coach expects them. The officer politely responds with, "I'm sorry. Without a pass, I can't let you in." Luckily, just as the producer is about to offend the officer, the general manager's secretary drives into the parking lot and tells the guard to let them in.

While the videographer and sound person set up their equipment in the coach's office, the producer chats with the coach.

> PRODUCER
> I thought we'd start with an interview. Then we'll just follow you around trying to catch what you do before the game. We hope you ignore us, or, if we're in the way, tell us.
>
> COACH
> Don't worry...I'm good at that.

Whether or not this interview is effective partially depends on how well the videographer and sound person do their jobs. However, unless the producer asks the coach questions that illicit interesting or dramatic or thoughtful responses, the scene will not be useful.

Interview Techniques

There are some interview techniques which the producer uses to make the coach comfortable and, at the same time, helps the videographer, sound person and the editor do their jobs. For example, the producer positions himself next to the camera lens so the videographer can compose full face shots of the coach looking in the direction of the camera. The producer sits three or four inches lower than the camera lens which forces the coach to look down slightly. This has two positive results. The coach's face is angled to evenly catch the light bouncing off the ceiling of his office avoiding harsh shadows under his eyes and nose. Also, the coach looks to be in control and comfortable from this lower angle.

The producer has a choice of four interview styles commonly used in nonfiction programs: 1) Off-camera/off-mic, 2) off-camera/on-mic, 3) invisible, and 4) on-camera.

Off-Camera/Off-Mic

The producer decides to use an off-camera/off-mic style of interviewing. In the final, edited documentary the interviewer will not be seen and will be heard off-mic. His questions will be picked up by the coach's microphone. This off-mic quality conveys the same "rough" quality as hand-held camera techniques, giving the impression that the interview was not thoroughly planned but happened by accident.

Off-Camera/On-Mic

Off-camera/on-mic is similar to off-camera/off-mic except the interviewer is not heard through the subject's microphone. The interviewer has his or her own microphone. This on-mic quality makes interviews seem more controlled, more "polished" than when questions are heard off-mic.

Invisible

The invisible interview style is one in which the interviewer is not seen or heard. This technique gives the impression that the subject is telling his or her own story without being lead by an interviewer. The absence of an interviewer does not necessarily mean a subject is telling his or her own story. In this style, as in the other three, producers and editors choose what to edit into a documentary and what to discard. They also decide how shots are ordered and what pictures are placed next to what sounds.

When the invisible style is used, the interviewer must make sure the subject's answers include enough information for the viewer to follow what is being said. For example, if a baseball player answers the question, "Did you ever play in the majors?" with "No, I didn't but I tried," his comments would not be useful. For this reason, the interviewer would ask him to re-phrase his response with some mention of the big leagues. An example of this is, "No, I never played for a Major League club but I tried out for the Cubs."

On-Camera

The on-camera style is most often used in news and studio based interview programs. It is the style the director of *In The Valley* will use in the studio portion of the program.

In on-camera interviews, both the interviewer and interviewee are seen and heard. Many times interviews photographed in this style include intercuts—shots of a person or persons listening, smiling, nodding, looking angry, and so on.

To shoot an on-camera interview in a studio, multi-camera setting, directors usually cross shoot two cameras. This means one camera is focused on an interviewer/host and another on the interviewee/guest or guests. A third camera is also usually included to provide a master shot; that is, a wide shot of the scene.

When producing programs with more than three people, some directors use four or five cameras. However, the most common way to cover interview/discussions with more subjects than cameras is to use camera movement and editing.

In this configuration, the director covers all five subjects with three cameras. For example, when the interviewer asks a question of guest X, camera #1 photographs the interviewer and camera #3 photographs guest X. When Y interrupts X, the director switches to camera #1 for a quick, inter-cut of the interviewer, and tells camera #3 to pan to Y. The director switches to camera #3 when it is framed on Y. Y talks on for a long time; Z and W become bored and fidgety. The director switches to camera #2 which has the master shot and tells camera #3 to get a two shot of fidgety Z and W. While Y continues talking, the director switches from the master shot to an inter-cut of Z and W.

An on-camera interview between an interviewer and guest can also be produced using a single camera. The first step would be to record the answers of the guest. This is done by positioning a camera and microphone over the shoulder of the interviewer. After the interview is completed, the videographer holds her position and records the guest listening (or pretending to listen) to the interviewer.

Then the videographer moves her camera to the master shot position and records a wide shot of the scene. She moves far enough away from the scene so that the viewer will not be able to see the subjects' mouths moving. This makes it possible to use the master shot at any point in the interview.

Next the videographer moves to a position over the shoulder of the guest and the interviewer asks the same questions that have already been answered. The interviewer asks the questions three times because he mispronounces a word in each of the first two takes. Then he pretends to listen to the answers. And finally he smiles, nods and frowns in the direction of the camera. During editing, the editor and producer decide which shots to use and in which order they appear.

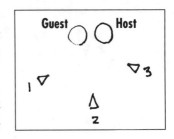

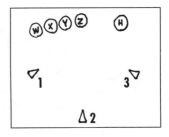

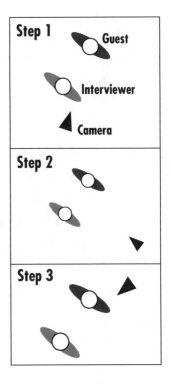

Choosing an appropriate interview style is important. However, it is not as important as having an effective, engaging interview. Good interviews usually result from the interviewer being well prepared. Genuine interest in what a guest is saying also contributes to the quality of an interview.

Good interviewers are good listeners. This describes the producer of the documentary about the coach. During their twenty-minute interview, the producer speaks three times. He begins the interview with the question, "How long have you been doing this?" Ten minutes into the program the producer asks the coach to "...tell us about your campaigns for City Council President." And, at twenty minutes the producer interrupts the coach and tells him how much he enjoyed the interview and how much he learned. In between the three times he speaks, the producer listens intently nodding, frowning, laughing or otherwise showing reactions to what the coach says. These reactions and genuine demonstrations of interest help or direct the coach as much as the questions asked.

Releases

After the interview, the sound person hands the producer a blank standard release form for the coach to sign. All featured persons in the documentary will be asked to sign such a release. It gives the production team and WORK-TV the right to use the picture and voice of a subject.

Secondary talent (fans, people on the street, ball players who are not interviewed but who are shown in the background) usually are not asked to sign releases. However, this is not the case in works of fiction where both primary and secondary talent are required to sign releases. If a production team does not get a release from its talent, the talent has the right to sue the makers of the program for using their picture or voice without permission.

PERFORMANCE RELEASE

WORK TV
(PAMDIGN LLC)

I hereby give my permission to WORK-TV, its agents, successors, assigns, clients and purchasers of its services and/or products to use my photograph (whether still film or television) and recordings of my voice and my name in any legal manner whatsoever.

NAME OF PERFORMER(Please Print):

_____

PERFORMER SIGNATURE: _____

DATE: _____

ADDRESS: _____   PHONE: ( ) _____

_____

PROGRAM:

_____

_____

DESCRIPTION OF ROLE:

_____

_____

Subjects of a news program need not sign releases. Producers of news programs are protected from being sued by the First Amendment. News reports are considered public events, to which the public has the right of access.

Additional Footage and Editing

The interview with the coach takes longer than planned so the producer skips pre-game interviews with the players and prepares to shoot footage during the game. As the videographer and sound person break down their gear and prepare to move to the stadium, the producer speaks to them about the next scene. During the game, because things happen so quickly, the producer will not be able to tell the videographer and sound person which shots and which audio to record. Most of the time they will be on their own so it is very important that they have a clear understanding of what the producer is "looking for."

Sequence I: 1-1/2 Minutes
Montage of close-ups of faces of fans at MacArthur Stadium.
    BILLY BONS, VOICE OF THE CHIEFS:
    It's the top of the ninth...Two men on.....One out.
Cut to CU of the Chiefs catcher giving a sign to his pitcher.
    BILLY BONS:
    There's the wind-up...
MS the coach in the dugout at the stadium chewing tobacco and spitting. He gives a sign to the catcher, scratches his head, takes off his cap, and spits again.
    BILLY BONS:
    And....Rogers strikes him out!
End sequence with MCU of coach. A slight smile of satisfaction lights up his face as he watches his pitcher strike out the batter.

Sequence II: 2 Minutes
Shots of the coach in the clubhouse congratulating his ball players on their victory as we hear him in voice over.
    The sequence ends with a close-up of Rogers, the pitcher.

After the videographer and sound person read this first portion of the extended treatment, they return to packing their gear while they speak with the producer.

VIDEOGRAPHER
I can certainly stick with the coach and get all the close ups of fans you need. But do you want me to worry about shots of the pitcher and the catcher? You can get those from WVXT. They're covering the game today.

PRODUCER
If we have to, we'll go to WVXT but I'd prefer not to. Their cameras don't match ours...and that could be a problem when we cut the scene together.

VIDEOGRAPHER
Ok...I can shoot the pitcher from the dugout. But I won't be able to cover the catcher. Do you mind if we set that up before the game. It's the only way we can get him from the pitcher's perspective.

PRODUCER
I can live with that.

SOUND PERSON
You want me to stick with the camera and catch as much as I can of the coach, right?

PRODUCER
Yea...also collect ambiance and sound effects...balls hitting bats and gloves, chatter among the players...vendors...you know what I need.

SOUND PERSON
OK. And how about the play-by-play. Do I need to worry about that?

PRODUCER
No, the radio station is taping it for me. Any more questions. We'd better get upstairs.

During most of the first two innings of the game, the producer, videographer and sound person cover the coach in the dugout. However, once in a while they turn their attention to the stands and to the game and pick up shots of the fans and players. During the third inning, they leave the dugout and walk through the stands recording close-ups of the fans and long shots of the playing field. During the fourth inning they position themselves behind the plate and get a number of good shots of the pitcher. They return to the dugout for innings five and six and spend the seventh inning in the bleachers before returning to the dugout for the end of the game. After the game, they run onto the field to record the end-of-game congratulations and follow the team into the locker room. They are especially pleased with the kind of shots and bits of conversation they catch as the team enters the locker room.

After the game the videographer, sound person, and producer stop for a late lunch at a restaurant around the corner from the stadium. During the afternoon's interviewing and shooting, the sound person numbered each tape and made quick, shorthand notes on the outside of each cassette and tape box. At the restaurant he rewrites some of these notes, making sure they clearly describe the content of each tape and that the counter numbers and date are easy to read.

After this task is completed he lists the general contents of the eight tapes on a videotape library record sheet. When he returns to WORK-TV he will hand the tapes and this form to the station's tape librarian. He will also photocopy the form for the producer who will need it when he views the tapes that were shot today.

For five days this three-member production team repeats this arduous routine. The following week, after the shooting is completed, the producer schedules a full day of viewing and discussion with the editor assigned to him. To prepare the editor, the producer sends a copy of the treatment to her so she can get a general sense of what the producer intends. This is a slightly different version of the treatment than the one which existed before production began, because after each day of shooting the producer returned to his office and modified the treatment depending on what was recorded that day. Sometimes he made these changes in long hand in the margins of the treatment; other times he made the changes on the copy in his word processor.

Sequence I has been changed from what it was before production began. As you recall, the earlier version begins with a montage of faces of fans at the stadium watching a Chiefs' pitcher strike out the final batter in the top of the ninth inning.

```
Sequence I: 1-1/2 Minutes
Montage of close-ups of faces of fans at MacArthur
stadium.
                BILLY BONS, VOICE OF THE CHIEFS:
            It's the top of the ninth. Two men on...
            One out...

Cut to close up of the Chiefs catcher giving a sign
to his pitcher.

                    BILLY BONS:
            The pitch...

MS OF the coach in the dugout at the stadium chew-
ing tobacco.
```

Here's how the sequence looks now. Note that this version contains references to specific shots and dialogue. These were added by the producer after he viewed the dailies of the documentary.

```
Sequence I: 2-2 1/2 Minutes
(Opening Title, white on black: "Triple
threat....Franklin Roberts, manager of the Landcaster
Chiefs.")

GENERAL AMBIANCE OF THE STADIUM—VENDORS, CROWD,
STADIUM ANNOUNCER

Cut to series of close ups of the runner on first, the
pitcher, the runner on third, players in the dugout
```

and the coach. (There are plenty of these types of shots in tapes 3 and 6.)

                      BILLY BONS:
The pitch, a high fly ball, it looks like an easy out. Oswald drops it! He drops it! Bracero, the runner at third, scores and, for the first time, the Chiefs take the lead.

Ten second montage of crowd going wild. (Tape 5, ten minutes in.)

MS the coach in the dugout watching the game, chewing and spitting tobacco. (Tape 3, first four minutes.)
(02:01:27 Tape 17, Voice of Romero over shots of coach)

    The most exciting time in my career was in Landcaster playing for Roberts. I don't really know why but he gave us the chemistry, the magic. We won the Triple A crown twice in a row… something no team had ever done before.

(03:04:39 Tape 11, Voice of B.B.Bonds over more shots of coach then to players in the dugout.)
End sequence with shots of fans. Tape 16, last two minutes.

                   B.B. BONDS VO:
He can be a son-of-a-gun. I remember the first day I met him.

The first thing the producer tells the editor at their initial meeting is to view the twenty-three tapes (260 minutes of material) shot so far and decide if she can produce a program like the one described in the treatment. He also tells her to list the contents of each tape so that it will be relatively easy to find shots and sound segments during editing and viewing. This is called logging tapes and the station has a special form for this purpose.

WORK TV LANDCASTER — TAPE LOG

PRODUCTION TITLE ___In the Valley___ TAPE # ___14 (Continued)___

PRODUCTION NUMBER ___001___ DATE _____

Scene/Shot	Take	Good	Bad	Time	Notes	HR	Min	Sec	Fr
D 1	4		X		too bright	—	46	13	10
	5	✓			use it – Coach talk	—	48	12	02
	1	✓			ext. Mac Stadium	—	53	34	04
	2	✓			" from car	00	57	22	10
	3	✓			" into stadium	01	00	38	01
	4		X		" rear view		01	02	11
	1	✓			Coach on field		02	47	40
	2		X		Sun glasses ↑		04	00	12
	3	✓			Coach w/ pitcher		06	30	08

It takes a day and a half for the editor to view all the tapes and log them. Afterwards, the editor and producer meet for two hours to view those portions of the tapes that they agree should be in the final cut of the program. They also discuss the treatment. The editor finds most of it workable. However, she suggests an additional segment about the coach's work with underprivileged kids and the producer agrees that this should be included.

As we said in the previous chapter, the work of the editor is certainly as important as that of the videographer and the sound person. And sometimes the editor plays a more important role than the other production team members. There are many examples of scenes that can convey very different impressions depending on how the editor does his or her job. This is especially true in documentary production. Certainly the way the editor works with the footage of Coach Roberts will determine the kind of person he appears to be. If sounds and pictures are ordered in one way, the coach will appear to be the spiritual leader of his players and the community; if ordered another way, he will appear to be an insensitive, cruel despot.

An example of this occurred in a scene of the coach speaking to his players one afternoon during batting practice. This is how the editor organized her shots in a rough cut.

Shot #1: Coach speaking to the team about their lack of concentration when at bat. ("You guys look like has-beens, losers, geriatrics.")

Shots #2, #3 and #4: intercuts of ball players listening while preparing to go onto the field, putting cleats on, doing stretching exercises, rubbing bats with pitch.

Shot #5: The coach finishing his speech.

Shot #6: Players hard at work hitting balls and running down grounders.

Shot #7: The coach sitting in a lounge chair, his pot belly flowing over his belt, sipping a cold drink, talking about working with young players. ("You gotta' be tough once in a while...for their own good.")

Shot #8: Continuation of shot #6, batting practice.

When the producer looks at this eight-shot scene, he tells the editor that he likes it up to shot #7.

PRODUCER
It makes Roberts look like a slob and a hypocrite. Use what he says as voice over of a shot of the coach in uniform at batting practice with the team, not sitting like an over-stuffed potentate.

After their meeting, the editor reads down her logs and finds on tape number eleven a series of shots of the coach at what appears to be batting practice. She replaces shot #7 with a medium shot of the coach shouting encouragement to a young player. At their next meeting the editor shows the producer the revised scene. He compliments her on her choice of shots but tells her that now it's a bit too long. This is a good example of the way professional editors work with producers and directors. The editor is given complete control over rough cuts, but ultimate control over what appears in the finished program rests with producer or director.

Sound mixing is the final stage of editing. Ideally it is done in a sound studio with multi-track audio record/playback machines interlocked with videotape machines as described in the chapter on sound. However, sound mixing can also be done in editing suites by using insert editing. After the picture portion of a program is completed, additional sound can be inserted into one or more audio channels. For example the editor of the documentary on the coach might want to add music and voice-overs to a scene of the coach talking to his players. She can do this by inserting the new audio onto a free audio channel.

While the documentary portion of the first episode of *In The Valley* is being edited, the producer meets with his director and hands him a schedule which includes all the activities leading to the live, multi-camera portions of the first episode.

STUDIO SEGMENT

DIRECTOR
Are you satisfied with the set and light designs we got last week?

PRODUCER
Yep, pretty much. But I want the lighting to be lower key than what is on the designs. They look like daytime television....not evening. It looks like there's too much light on the backgrounds.

DIRECTOR
That's not a problem. I'll pass that on. How about cameras and sound. Are there any changes there?

PRODUCER
No, I'm satisfied with what we laid out in our meetings last week. How's the set coming along?

DIRECTOR
I was down in the scene shop this morning. I liked what I saw. It's coming along nicely. They promise it by the end of the week.

Another important document in a multi-camera program is the facility requisition. The director of *In The Valley* fills out two of these forms: one to reserve studio A for assembling the set

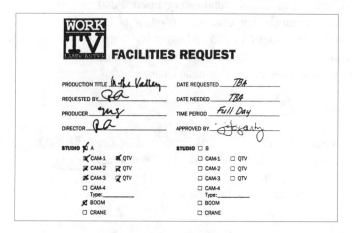

and lighting it, another to reserve the same studio, its control room and three videotape machines in master control for one day of rehearsals and one day to tape the studio segments.

In addition to filling out facility requisition forms, the director has his assistant fill out crew assignment sheets for the three

CREW ASSIGNMENTS

PRODUCTION TITLE _In the Valley_   WORK DATE _T.B.A._

DIRECTOR _R.A._   UNIT MANAGER _Sean Fogarty_

Time In	Time Out	Name	Position	Location & Comments
		N. Rawdin	set / lights	STD A
		R. Killeen		STD A
		M. McGhghy		STD A
		J. Gios	cam 1	STD A
		C. Dupes	cam 2	STD A
		T. Elkard	cam 3	STD A
		K. Hornig	boom	STD A
		V. Ayed	floor mgr	STD A
		K. Viturro	gaffer	STD A

days he will need crew for set-up, rehearsal and taping. He requests a three-person crew for building the set and lighting it and a ten-person crew for rehearsal and production.

   The job of the camera operator is to pan, tilt, zoom, dolly, truck and pedestal cameras and compose shots in accordance with the commands given by the director and the assistant director (AD). Sometimes directions are written on shot sheets, which are lists of each camera operator's responsibilities. These sheets are clipped or taped to the back of cameras so operators can read and, when necessary, modify them. These shot sheets are only guides to aid camera operators. The precise composition and camera movement expected of operators comes directly from verbal cues spoken by the director and the assistant director during rehearsal and taping.

The camera operator, like the other members of the crew, is in direct communications with the director and AD. During set ups and rehearsal they can speak directly to one another through the headset/microphone combination they wear. However, for obvious reasons, they must just listen and not speak during rehearsals and taping of "live" productions.

ASSISTANT DIRECTOR
Stand by....Camera three. Tighten up....I'm changing your shot.....move to an extreme close up. Ready....

DIRECTOR
That's a little too tight, three. Good...and dissolve to three.

The boom operator, like the camera operator hears commands from the control room through a headset. However, the boom operator's headset also contains the program line, the sound being recorded or broadcast. This, along with the commands by the director, AD and audio person, helps the boom operator determine whether he is doing his job effectively.

ASSISTANT DIRECTOR
Boom be careful, there's a boom shadow behind the host.....

AUDIO PERSON
Bring the boom down closer to his head, you're losing him.

DIRECTOR
I need that shot! Hold the boom there, shadow or no shadow! Take three.

The floor manager cues talent to begin and end a scene or a program, informs the talent when a videotape or film insert is about to be rolled in, gives and take props to talent and places graphics cards in front of cameras. Also, floor managers are the director's representatives in the studio during rehearsals and taping. This requires initiative, quick thinking and sometimes diplomacy.

DIRECTOR
Be careful! If he moves another step to the left he'll knock over the set.

FLOOR MANAGER
I've got it.

DIRECTOR
She looks like she's going to explode. Next chance you get tell her how well she's doing or tell her a joke....do something.

FLOOR MANAGER
It's done.

DIRECTOR
We're out of time. Give him the wrap up signal.

Directors call upon their assistant directors or ADs to perform a number of jobs including directing roll-ins of videotapes or films; readying cameras, music, and sound effects; and keeping track of time cues.

ASSISTANT DIRECTOR
Stand by. Ready in the studio, one minute to air...thirty seconds...fifteen...five, four, three, two, one.

DIRECTOR
Mic and cue talent.

ASSISTANT DIRECTOR
Master Control...ready to roll tape five...and roll it....three, two, one...

DIRECTOR
Dissolve to tape.

The technical director (sometimes called the TD or video switcher) implements the director's editing and transitions. This is accomplished with a video switcher. Switchers allow the TD to do the following:

1. Select video sources (cameras, film, videotapes, and so on.)

2. Select transitions (takes, fades, dissolves, wipes, and so on.)

3. Mix more than one video source at one time (split screens, superimpositions, chromakeys, keys, mattes, and so on.)

The job of audio operator is similar to that of the TD. However, instead of mixing and editing pictures, audio operators edit and mix sounds at an audio console.

During production, the audio person has three primary responsibilities: sequencing, mixing, and monitoring levels.

The director gives commands to bring in music, open mics, mix music with voice, and so on. These commands have been indicated in the director's script at the exact time and in the precise sequence needed. It is the audio person's responsibility to execute these commands as they are given.

The audio person carefully monitors the level of each audio source by watching the VU meters on the console. What one hears from the expensive sound system in a control room can be misleading. Over-modulated signals may sound normal in the control room but when reproduced later on a television set in the home or schoolroom are heard as distorted.

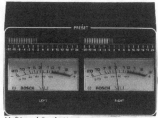

V/U and Peak Meters on an audio console

While watching the levels displayed on VU meters, the audio person must also listen carefully to the mix of different audio signals. This is done to be sure that they are correctly balanced: background music must not drown out someone who is speaking, the sound effect of rain falling softly must not sound like a raging river.

ASSISTANT DIRECTOR
Ready to mic and cue host and ready to fade in music.

AUDIO PERSON
Ready.

Another key member of the crew is the lighting designer. Before rehearsal and taping, his primary responsibility is to light the set according to the designs approved by the director and the producer.

Lighting designers normally use a dimmer board (or lighting console) that performs functions similar to those performed by the video switcher and audio console: lighting instruments can be turned on, faded out, or mixed with other instruments.

The dimmer board provides a way of controlling the intensity of each light when setting up a lighting design and when making changes during a program. For example, the dimmer board is used to change from normal lighting to a silhouette or a cameo effect during a program. During rehearsal and taping, a production assistant will make the lighting changes asked for by the director or the assistant director.

The camera control operator is responsible for the quality of the camera's output. The general term used for this job is shading. To shade a camera is to adjust contrast, color, light, sensitivity, and fine focus. The job of camera control is essentially to provide the type of pictures that support the program's lighting design. If the design is intended to be bright and even, the camera-control person adjusts cameras to be sensitive to the full spectrum of light. When lighting designs call for uneven lighting with dramatic contrast, cameras are adjusted to render only dark and light areas of the scene. When a scene is designed with a specific tone (blue for sad, melancholy; yellow for happy, bright; sepia for scenes with a dated, antique look) cameras are adjusted to be more sensitive to one portion of the color spectrum than to others.

The camera-control operator is usually stationed in master control and is in communications with the control room. This allows the operator to hear the AD's ready commands. For instance, when the operator hears the AD say "ready camera one," he shades camera one before the director uses the camera. Also, if a camera is not functioning properly, the camera-operator interrupts the AD's ready command.

The videotape operator is responsible for the machines that both record the program being produced and play back any material which is meant to be inserted into the program. Before rehearsal, the assistant director hands the operator a videotape onto which to record the program. He also hands him a list of the videotape inserts that will be rolled-in to the program and the videotapes themselves.

The last member of the crew is the supervising engineer. This person oversees all the facilities assigned to the production. If a technical element of the production does not work properly, the supervising engineer is called. Because master control is the center of the production facilites, and because there is more equipment in master control than in any other locale, the supervising engineer is stationed there during rehearsal and taping.

On Tuesday at 9:00 A. M. two production assistants roll in the pieces of the *In The Valley* set and begin to re-assemble it. This takes two hours. The lighting designer and two assistants work ten additional hours to light the set. The following day, when the rehearsal is scheduled, the director sees for the first time the fully lit set.

> **DIRECTOR**
> *I really like what you've done, except the backgrounds are still too flat. I want more shadows back there. Also the key lights are too hot.*

While the lighting designer makes this change, the director calls a meeting with his crew. While the director and his production team have been working for weeks on the details of *In The Valley*, the technical crew knows little about the program.

> **DIRECTOR**
> *Can I have your attention for just a second? Let me give you a brief description of what this program is all about. The station has decided to do something very new and, I think, exciting. In The Valley is a weekly, totally local program that combines documentaries about local people with live interviews. The intros and outtros to the documentary, commercial breaks and the interview will be done here, live. Today, because this is our first program, I want to do a run through. Any questions before we begin?*
>
> **CAMERA OPERATOR**
> *You need anything special from us?*
>
> **DIRECTOR**
> *Just in the opening: I want a long dolly in as if through the studio door. Then you'll cover the interviews. I'll get the audio person the carts with the theme music. You have the list of microphones?*
>
> **CHARACTER GENERATOR OPERATOR**
> *Can I have your list of graphics, so I can get them typed into the C.G.*
>
> **DIRECTOR**
> *Yes, here it is. Anybody need anything else? Ok, then, why don't you go to your positions and we'll start the run through in ten minutes.*

The character generator operator takes the list of credits from the director and immediately begins typing them into the character generator.

While the credits are being entered, the other members of the crew go to their positions and prepare for the rehearsal. At the same time, the director looks at his version of the script, appropriately called director's script. This document is a guide for the director when producing the program "live" from the control room. In essence, the director's script serves the same function in multi-camera production as edit decision lists and sound rundown sheets in single camera. It contains a list of shots, camera movements, sound, and graphics. Its multi-column format helps indicate the time and space relationship among all these elements which make up the program.

TIME:	VIDEO:	AUDIO:
00:00- 00:15	OPENING GRAPHIC (1A).	MUSIC UP AND UNDER (CART #1).
00:15- 00:55	ANIMATION SEQUENCE, LANDCASTER FROM SPACE (TAPE #2).	

ANNOUNCER:
(VO, CART #2)

| 00:55-
01:30 | FOOTAGE OF
ROBERTS ON
PLAYING FIELD
(TAPE #3). | In The Valley, featuring the events
and people who make the news in
Landcaster. This evening we meet
Franklin Roberts.
For fourteen years the coach of the
triple A Chiefs and twice candidate
for City Council President. |

MUSIC OUT.

| 01:30-
02:30 | COMMERCIAL BREAK
#1. | SOUND ON TAPE(SOT) |

STRUM:

| 02:30-
03:15 | MCU HOST.

ZOOM IN TO CU OF
HOST. | Today we begin an experiment. We're
going to try something that most
everyone in television thinks cannot
be done. We're going to produce a
full-blown early-evening program about
local issues and events. We think our
city deserves this kind of attention.
If you agree...we're in business! If
not, then it's back to Entertainment
Tonight and the rest of those programs
that are really not about Landcaster
and don't help you know your city. |
| 03:30-
10:15 | DISSOLVE TO:
DOCUMENTARY,
SEGMENT #1 (TAPE #3). | |

During rehearsals and taping, the director must pay attention to what is actually happening in front of the cameras and microphones as well as to what should be happening, which is described in his script. The director's script is designed for this purpose because it can be read at a glance.

Directors scripts are guides; they usually cannot be followed to the letter. There are some things that just will not work out as they were written before production. Because of this, one of the skills of successful directors is the ability to continually adjust their scripts during the production process. This is especially true for programs like *In The Valley*. For example, during rehearsal the director notes that the host's on-camera welcome is stronger and more convincing than expected. This leads him to decide to change the script so the host's welcome becomes the program's first sequence, not the second sequence as it is on his script.

DIRECTOR
OK, let's run through the new opening. We start with Bill in the studio instead of with the roll-in.

ASSISTANT DIRECTOR
Ready in the studio, ready in the control room, ready to roll tape #3. Ready to fade to camera one.

FLOOR MANAGER
Check....

ENGINEER IN MASTER CONTROL
Ready...

ASSISTANT DIRECTOR
This is a rehearsal.....In thirty seconds.

DIRECTOR
Camera one, tighten your shot up. Fine.

ASSISTANT DIRECTOR
Ten, nine, eight...

DIRECTOR
Ready to mic and cue talent...

ASSISTANT DIRECTOR
Three, two....

DIRECTOR
Mic and cue talent!

HOST
Welcome to this the first program of In The Valley ....

ASSISTANT DIRECTOR
Ready to roll in tape #3. And,roll...five, four, three...

DIRECTOR
Dissolve to tape #3....sound, where's the sound?

AUDIO
I don't have it here.

DIRECTOR
Cut! Sorry....relax everyone....

FLOOR MANAGER: (IN STUDIO)
Relax....there's been a technical problem.

AUDIO: (TO MASTER CONTROL)
What channel is the sound on?

ENGINEER
Three.

AUDIO
OK. Now I have it.

ASSISTANT DIRECTOR
Stand-by....here we go again.

After the rehearsal, the director and his assistant compare their scripts. Both contain handwritten notes describing the changes they made during rehearsal. After making sure that her script has all the changes, the AD returns to her office and revises the script for tomorrow's "live" production.

The next afternoon, as the program is being broadcast to thousands of homes in the Landcaster community, the coach decides to show the host that he still has the form to slide into second base and he gets up out of his chair and demonstrates. This forces to director to change camera blocking on air. He also has to make on-air adjustments of the boom microphone.

DIRECTOR
Camera two pull back....cover the coach as he stands. More to the right. OK hold it there! And one, get a tight shot of Strum. Good hold it.

ASSISTANT DIRECTOR
Camera one, a wide shot. Three, cover the host. Boom, watch it. You're in the shot.

The director does control most things quite well during the production of this and the other twelve programs in the program's first season. The team stays on schedule and close to budget and, more importantly, becomes popular enough for the sales department to sell time slots to local businesses and locally owned franchises at a rate high enough to cover production costs. Also of importance to the station is the good publicity the program has generated for the station.

WORK-TV BREAKS NEW GROUND WITH OLD FORMAT
Three cheers for WORK-TV. On Wednesday evenings at 7 P.M., WORK-TV, Landcaster's newest television station is going back to basics. They are producing a local program worth watching.

HATS OFF TO WORK-TV!
Our hats are off to the team at WORK-TV for doing what local media should be doing but seldom do. "In The Valley" combines the best of both worlds—solid documentaries and intelligent interviews.

Sure of the quality of their program, WORK-TV places a full page advertisement in the local newspaper.

WORK-TV'S
IN THE VALLEY
FRIDAYS AT 7PM

It's About Landcaster
and
its People

WE'RE THE
COMMUNITY MINDED
STATION THAT CARES.

The General Manager of WORK-TV schedules a meeting in his office with the station's production manager and the producer of "In the Valley" the day after the thirteenth program, the final episode of the program's first season.

GENERAL MANAGER
The series has done more than any of us thought it would do. We actually are breaking even on the thing. And, if it continues to get the ratings, we'll make money on it next year. But even if it doesn't, our marketing people believe it will help us win loyal viewers for WORK. Bottom line...you guys did a great job.

PRODUCER
Thanks.

PROGRAM DIRECTOR
I thought I would never hear that from you.

GENERAL MANAGER
There is one little favor I do want to ask of you two.

PROGRAM DIRECTOR
Here it comes....

GENERAL MANAGER
Seriously, would you put together a twenty-minute collection of the best of In The Valley for the affiliates meeting next month in Dallas. The network is very impressed and want us to show off what we've done to the management of other stations.

Chapter 16

Bergen

REHEARSALS The nerve center of IPW's production of *Bergen* is a rented suite of offices on the twelfth floor of a Manhattan skyscraper. The producer, unit manager and the director each has a small room with a desk and telephone. In one of these rooms, the director and unit manager are seated around a table with a copy of the director's, discussing scene 11.

11.1. INT. THE BOWLING ALLEY. LS, LOW ANGLE as though looking through the pins to the scorer's table. Robin and Bergen are seated, putting on bowling shoes. As they talk, camera slowly dollies into eventual MS.

                    ROBIN:

You remember Ramos? He used to come here bowling with us when we were kids.

                    BERGEN:
I remember. Pop says he's turned into a no good bum.

                    ROBIN:
That's only 'cause Pop don't like me goin' out with him.

                    BERGEN:
If he's not a bum, it's none of Pop's business.

11.2. INT. BOWLING ALLEY. MS, LOW ANGLE. Bergen reaches down to pick up bowling ball.

                    BERGEN:
So what's the story. Is he a bum?

11.3 INT. BOWLING ALLEY. MS of Robin as she looks back over her shoulder to see Ramos and DeGatta walking towards them.

                    BERGEN:
(LOOKS DISGUSTED.) Damn. (DOESN'T TURN AROUND.) So, answer me. Is Ramos a bum?

11.4. INT. BOWLING ALLEY. LS from pins POV of Bergen throwing the ball. He stops at the foul line and waits to see the result of his throw.

11.5. INT. BOWLING ALLEY. MS over Bergen's shoulder of Ramos, Robin and DeGatta.

> RAMOS:
> Who wants to know, Slick?

11.6. INT. BOWLING ALLEY. REVERSE ANGLE over Ramos's shoulder to MS of Bergen as he slowly turns around. He's surprised to find Ramos behind him, but not afraid.

> ROBIN:
> He didn't mean nothin', Baby. We was just talkin'.

11.7. INT. BOWLING ALLEY. REVERSE ANGLE over Bergen's shoulder to MS of Ramos.

> RAMOS:
> I wasn't talkin' to you, Kid. Sit down
> and shut up.

11.8. INT. BOWLING ALLEY. REVERSE ANGLE over Ramos's shoulder to MS of Bergen.

> BERGEN:
> Hey, Rickie, that's not a very nice way to talk to my sister.

The unit manager uses this director's script to make a list of the crew, cast, set, prop and equipment needs for each of its forty scenes. He keeps track of all this information on a script breakdown form.

Using this breakdown of the script, the unit manager, the director, and other members of the production team can clearly see which scenes will be shot in the same locations, which scenes require the same cast members, and which scenes have similar crew and equipment needs. This breakdown of the script serves as the basis of the production schedule.

BREAKDOWN SHEET

PRODUCER: R. SABOR
TITLE: "BERGEN"
DIRECTOR: SANDERS.

PAGE # 1 OF 40
SHOOT DATE: 3/12
TIMES: 5:00 AM - 9 PM

SCENE #	PAGES	LOCATION	INT/ EXT.	DAY/ NIGHT	CAST	CREW	PROPS	NOTES
11	101-104	BOWLING ALLEY (FLAMINGO BOWL 1432 19th St.)	Int.		~~Rob Bennet~~ Rob Bennet BETSY MILGAW JUAN BENGO HERB HANSEN ANGEL BOYD SUE TOTH	B. WOODS J. FLOYD H. LUISON B. KANNT S. ROBERTS J. MIGUEL F. VANOVER J. KUBLICK D. KUBLICK J. SCHLUDER	4 BOWLING BALLS 1 JACK KNIFE 6 BEER BOTTLES	WE NEED 4 ~~~~ SETS OF PROPS AND GRAPHICS FOR FINAL SHOT IN THE SCENE. THE FIGHT

When shooting single camera style, the order in which scenes are scheduled to be shot is not the same as the order in which they appear in the script or in the completed program. Scenes are shot in an order which makes the most efficient use of locations, cast, crew, and equipment. In the *Bergen* production, all shots which take place in the bowling alley are scheduled for a four day shooting period. Then, all the shots which take place in the Munoz living room are scheduled for another time period.

The availability of talent—especially high salaried, well known talent—might in some instances be an even more important scheduling factor than location. The actress playing Ms. Munoz in *Bergen* is only available during the daytime because at night she is staring in a hit Broadway musical.

DIRECTOR
Remember, Larry, Betsy's got to be done no later than noon. The union says she's got to be off five hours before she goes back to the theater. And she's got a 6:00 call for make-up there, so that would put us right at her limit.

UNIT MANAGER
I had planned to do all her scenes on Monday, when the play's dark.

> **PRODUCER**
> No deal. I talked with the union about that and they insist she have that day off. So it's mornings for everything with her.
>
> **UNIT MANAGER**
> Well, we have a problem then. There's two scenes when she's standing by the bridge in the middle of the night.
>
> **PRODUCER**
> Can't we shoot those day for night?
>
> **DIRECTOR**
> We could but I'd prefer doing them on a sound stage with a traveling matt.
>
> **PRODUCER**
> I thought you wanted a documentary look. Matts look like they're shot in the studio. We have no choice. Schedule the river scenes in the morning and shoot them day for night.

By the end of the week, the director and her unit manager have "stripped" or reordered the script into a ninety-page book. Each page lists the details of each shooting day.

PW

| 96 | EXT | CANTERBURY HOTEL | DAY | 0 2/8 |

SCENE #s	ATMOSPHERE	ANIMALS/VEHICLES
34, 42	2 S.I.	5 Taxis
	10 Atmos. w/ cars	
Bergen spots Tracy	Bellhop	
CAST	5 Cabbies	
2 BERGEN	Hot dog vendor	
4 TRACY PHILLIPS	Hotel doorman	

| 97 | EXT | CANTERBURY HOTEL | DAY | 0 6/8 |

SCENE #s
35-41

Bergen hit by cab

CAST	ATMOSPHERE	ANIMALS/VEHICLES
2 BERGEN	2 S.I.	5 Taxis
4 TRACY PHILLIPS	65 Atmos.	
16 CAB DRIVER		**STUNTS**
		5 Taxis

| 119 | INT | HOTEL SUITE | NIGHT | 2 6/8 |

SCENE #s
43-44

Michael attacks Bergen

CAST	ATMOSPHERE	PROPS
2 BERGEN	3 S.I.	CANE
4 TRACY PHILLIPS		CHAMPAGNE
5 MICHAEL BEAN		GUICCI LUGGAGE

CONTINUED NEXT PAGE

As precise as this production schedule might appear, the wise director prepares for the unexpected. Contingency plans must be made to assure that precious shooting days are not lost to the accidents of nature or man.

DIRECTOR
I'm worried about all these shooting days in April. What if it rains?

UNIT MANAGER
We've covered ourselves there. Remember, we have all these atmosphere shots of the lower East Side in scenes 12, 44, and 178. We can shoot those in any kind of weather. Also a little rain would help those early shots of Bergen driving into town.

After the script has been "stripped" for shooting, the director has three days of rehearsal with the primary actors. For these sessions, the producer has rented a rehearsal hall.

The director uses these rehearsal days to convey to the actors her vision of the final product. Because the production will be shot out of sequence, in long days of takes and retakes of disconnected moments, it is important for her to establish what she intends the finished program to be. In the first rehearsal, there is a read-through of the entire script, in sequence. The director will talk to the cast about the story and the characters. This will be the only time when she will have all the cast members together in one place without the usual distractions of crew and equipment. It is also an opportunity for the writer to express his feelings about the work and for the director to hear what the actors think about their characters.

DIRECTOR
Good morning, everybody. I hope you all have your coffee and helped yourself to those donuts.

CAST
Yes... Thanks they're great for my diet..What's for lunch?

DIRECTOR
I want to begin by saying Bergen is a very important project for me... I've been in love with the story since I saw it as a stage play two years ago. I like what it says about the strength of the American family. And Fred's—stand up Fred—adaptation for the screen is marvelous. We're setting it in the rougher neighborhoods of Newark which should give it an authenticity... a documentary look.

ACTRESS
Kind of raw and naturalistic?

DIRECTOR
Absolutely. But there are also some wonderful cinematic moments of fantasy which I also don't want to miss. But why don't we just start reading through it and you'll all have a chance to see who these characters are and what pushes them to the brink of disaster. I'll read the

set ups. Here we go. "Scene One. View through windshield of moving car. Late afternoon. Willie Nelson is heard through the roar of traffic......."

After a lunch break, the cast comes back together to study each scene in more detail with the director. This is an important opportunity for the actors to ask questions, explore their characters, and begin to get a sense of the story's textures and subtexts.

ACTRESS
"So come on, Ramos, let me see if you're man enough..."

DIRECTOR
Let me interrupt here for a moment and ask you to be more vulnerable... softer.

ACTRESS
That doesn't feel right. I see her as a tough old broad.

DIRECTOR
Eventually... but let us discover that... that she's really a gutsy lady underneath all those aprons and mothering.

ACTRESS
That makes sense.

In a bare rehearsal hall without lights or cameras, there's obviously not much value in rehearsing action scenes or scenes which involve large numbers of extras. The director uses the remaining days of rehearsal to work on those scenes with extended dialogue between two or three characters. She takes advantage of these quieter, more leisurely hours with her actors to develop their characters and establish in their minds the blocking she has planned. She also uses this time to talk about scenes in which the actors are not involved.

In most instances, the director tries to keep her actors informed about how their performances will fit into the final, edited product. However, sometimes it is not useful for the actors to know everything that is going on or how their scene will be cut.

The relationship between a film/television director and actors is quite different from that of the stage director and actors. In the theater, the actors are much more in control of communicating the writer's and director's intentions to the audience. Their position on the stage, their interaction with other actors, their intonation, gestures... all of these important elements of the theater language are manipulated *primarily* by the actor's voice and movement. But in television, as we have seen, the producer, director, videographer/cinematographer, editor, and sound designers are the manipulators, not the actors. To do their jobs, the actors do not always need to know everything that is going on. And there are instances in which actors give more believable performances when they do not know how they are being shot, or how their gestures or spoken lines will be edited or what type of music will be mixed under their performances.

To help the actors get the feeling for the places where scenes will be shot, the director shows slides of some of the film's locations—the bowling alley, Bergen's home, the factory and the main street of town. She also asks the costume designer to show the cast sketches of their costumes.

During these rehearsals, the actors begin working with hand props. In one scene, an actor holds a pistol behind his back while another tries to hide a half empty bottle of whiskey in his jacket.

DIRECTOR
Okay, now this scene takes place in the kitchen. David, you're up leaning against the sink with your gun and Brian, you're seated with your head on the table. Betsy, you come in from the hallway over there and stop in the doorway.

ACTRESS
What was I doing in the previous scene?

DIRECTOR
Remember, you'd sealed the letter in the envelope and put it on the table in the dining room.

ACTRESS
Okay, so I come in here and then what?

DIRECTOR
You're surprised to find them here at first. But notice that your first line is, "Are you sick, Ramos?"

ACTRESS
So I'm really not mad or frightened... I'm worried about him. Why would I assume he was sick? Why not just say, "What's the matter with you, Ramos?"

DIRECTOR
Fine with me. Fred?

WRITER
I like that even better.... it's not so specific. And it suggests she suspects something right off the bat.

DIRECTOR
That's right. Okay, and then when neither of these guys says anything, you're even more suspicious. And you come right down to the other side of the table there and grab Brian by the hair and jerk his head up.

ACTRESS
Oh, good, I'm going to like that.

While these rehearsals continue, the associate producer, unit manager, lighting and set designers and their crews are hard at work preparing the location for the first day's shooting. All of the scenes in the bowling alley will be shot over a two day period. A location scout has found a small, neighborhood bowling alley in Brooklyn which has the character needed for this scene.

The producer has leased this alley for four days: one to set up and light, one to shoot, one for "protection," and one to *strike* (or dismantle). The protection day is important because it relieves the pressure of feeling that everything must be completed during the scheduled shooting day. The director feels she can take more time with each shot. She can rehearse the actors and have opportunities for re-takes when she knows there is another day which can be used without straining the schedule or the budget.

These first four production days will test the organizational and artistic skills of everyone working on this production. The scene involves a fist fight which spills out into the street, stops traffic, draws a large crowd of curious passerbys, and requires three police cars. There are several production assistants needed to handle the large number of extras who will play the passerbys. One assistant director has been assigned the job of working with the New York City police who have agreed to block off the street outside the bowling alley and loan the production company the use of three cars on the second day of shooting.

More modest productions may not have the same large number of staff to oversee production logistics as a project like *Bergen*. However, every possible contingency must be someone's responsibility. Someone will have to make sure all the necessary camera, lighting, and sound equipment is set up and working. Someone has to secure permission to use rooms, close off streets, or take over a section of a public park.

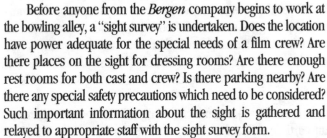

SIGHT SURVEY

PRODUCTION: Bergen
SURVEY BY: M. Larson
PRODUCER: R. Sabor
DIRECTOR: Sanders

DATE OF SURVEY: 2/12
DATE(S) OF PRODUCTION: 3/12 - 3/14
TIME PERIOD(S): 5 A.M. — 9 P.M.
APPROVED BY: LJP

Location address: FLAMINGO BOWL
1432 19th St

Location contact 1: A. Fenner   Phone: (212) 555-2967
Location contact 2: D. Weiss   Phone: (212) 555-1027

Power: _____ 120V. _____ 220V. Available Amps within 700 ft.: _____

Location of main power box: Basement

Nearest Telephone(s): on Premise

Microwave/satellite path notes: NA

Contractural or inherent limitations: None

Alterations required: None

NOTES
See R. Jensen for Parking Permits

Before anyone from the *Bergen* company begins to work at the bowling alley, a "sight survey" is undertaken. Does the location have power adequate for the special needs of a film crew? Are there places on the sight for dressing rooms? Are there enough rest rooms for both cast and crew? Is there parking nearby? Are there any special safety precautions which need to be considered? Such important information about the sight is gathered and relayed to appropriate staff with the sight survey form.

The day before the shoot at the bowling alley, the lighting director is there, supervising the work of six gaffers. These are union electricians who will hang and focus the 20 lighting instruments needed to fulfill the lighting designer's plan.

The scenic designer and cinematographer are also at work inside the bowling alley supervising the work of several grips. These are union laborers who erect scaffolding, platforms or tracks for the twelve different camera locations which are required to get the shots the director has specified in her shooting script. They will also assemble a break-away table and break-away window pane which will be used in the fight when Bergen pushes one of his attackers onto the table and out through the window.

Helping the grips are nine production assistants (PAs), recent college graduates working for minimum wage. Their job is to be "gophers"—they go for coffee, script revisions and lunch.

On the eve of the first day of shooting, the director and the other key members of her team sit down to box lunches around a table in the *Bergen* production offices. The unit manager is the first to report on the progress of plans for the next day's shoot. He makes an important announcement:

> *UNIT MANAGER*
> *All right everybody, be sure to remind your people the crew call is 5:00 a.m. tomorrow. Actors are at 6:00 and extras we don't need until noon. No one parks on the street...we've got a lot for the whole weekend two blocks away from here on 7th and Broad.*
>
> *DIRECTOR*
> *Frank, do you have enough bull horns for all your PAs? Once we start shooting outside tomorrow afternoon, we need super crowd control from those guys.*
>
> *ASST. DIRECTOR*
> *It's all taken care of: each PA has a bull horn and a walkie talkie.*
>
> *DIRECTOR*
> *Francis, I've switched the order of the first shots inside. Did you get that? All those shots from the end of the alley back up to the bar go first because if we wait until after Ramos and DeGatta approach Bergen, the place will be a shambles.*
>
> *CINEMATOGRAPHER*
> *No problem. My first camera location is a high craning shot down by the pins. Right?*
>
> *DIRECTOR*
> *Yep.*
>
> *ASSISTANT DIRECTOR*
> *Linda, Betsy tried on her costume for scene 26 and it's too tight. She asks you to let it out about an inch.*

And so the meeting continues until late in the afternoon when every last detail on everyone's list has been checked. The unit manager returns to his office to write in the changes which have been made in the production schedule. The writer returns to his word processor to rewrite several pages of dialogue from a scene which did not work right in the last rehearsal. The director and associate producer drive to Brooklyn to take one last look at the bowling alley before the next day's shoot begins. As they carefully step over cables and around light poles, the director refers to her script and some rough storyboards she has sketched of the shots she plans for the next day.

SHOOTING

Shooting Day #1, *Bergen*

5:00 A.M. All of the crew assembles the next morning at the bowling alley in time for coffee and donuts and a production meeting with the unit manager. He goes over the day's shooting schedule and breaks the gaffers and grips into two separate teams. One team will work with the director and her assistants on the shot being filmed. Another team will work with the unit manager preparing for the next shot on the schedule.

5:30 A.M. The cameraman and his assistants work with the grips to set the bulky 35mm film camera on its mount for the first shot of the day. One Assistant loads the camera with a film magazine and checks to make sure it has the right lens for the shot the director has described in the script. Another assistant asks two production assistants to stand in the place where the actors playing Bergen and Robin will stand for the first shot. He then uses a long tape measure to determine the exact distance from the face of the lens to the face of the person standing in for Bergen. Knowing this distance will assure the actor will be in focus for this first shot.

The lighting director also uses the two stand-ins to focus the three fresnels which serve as the key and fill light for Bergen and Robin. He also checks to see if the lights concealed in the ceiling cast enough back light on their shoulders to separate them from the background of this scene: the dimly lit lighted bar of the bowling alley.

The sound designer for *Bergen* has been concerned about how to mic the actors in this scene since he first saw the script. "A bowling alley is an invitation for sound disaster," he has complained. "Bowling alleys make great echo chambers." He has decided to solve the problem by giving each principal speaker (Bergen, Robin, Ramos) a wireless body mic which will be concealed in their clothing. This will give him maximum control over each character's level and reduce the room noise and reflected sound from the alley's hard, flat surfaces. However, there may be a problem with the body mics during the fight scenes. The actors may inadvertently hit a mic or the mics might rub against clothing. If this is the case, the sound person is prepared to switch the body mics for highly directional, boom mounted instruments.

Because the sound person recorded ambient room sound a week ago, he won't have to stop production for that purpose today. He knows he has a good fifteen minutes of a typically loud Friday night bowling league ambience.

The bowling alley's locker rooms make perfect dressing rooms for the principal actors. The costumer has unpacked each character's costume and hung them on racks. She has a set of clothing to cover the needs of the three different scenes which will be shot at the bowling alley. She has brought five identical versions of one shirt for the actor playing Ramos. She knows he will be covered with fake blood each time he is thrown through the window into the street by Bergen. She anticipates that several retakes of this shot will be needed. With five shirts, she's well prepared.

The make-up and hair designer for *Bergen* has hired an assistant for this shoot. He is a specialist in effects make-up and will be responsible for making Ramos' face look bloodied and cut after going through the window.

6:00 A.M. The actors arrive and go immediately to the locker rooms for make-up and wardrobe. The production schedule has allotted one hour for this important work.

6:45 A.M. A bulb in one of the fresnels which will be Bergen's key light burns out. The unit manager tells the director it will probably be another ten minutes before they can begin. The assistant director tells everybody to "relax, but don't fall asleep."

7:15 A.M. The bulb is replaced. Everybody resumes work at a faster pace to make up for lost time.

8:10 A.M. The actors playing Robin and Bergen Munoz take their places behind the scorer's desk at alley number five. The director makes sure the cameraman knows how she wants the first shot composed and the speed of the dolly down the alley. She then walks down the alley and moves the actors to their spots behind the desk and calls back down to the cameraman.

DIRECTOR
Got them framed, Gabe?

CAMERAMAN
*Nope. . . Betsy's got to move just a little to her right. . . There, hold it.
That's good. Derek, step upstage of her about a foot. Good. Hold it.
That's it.*

DIRECTOR
*Okay, mark those spots and let's walk through this a couple of times.
Remember, you've got to stay pretty much right on those marks until
Gabe's all the way up here with the camera.*

BETSY
*This mic's really uncomfortable tacked down in my blouse here. I feel like
it's going to fall out. Can't we put it up in my hair?*

DIRECTOR
*Why not? Tony, can you fix Betsy's wireless in her hair and still have her
on mic?*

AUDIO PERSON
Sure, but it will take a couple of minutes.

*DIRECTOR: That's okay. Gabe, while Betsy's getting set, why not dolly up
here once or twice and see how it looks.*

After the microphone is repositioned, the audio person checks the sound level on both actors. The make-up assistant in charge of Betsy touches up her forehead and rearranges her hair to make sure it completely conceals the tiny microphone. The lighting director notices that Betsy is no longer in her light and adjusts a fresnel.

8:30 A.M. The director now asks for "quiet on the set" and turns her attention to the two actors. She asks them to go through their lines while the cameraman and his assistants dolly the camera from a long shot to a medium two shot. In the first run through, the actors finish their dialogue before the camera finishes its movement. The director does not want to increase the speed of the dolly because that would make the shot more dramatic than she intends it to be. So she asks the actors to pace their lines more slowly and to make the tone more casual and conversational. After experimenting with this delicate relationship between the delivery of the lines and the speed of the camera movement, she's satisfied with the technical quality of the shot. The camera movement and the speed of the delivery of the dialogue are now coordinated. However, the dramatic quality of the scene is not "there" yet. The actors are not believable. They appear to be actors playing parts; they have not yet become the characters in the film.

DIRECTOR
(TO HER ASSISTANT) Let's give the crew a half hour break. I want to work with the actors with the set cleared.

ASSISTANT DIRECTOR
Ok. Attention everybody! The crew has a half hour break. Please clear the area. The caterers have set up in the back . . . there's Danish and coffee. And for those of you from California, herbal tea and whole grain oat bran muffins.

DIRECTOR
(TO THE ACTORS) Ok. Let's go through the lines this time without worrying if you're right on the script. Also, as you deliver your lines, look

One of the jobs of the assistant director is continuity: keeping a log of each take of each shot and noting which takes are thought to be good at the time of the shooting and which are thought to be unusable. This will help the editor when he begins putting together the rough cut.

One factor that determines whether a take is usable is whether it contributes to the appearance of continuity. For example, in the fifth shot Ramos is smoking a cigarette. If attention is not paid to this detail, the cigarette might appear to grow longer instead of shorter when we see it in shot six. Another example where the appearance of continuity might be lost is in the ninth scene when Bergen walks through the city. Because this scene is scheduled to be shot on five different days, the assistant director makes sure the actor is dressed exactly the same on each of these days.

11:30 A.M. It appears to be time to actually expose the first foot of film on *Bergen*.

Suddenly the actor playing Bergen complains that the bowling ball, is too heavy. The assistant director asks the property manager to find him a lighter one. The director reminds Bergen that he doesn't actually lift the ball until the next shot, which they aren't shooting until later in the morning. She gently suggests that everybody should concentrate on the shot at hand for now.

DIRECTOR
Okay, everybody. Let's do it.

ASSISTANT DIRECTOR
Quiet on the set. . . Sound.

Another assistant holds up a slate in front of the camera which indicates the date, time, scene and shot number and the number of the take.

ASSISTANT DIRECTOR
Sound. . .

AUDIO PERSON
Rolling!

ASSISTANT DIRECTOR
Camera. . .

CINEMATOGRAPHER
Speed!

ASSISTANT DIRECTOR
Slate.

The assistant holding the slate reads the date and shot number. He then raises the top of the slate and drops it, making a loud "clack" which will be recorded and used when the film is being edited to synchronize the sound and picture.

DIRECTOR
And... action!

ACTRESS
"You remember Ramos? When we were kids?"

ACTOR
"I remember. Pop says he's turned into a no good bum."

ROBIN
"That's only 'cause Pop don't like me goin' out with him."

BERGEN
"If he's not a bum, it's none of Pop's business."

DIRECTOR
And... cut. Okay, that was all right, but Betsy, don't look at him. Look down the alley, like this... and then back over your shoulder... I want you to appear a little more apprehensive. How was that for you, Gabe?

CAMERAMAN
Looked good. Nice and smooth.

DIRECTOR
Good. We're going to take it again now, quiet everybody. Ready for take two.

As each shot is rehearsed, taken, and re-taken, the cast and crew begin to work more effectively as a team. As this happens, the director relaxes and begins to feel free to experiment and improvise some shots which she hadn't planned. She takes advantage of opportunities which only would have become apparent to her with the actors in place and the camera at her side.

> **DIRECTOR**
> *I saw something here, Betsy, in the way you looked at him in that last take. But I don't want the camera moving... so let's just bring it right in close here on Betsy and do the entire shot just on her. Okay, Gabe?*
>
> **CAMERAMAN**
> *Looks good except for her light... there's a heavy shadow in the background. And her hair...*
>
> **ACTRESS**
> *I beg your pardon.*
>
> **CAMERAMAN**
> *I love your hair. It's just out of place.*
>
> **ACTRESS**
> *That sounds better.*
>
> **ASSISTANT DIRECTOR**
> *Gabe. Please take a look at the light here. And Marg, I need Betsy's hair combed back...*

Betsy's make-up assistant quickly pushes an errant strand of hair back in place. The cameraman and his assistants move the camera into place as the lighting director adjusts Betsy's key light. It's now noon and *Bergen* is becoming a reality.

Before the second day of shooting begins, the production team looks at "dailies" or "rushes." This is the footage from the previous day, screened in the order in which it was shot. It's the first time they know for sure whether any of the material they shot will be usable. There is a sense of excitement as these brief flickerings on the monitor are scrutinized by the producer, director, camera person, editor, and writer. This is more than a ritual. Viewing the dailies gives the production team a sense that the intended continuity and "look" of the project is or is not being achieved. It is especially valuable for the editor who can check what he sees with the notes on the tape logs. This will be very useful when he begins to piece the scene together. Of the 53 different takes of the seven shots in the first scene in the bowling alley, the director and editor agree that 10 will probably not end up on the legendary cutting room floor. The shooting ratio for the first day then works out to be about 5 to 1. After the first day of shooting, about two minutes of *Bergen* is "in the can."

For the next two weeks the cast and crew settle into the routine of their production schedule. By the time all location footage has been shot, they will have accumulated thousands of minutes of pictures and sounds. Now begins the work of making all of these disjointed pictures and sounds look like one continuous narrative. *Bergen* is scheduled to premiere on prime time television in just six weeks.

EDITING & MIXING   Based on notes made during the shooting and viewing of dailies, the editor and director have already cut by more than half the choices they must make among different takes of different shots. The editor's first job is to find and group together all the shots which make up each scene. A tremendous aid in this are the slate identifications which he finds at the beginning of each take and the daily shooting log made by the assistant director. At the editing console, he then builds each scene from its various shots, using the director's script as his guide. The first time he assembles a scene, it will be a very rough version, meant only to be shared with the director. He and the director will then refine this rough cut until the scene has the exact pace, flow, and impact desired.

DIRECTOR
Okay, I like the way that scene builds, but you give too much emphasis to Bergen's sister too early with that close-up. And I don't like breaking those first lines of dialogue up into three shots. It makes it too busy.

EDITOR
I can use more of this first shot and then go to the two shot instead of the close-up on her.

> DIRECTOR
> That's the idea. Then, when Ramos comes in and she becomes the focal point of that moment, put that close up of her back in.
>
> EDITOR
> Is there going to be music under here?
>
> DIRECTOR
> No, just the room noise.

Each day the editor builds another two or three scenes and shows them to the director. Slowly, scene by scene, the story begins to take shape. At the end of the third week, both the director and editor agree that they are ready to share a rough cut of the entire program with the executive producer, producer, and writer. This rough cut does not have music, sound effects, special visual effects and transitions, titles, or credits. It is also six minutes too long. These important refinements will be made after the producer and director are satisfied with the rough cut.

Everyone gathers in the executive producer's office at the IPW corporate center. A videotape play back machine and monitor have been set up at one end of the room. The director reminds them that what they are about to see is only a rough cut. The lights are dimmed.

About 78 minutes later the lights come up and there is an uneasy stir in the room. The executive producer clears his throat and looks to the producer.

> PRODUCER
> Well. . . frankly. . . I like it. I was really moved.
>
> EXECUTIVE PRODUCER
> I have to agree with Claude, and I think we may have a real winner here.
>
> PRODUCER
> I mean, it's not perfect. . . there's a way to go yet and I can't wait to see

it with Charlene's music. But we're very close here.

EXECUTIVE PRODUCER
That scene by the river seems a bit long and it's hard to see all those people in the dark. Anything you can do about that?

DIRECTOR
Well, we can take a look at it.

EXECUTIVE PRODUCER
And I don't know why you spend so much time looking at that dead body in the end there. I don't think the network's going to buy that anyway.

PRODUCER
That's where you can pick up some time. You've got to trim about six or seven minutes, right?

EXECUTIVE PRODUCER
Seems to me you could lose that whole scene by the river and not lose any of the story, am I right, Claude?

The discussion and critique continue for more than an hour and by the time it's over, the director and editor have several pages of notes. They too see opportunities for changes and refinements. They will now return to the editing console and make the changes they feel are mandatory and experiment with some modifications which might further strengthen the story. They work with the knowledge that the time for flexibility is growing shorter and shorter. In less than a week they must screen the completed film for the network. By then, the music must be recorded and laid in, the soundtrack "sweetened" with sound effects, and the titles and credits added.

It's past midnight and the director and editor have been working at the editing console since 3:00 in the afternoon. The final scene, when Bergen is discovered shot in the face outside his parents' home, has been re-edited five different ways. But neither the director nor the editor is satisfied.

DIRECTOR
I know Larry doesn't think the network will let us get away with the long zoom out from his battered face. But that's really what the final image has to be.

EDITOR
But it could be stronger if we just suggest it. Let's try this: we show his face, then cut to his mother's reaction. Then we've got his father coming out of the house... we see it on his face. Then the sister... she's looking out the window upstairs and we've got a beautiful shot of her face through the curtains.

DIRECTOR
But then hers is the last face we see... it's not her story.

EDITOR
Let me finish! Slow dissolve from her face... to the long overhead shot with him on the lawn and everybody running out to him. Then, blam, we cut to black and roll the credits.

DIRECTOR
No, not a cut to black. Freeze it, then pull all the color to a black and white and then credits.

EDITOR
A little showy for my taste.

DIRECTOR
I think I like it, but let's see what it looks like.

The director leaves the editing suite while the editor makes the changes they discussed.

The next day, the director, confident that the picture side of *Bergen* is just about complete, turns her attention to the sound track.

Her first decision is to make use of "found" music rather than commission a composer to write an original score. She makes this decision because she wants the sound track to be filled with contemporary country music, the one thing Bergen has in common with the family and friends he left behind when he moved away. He no longer works in a factory, does his own car repairs, or bowls but he still listens to Willie Nelson, the Oak Ridge Boys, and Tanya Tucker.

The first step in building the movie's sound track is a meeting with the sound designer, editor and the director to review the script and the rough cut. The meeting is in a conference room with a videotape machine and a television monitor. Everyone has copies of the script in front of them.

DIRECTOR
By early next week all the music has to be selected. That will give the legal department enough time to negotiate fees, and make sure we can get rights to everything you select.

PRODUCER
We certainly don't want to go into the mix with something we don't have the rights to.

DIRECTOR
The way I see it there are slots for about fifteen songs and ten or so solo guitars or harmonicas. Let's go through the rough cut so we can discuss how I see the music being used. Feel free to ask anything as we view it.

SOUND DESIGNER
Is the script accurate? Does it follow the rough cut?

EDITOR
Pretty much. Only scenes five and twelve have been changed from the script.

SOUND DESIGNER
That's good to know. Ok. Let's see what you've got.

EDITOR
Here goes.

THEY VIEW THE ROUGH CUT.
EDITOR
In this first scene, the script calls for a Willie Nelson number.

DIRECTOR
I'd like "Detour" or "Let The Rest of The World Go By."

SOUND DESIGNER
I'll buy that. Either would work in that slot.

EDITOR
Then here in shot three after his battle with the tractor trailer, we'll need something strong.

DIRECTOR
In shot six, I want either a solo harmonica or a song with soft lyrics. McEntire's "You Must Really Love Me," or "So, So, So Long" might do it.

SOUND DESIGNER
Why?

DIRECTOR
Because this guy has cut all his ties. . . he's a corporate loner.

SOUND DESIGNER
Ok. Although I'm not sure McEntire's right there.

DIRECTOR
Fine. I expect you to come up with what you think is right. Then we'll compare notes.

After this meeting, the designer listens to thirty-three CDs and fifteen audio cassettes and develops a long list of songs and instrumental cuts that seem to have what is needed. To help make his final selections, he calls upon the editor.

It takes an entire afternoon and half the next day of listening to music while viewing the rough cut for the sound designer to decide which songs and which instrumental pieces work best with the edited scenes. He delivers a list of his selections plus information on who has to be contacted concerning purchase of the rights to the director. He also faxes the director a copy of the script with indications as to which cut of music goes with which scene.

1. VIEW THROUGH WINDSHIELD OF MOVING CAR. LATE AFTERNOON

WILLIE NELSON'S "DETOUR" is heard through the roar of traffic. The view through the windshield is very confusing because there are many exit signs from which to choose coming upon the driver very quickly.

TITLE OVER WINDSHIELD.

The title fades and we cut to ECU of Bergen as he tries to decide which exit to take. This is unfamiliar territory. He may have decided too late.

2. LS OF CAR RACING TO GET IN FRONT OF TRUCK SO HE CAN MAKE HIS EXIT.

Music continues until loud roar of trailer's horn drowns it out.

3. MCU OF BERGEN.

He is slightly shaken but pleased with his victory
and celebrates by turning up the music—**I SAW THE
LIGHT**.

4. LS FROM MOVING CAR OF FACTORY WITH PICKET LINE
IN FRONT.

Hold as camera picks up individual strikers and
dollies past. Then stops.

5. CU OF BERGEN.

He is uncomfortable, turns.

6. (CROSS FADE OUT **"I SAW THE LIGHT"** TO SOLO HAR-
MONICA). MLS OF BERGEN'S PARENTS OPENING FRONT DOOR
GREETING HIM.

The director looks over the list and immediately calls the
sound designer and compliments him.

> *DIRECTOR*
> *I like what you put together and I'll send the list over to legal. They'll take
> care of getting the rights. In the meantime, I want you to move on. Begin
> building your tracks and let's plan to see a scratch mix in three days.*

For the next two days the designer records nineteen separate sounds tracks onto one audiotape. Four of the tracks contain "sync" sound, six contain voice overs, two contain ambient tracks, three contain music, three contain sound effects and
one contains SMPTE time code.

As you recall from our discussion of sound mixing in Chapter 11, time code serves three functions. First, it aids the sound
designer in preparing the multi-track audio tape for sound mixing.
For example, the sound designer views the videotape and sees
that smoke comes out of a gun at 01:02:18:22 (one hour, two

minutes, eighteen seconds, and twenty-two frames). Knowing this he runs the audio tape on the multi-track machine to 01:02:18:22 and records the gun shot at this precise point.

The second use of SMPTE time code is to interlock the videotape and the multi-track audio machines so they can be used together. The sounds coming from the multi-track audio playback will be heard as if they are part of or "locked" to the picture which comes from the videotape playback machine. A gun shot on the audio tape will be locked to a picture of a gun with smoke coming out of it; the music of Willie Nelson will be locked to the opening frame of the film.

The third use of SMPTE time code is in the preparation of rundown sheets which are used during sound mixing. The rundown sheets list the contents of each line or track of music and when it is to be heard. For example, the sheet below indicates that Willie Nelson's song *Detour* must be faded in at three minutes, five seconds and one frame or SMPTE number 00:03:05:01.

Sound Mix Rundown	Client: IPW Job: Bergen Engineer: Jon Adelman				
Page 2 of 21					
Action	Sound Cue/ Designation		Mixer Note	T. C. In	T.C. Out
Driving Scenery: Truck enters township	W. Nelson: Detour	I	Fade In	00:03:05:01	00:05:46:00

With the rundown sheet, the audio tape containing the eighteen separate elements of sound plus time code and the videotape containing the video portion of the movie, the sound designer is prepared to produce a scratch mix of the sound track for the director. He does this at the facilities of a sound house which specializes in sound mixing. An employee of the sound house, a sound engineer, will do the actual sound mix using the rundown sheet as a guide. Also, the sound designer sits next to the sound engineer to answer questions and help interpret the rundown sheet.

> ENGINEER
> As I read your rundown sheet, in the first scene you fade up on tracks G and H with ambiance then they go under for the first cut of music, until the truck horn on track J.
>
> SOUND DESIGNER
> That's it exactly.
>
> ENGINEER
> Let's give it a try.

During the mixing process the sound designer will hear for the first time how the composite track actually sounds. If a portion of the track does not work out as planned or if the engineer interprets the rundown sheet in a way with which the designer does not agree, the designer will ask the engineer to redo the mix. This is common and does not offend the engineer. It's part of the creative give-and-take in sound mixing.

> SOUND DESIGNER
> The music on the last scene is too hot. It drowns out the voice over, can we try it again?
>
> ENGINEER
> Sure, let me reset my levels. . . and here we go.

This scratch mix takes fifteen hours, which means the director does not get her hands on it until a day after the deadline. The production is now behind schedule and the final screening for the network is less than a week away. Realizing this, the director schedules a review of the sound track with the producer, the executive producer, the editor, and the sound designer in the evening.

Over dinner in the conference room at IPW, the four watch the movie while listening to the mixed sound track for the first time. Both the director and producer have pen and paper and make notes for themselves as they listen and watch. The producer writes very little while the director fills up ten pages.

After the final image of Bergen dead in front of his parent's home, the music fades and the screen fills with video snow. The room is silent. The sound designer's heart is pounding. He knows if the producer and director are not satisfied, he'll be working throughout the night under great pressure. Then the producer opens his mouth and all eyes turn to him.

PRODUCER
Yes... a big fat yes!

DIRECTOR
Great. It really works. I mean it's much stronger than I ever imagined.

SOUND DESIGNER
You like it?

EDITOR
Sounds to me like they really like it... congratulations.

DIRECTOR
I made a bunch of notes, details on when ambiance is too hot, music too dominant... that sort of thing. But, these are easy to clean up. The bottom line is it works.

SOUND DESIGNER
I'm really pleased and I'm really tired. Can we get together tomorrow for your comments and I'll make arrangements for the final mix on Wednesday?

DIRECTOR
Sure, let's meet tomorrow at 11:00.

After their meeting the next day, the sound designer revises his rundown sheets and returns to the sound house to do a final mix with the same engineer he worked with earlier. The director sits in on these sessions.

> DIRECTOR
> The background has got to sneak under fairly quickly because you're burying her first line.
>
> ENGINEER
> Ok, that's easy to fix... anything else?
>
> SOUND DESIGNER
> Can you filter out any of that high frequency in the second background music. It's annoying.
>
> ENGINEER
> Let me take a look.

This sound mixing takes two full working days. When it is completed, the director and producer are satisfied with their product and call the Executive Producer at IPW to tell him it's almost time to show the finished work to the network. The titles and credits need to be added and the director and producer want to write a brief dedication to the American laborer to serve as an epilogue.

SCREENING

The afternoon of the screening for the network executives arrives. The director, executive producer, and producer meet in a plush screening room on the twenty-fifth floor of the network's corporate offices. They will watch the film with the Vice President of Special Projects, the President of Night Time Programming, and the Vice President for Sales and Marketing. After the usual introductions, casual conversation and the serving of refreshments, the lights are dimmed and the screen fills with the first image of *Bergen*.

Seventy minutes later, the lights come back on. The network executives are generally pleased with *Bergen*. They are aware that a small but eager audience has already been created for it based on the reputation of the stage play. It has been scheduled to be shown on a Sunday night and will be promoted as "a serious drama about the passions of a family threatened by an America they no longer understand." Arrangements are made with the producer to screen an advanced copy for New York and Los Angeles critics two weeks before it appears on television. The network promotions department also schedules the two stars to appear on national and local television talk shows.

TV GUIDE

Sunday, 8:00. CH 6. Bergen, network special about a poor boy who leaves home and comes back rich and misunderstood. Powerful performances from Derek Blains and Betsy Wagner.

TALK SHOW HOST
*Betsy, you were appearing every night in **Days of Darkness** on Broadway at the same time **Bergen** was being shot. How did you manage that?*

ACTRESS
It was a nightmare... but I felt so strongly about this script... And I wanted to work with Nancy Corcoran. She's a tremendously talented director.

TALK SHOW HOST
Let's take a look at one of the scenes. Tell us what's happening here, Betsy.

ACTRESS
Oh, this is the kitchen scene, one of my favorite moments in the film.

Bergen is that rare event on commercial television: thoughtful and cinematic. It has the look of those landscapes that were carved into the American psyche by such photographers as Evans and Reuter. It feels and sounds authentic, like passages from *Let Us Now Praise Famous Men* or John Dos Passos' trilogy.

—THE NEW YORK TIMES

If you were fortunate enough to see the play during its short New York run, you will find much that is new in this television version of *Bergen*. But the gritty John Raymond script is intact and the performances of Betsy Wagner and Derek Blains will surely earn them same attention at this year's EMMY's as they received at last year's TONY award ceremony.

—L.A. TIMES

The night *Bergen* is broadcast, the executives of IPW invite the cast and the production team to a party at a downtown restaurant. Along the walls of the crowded room, there are three large television sets where the guests will view the movie as it airs.

The director is the only member of the production team unable to attend. She had scheduled a visit with an old college roommate long before she knew when *Bergen* would be shown. Her friend is a housewife living in a small community ninety miles from the city. So, while the writer, producer, editor, sound designer and other members of the production team and cast watch *Bergen* as they drink champagne, the director watches in the living room of a home in a typical American small town sipping coffee with her college roommate and her roommate's elderly parents.

In the Manhattan restaurant, after the final shot of the final scene, everyone studies the closing credits and cheers loudly when his or her name appears. Ninety miles away in the living room, the family begins talking after the final shot and ignores the credits. Only when the director's friend shouts, "Look there's your name!" does anyone begin to pay attention.

In the Manhattan restaurant, immediately after the final credit, the cast and crew begin to analyze what they saw. "I think the lighting really looked great on that screen." "I wish the pace had been faster in the last two scenes." "The frozen frame at the end was the wrong way to go."

In the living room, as the director is saying good-bye, her friend's elderly mother comes up close to the director and shyly says, "I loved your little program. It reminded me of when I was young and how important we all were to each other."

A month later, the director joins the writer, producer and executive producer at the offices of IPW for a "post mortem" or project evaluation of *Bergen*. Other executives with IPW are seated around the table.

EXECUTIVE PRODUCER
Our numbers were pretty good. The ratings were high enough to keep the network happy. Also we got some great press.

MARKETING VICE PRESIDENT
Also we struck a deal with Bismark who will sell it in Europe and Videomask who will distribute on cassette.

EXECUTIVE PRODUCER
Mark also got us a rerun this summer.

The director knows these positive results will certainly aid her career. Because IPW did so well with *Bergen*, she will inevitably have other production companies offering her lucrative directing jobs. It has taken her many years to reach this position and she savors her success: her direction resulted in solid ratings, an overseas and cassette distribution contract, and an Emmy nomination. It also, she proudly recalls, meant something to her friend's elderly mother. And to her surprise, the woman's comments mean as much to her as the good ratings and the Emmy nomination.

Four months later. It is past midnight, in an office at IPW. The executive producer of *Bergen* turns the last page of a murder mystery he has been reading for the last week.

He puts the book down and stares at the ceiling. The story of murder and deceit he has just read has taken hold of his imagination. He sees it in his mind, scene by scene, shot by shot, frame by frame. He sees it as an opportunity to take advantage of the books' best-selling reputation. He knows of an actress who would be perfect for the leading role. But best of all, he knows of a young director who is just right for this project. Before he leaves to go home, he picks up his mini-cassette and dictates a reminder for tomorrow:

EXECUTIVE PRODUCER
*Call Nancy Cocoran. Tell her to read **Blood at Midnight** and call me when she's done.*

Appendix A

Production Paperwork

Throughout our description of the three stages of the production process, you have seen the production team preparing a variety of documents: scripts, lighting plots, budgets, edit decision lists, etc. Here we will discuss the purpose of each of these documents and present examples to use in your own production work.

Paperwork should not be seen as an end in itself. A production book which is neatly typed and bound in a leather portfolio does not guarantee the resulting program will be a success. But, planning on paper and communicating clearly those plans to collaborators usually leads to successful productions.

The kinds of paperwork and the way they are used in television and film production varies from one setting to anther. There are two reasons for this. First, as we have seen, different programs demand different preparation and planning. The producers of a nightly newscast draw up one set and lighting design which is used every night for a year. Their counterparts at an advertising agency create a detailed storyboard, set and lighting design for each of the fifteen shots of a twenty second commercial. The script for an instructional program produced multicamera in a studio is written in a split page format while a made-for-television-movie shot singlecamera on location is written in a single column.

The second reason for the confusing look of production paperwork is that television production is carried out in a variety of environments. Each has its own needs and requirements. At a large production house, such as the one which produced BERGEN, there are hierarchies of management and job specialization with rigid paperwork requirements. In an institutional setting such as Mammoth Oil where writing, design and direction might be the responsibility of one or two person, documents are more informal: requests for equipment are handwritten on a piece of note paper instead of on a pre-printed form.

PROPOSALS

The early stages of most productions are concerned with writing proposals. In some settings, proposals are in the form of letters or memos. In other settings, they are more formal: one or two page descriptions of the intended program and what it will cost in facilities, time and money to get it done. Professional proposals contain all or most of the following.

1. A brief description of the program's purpose.
2. A summary of the program's content.
3. A description of the target audience.
4. A statement about how the program will be used.
5. A proposed budget, production schedule, an estimate of facilities and personnel needed.

Purpose

A statement of the program's purpose should be clear and simple. If it's not, it may be the first indication that trouble is in store in the design and execution stages. A purpose statement might be as simple as saying the program "will provide a showcase for Mr. Smith's talents." For educational and informational types of programs, the purpose statement should identify exactly what an audience should be able to do after viewing the program.

Content

A statement about the content should contain a brief description of what the viewer will see and hear and in what order when the program is complete. It may be the plot of a dramatic program. "It is about an old policeman near retirement and a young policewoman who chase a jewel thief across Australia. The first sequence is the robbery; the second the assignment of the two officers to the case; the third and forth show their adventures in the outback..." Or, a content statement may be the outline of an instructional program. "In the first sequences we demonstrate how to unpack the X93. In the second sequence we show how to stand it on end...."

Style

One way to describe style is to place the intended program into a program or film category: sitcom, journalist documentary, quiz show, music video, film noire, etc. Another way to describe style is to compare the intended program to an existing program or film. "We plan to use The Sixty Minutes style." "It will be structured like Midnight Run but have the look of a Bogart film."

Target Audience

The target audience for a program should be defined as clearly as possible. For broadcast programs, the target audience is usually described in terms of broad demographics (early teens, young mothers, males over thirty-nine.) For many programs distributed on cassettes, satellite and cable, the audience can be more narrowly defined (plant managers, corporate lawyers, dog owners, sixth graders, etc.)

How the Program Will Be Used

Again this element of the proposal varies depending on whether the intended program is to be broadcast or not. If it is to be broadcast, the usage statement might take the form of a marketing plan or strategy. If the program is not for broadcast, a description of where the program will be seen, under what conditions and if there will be any immediate follow-up activity (such as a question and answer session or a demonstration) should be included in this section of the proposal.

Budget, Schedule, Facilities & Personnel

Somewhere in the proposal should be a statement of the anticipated needs for the production. There might be four categories of needs to address: money, time, facilities and people. Clearly the value of a needs statement is to alert those who are going to pay for a program what resources will be required.

HOMETOWN is a two hour documentary about Centertown, Washington. The program will be broadcast on PBS. In addition, we envision cassette distribution to universities and high schools for use in Sociology and American History courses.

Until the mid 1970s, Centertown is where the Hometown "Rhino Truck" was made. When the factory closed many Centertown residents felt the town was doomed. They were wrong. The town survived. However it is a very different place to work, live and grow up in than it was before April 6, 1977, the day the factory closed.

In many ways Centertown survived this loss very well. Today there are plenty of jobs. The community banded together and won a political battle with the State in halting plans to create a low level nuclear dump site in a nearby community. However, on that fateful day when Hometown closed, Centertown was threatened with becoming another faceless American town.

Today there are openings at the Wendy's, McDonald's and Holiday Inn at the Interchange, sales and clerical jobs at the two large malls in town, and assembly line positions at Jones & Jones and Tupperware. But none of these employers are locally owned and run like Hometown was for many years.

This documentary, then, is the story of the Hometown closing and how it threatened to transform Centertown into another of the hundreds of America towns that are owned and operated by outsiders.

The story will be told in a reflexive style -- members of the community will tell their story through interviews, photomation, songs written about Hometown trucks and newsreel footage. The film will also include events like the annual reunion of Hometown employees, a visit with the retired CEO of Hometown in his compound in Arizona, football practice at the High School and an afternoon at a truck stop speaking and driving with Hometown aficionados.

The documentary will contain two contrasting styles. Key interviews and photomations will have a polished, highly produced look like that used in the interviews in the "Thin Blue Line." In contrast, the events like the football practice and the afternoon at the truck stop will be shot in a verite style similar to that used by filmmakers like Wiseman and the Maysles.

We have received funding for about $75,000 of our budget of $200,000. We will use these funds to begin shooting some of the scenes outlined in treatment. We hope the remainder of our budget will come from the Open Solicitation Fund of CPB.

Treatments are general descriptions of the intended program organized into scenes or sequences. Assume you have watched the completed program. Then, write a summary of what you saw in the present tense.

B. SAMPLE TREATMENT

Treatment for Syracuse Historical Video

A. A day in the life of late nineteenth century Syracuse. Audio is music of the day, natural sounds, actors dialogue with some set up and transitions by narrator. James Geddes wakes up and begins his day. A school boy makes his way to school. We see workers waiting to unload canal barges and then another set unloading a train. We learn that a family is secreting a black slave from the South in their farm house. We see the work on the farm parallel with work at one of the early industries. A student leaves a building at Syracuse University. Families sit down for the evening meal, eating foods of their native lands. Some families are seen headed for an opera, others to the vaudeville show and others attend an abolitionist meeting to hear Sam May.

The concept here is that we see the details of daily life: how people dressed, the architecture, the rich diversity of the city and surrounding farmlands. We see some of the luminaries from this period working and living side by side with the common man. All four categories of content are woven together to demonstrate that they are dependent on one another: transportation serves the growth of business and capital; transportation brings a diversity of people and contact with the wider world and ideas of progress and reform; transportation brings a diversity of people and contact with the wider world and the consequent flowering of culture.

B. A day in the life of late twentieth century Syracuse. We see the same patterns of daily life. Audio is music of the day, natural sounds, actors dialogue with some set up and transitions by narrator. The day begins with workers entering buildings like the refurbished New Process Gear factory or the Syracuse Savings Bank building. We see workers in the farmlands in parallel with those at the Science and Technology Center at the University. We see people enjoying the art museum, the zoo, Syracuse Stage, the balloon festival. Routes 81, the Thruway and the airport have replaced the canal and the railroad. We see shoppers at the Galleries and Armory Square. Again, we see people enjoying life in their homes but also eating at good restaurants. We see some of the rituals of life: births, marriages, graduations, etc. Throughout, the emphasis is on the way Syracuse has built upon its past in the most positive ways and how it remains a cross roads of ideas and cultures.

A script is a recipe. It gives instructions about how characters should perform, what they might say, what elements of the visual language should be mixed together, in what sequence and, sometimes, for how long.

The basic visual element of a script (and the resulting program) is a shot. A shot is defined as the frames between two transitions. During that time, the content and composition of the frames may change. The camera might zoom from a long shot to a close up or a character might walk out of the frame. But once a transition is made—a cut, a dissolve, wipe or fade—one shot ends and another begins.

A scene is made up of a series of shots that are related to a common theme, image, action, or narrative cue. Theme: several shots of the facade of a tall building which, when seen together, show the power and reach of the corporation housed within. Image: several shots (starting in extreme close up and progressing to a long shot) of the parts that make up the latest Detroit sports car. Action: a murderer picks the lock on the door, opens it, crosses the room, takes a dagger from his pocket and raises it over a sleeping figure. Narrative cues: it's fall at the university, the students are back on campus; it's late at night and the noise in the bushes might be the monster.

The name of the larger structural units made up of several scenes varies depending on whether the work is fiction or nonfiction. In works of fiction, one or more scenes are grouped into acts. A half hour situation comedy usually has a two act structure. Hour long television dramas and films usually follow the traditional three act structure of the well-made play. Often this structure will be modified to include a prologue at the beginning and/or an epilogue at the end.

In documentaries, news programs and other works of nonfiction, a number of scenes make up a sequence. The change from one sequence to another is determined by a number of factors such as change of time, place, topic or tone.

Script Forms

There are two basic types of scripts which you have seen in this book: writers' scripts and shooting scripts.

WRITER'S SCRIPT These scripts, usually based on treatments, are often referred to as "master scene" scripts. They contain dialogue, narration and a general description of what will be seen or what action will be contained in the finished program. In most instances, writer's scripts do no indicate sound effects, music, camera shots or other technical elements. In such a script there will be more attention to the details of structure and content. It is not broken up into individual shots. How to technically achieve the program—precise composition of shots, the exact relationship between sound effects and music, etc.—should not necessarily be the concern of the writer in a writer's script.

SHOOTING SCRIPT These scripts are also referred to as "technical" or "director" scripts. They contain the dialogue, narration and action in the writer's script plus shot descriptions, transitions, sound and music cues and other technical elements. In many instances, shooting scripts also indicate the time within the program of each of these items.

The style in which a shooting script is written can vary from one production setting to another. However, there are conventions used by the majority of professional writers and directors. We detail these conventions below.

Sight Usually written in UPPER CASE, single spaced.
   WHAT IS SEEN What is the subject of each shot.

>   MARY'S FACE IN PROFILE.

   HOW IS IT SEEN What is the composition of each shot (LS, MS, CU) and how does the composition change (if it does) throughout the duration of the shot.

>   CU OF MARY'S FACE IN PROFILE.

   TRANSITIONS What is the transitional device (dissolve, fade, wipe) to be used from shot to shot. The most commonly used transition is the cut and it therefore does not need to be specified. Transitions are usually underlined.

```
CU OF MARY'S FACE IN PROFILE.
DISSOLVE.
LS OF MARY LOOKING INTO THE
SUNSET AS JACK WALKS IN
FROM FRAME LEFT.
```

Sound Usually double spaced.

WHO SPEAKS Identify the person speaking. This is usually in UPPER CASE and set off in the center of the column punctuated by a colon.

```
                MARY:
```

WHAT IS SAID The lines of dialogue or narration which the person identified speaks. This is usually in lower case. Punctuation used in writing dialogue and narration has specific and important meaning for the talent. It gives clues about how lines are to be delivered. Ellipsis (…) are used to indicate that a person has failed to complete a thought. The dash (--) is used to indicate that one person has been interrupted by another. Exclamation points should be used sparingly; only when a line is to be spoken with extreme intensity. The semi-colon should be avoided as it creates ambiguity for the spoken word.

```
                MARY:
        I didn't think you were coming
        today. You should have—

                JACK:
        I should have what? Sent you a
        telegram?

                MARY:
        You could have phoned or... No,
        you would never think of that!
```

HOW IT IS SAID Directions about how lines are to be delivered should be given only when absolutely necessary. Well written copy or dialogue should convey tone without prompting

Action Stage directions for actors and acresses are usually written in UPPER CASE and enclosed in parentheses.

  INDIVIDUAL Action instructions which relate to what a single character is to do are placed inside that character's dialogue or narration.

```
                         MARY:
             How could you treat me this way?
             (SHE STANDS AND TURNS AWAY, HER
             HAND TO HER FACE.) I trusted you.
```

  ENSEMBLE Action instructions which relate to more than one character are separated from dialogue or narration.

```
                         MARY:
             Don't ever speak to me again.
             (MARY TURNS AROUND AND SLAPS JACK
             HARD ACROSS THE FACE. HE
             STUMBLES BACK AND FALLS OVER
             THE CLIFF.)

                         MARY:
             Oh, Jack, what have I done?
```

Timing Some programs require exact timing. There are two types of time which might be indicated in production scripts. Such times are indicated in total seconds and minutes.

  SEGMENT TIME The time (estimated or exact) of discrete program elements such as one news story in a half hour news cast, a demonstration used in an educational program, a romantic montage in a drama, etc..

  RUNNING TIME The time which is the accumulation of each succeeding segment time. Ideally, the total running time of a program should equal the total of all the segment times.

Act, Scene & Shot Numbers When appropriate, singlecamera production scripts should indicate clearly the hierarchical sequence of each shot. Acts are usually designated in roman numerals. For example, II.3.45 would indicate shot number 45 in scene three of act two.

Page Slug or Header At the top of each page should be the title (or a shortened version of it) and the page number. Some scripts (like newscasts) should indicate both page number and the total number of pages for the entire script.

```
SIX O'CLOCK NEWS        PAGE # 3 OF 22.
```

The format of a shooting script depends on the production style: multi- or singlecamera. Split page scripts are most often used in multicamera environments. Single column scripts are most often used for programs shot singlecamera.

C. MULTICAMERA SCRIPT

BUILD A CITY

VIDEO:	AUDIO:
BLACK.	SFX: BIRDS, WIND THROUGH TREES.
SLIDE #1: EARLY MORNING SCENE, EMPTY MEADOWLAND.	
DISSOLVE TO:	
SLIDE #2: XCU, IN THE GRASS, LOOKING ACROSS THE MEADOW.	
DISSOLVE TO:	SFX: UNDER, HOLD.
SLIDE #3: XCU, THROUGH BRANCHES OF TREES ACROSS MEADOW.	
INSERT CHROMAKEY OF MS NARRATOR IN SLIDE #3.	NARRATOR:
	What do you need to build a
	city? Well, you need a place
	where people can find shelter
CU OF NARRATOR IN SLIDE #3.	and feel secure. And there
	has to be a reason for those
	people to want to stay and
	raise families.
	SFX: HAMMERING, CONSTRUCTION.
MS OF NARRATOR IN STUDIO BESIDE MODEL OF FIRST CITY HALL STRUCTURE.	There must be work for them to
	do. And there must be the
	promise that the place will
	sustain itself, grow and
	prosper.

==CONT.==

21.

CONTINUED:

We see Ellen and Gerald in earnest conversation in a corner, going over some printouts. Barry is still busy with his camera.

CLOSE ON ELLEN AND GERALD

as they go over the printout.

> **GERALD**
> I think we have to offer special overtime incentives to meet these delivery schedules.

> **ELLEN**
> You're better off staffing up permanently. We're in for at least a seventeen percent upswing...

Adam arrives with two plates of cake.

> **ADAM**
> You guys are going to take time out to help celebrate.

> **GERALD**
> (taking the plate)
> Only thing I can't resist is temptation.

> **ADAM**
> (putting an arm
> affectionately around
> Ellen's waist)
> Me too...

CLOSE ON SPOON AND GLASS

A SPOON CLINKING ON A GLASS for attention. CHATTER CONTINUES. The SPOON CLINKS AGAIN, LOUDER.

WIDER - ELLEN'S OFFICE - MARIE, ELLEN, ADAM, GERALD, BARRY, OTHERS - DAY

It is Ellen who raps the glass for attention.

> **ELLEN**
> If I could... hello?
> (more glass clinking,
> they turn to her)
> If I could have your attention...
> We have one announcement I think will interest you all, especially our guest of honor. Marie...

(CONTINUED)

A special form of shooting script is the storyboard. These are useful for productions or sequences within programs which require specific visualization before execution. Advertising agencies use storyboards to "sell" the idea of a commercial to clients. Some productions with expensive special effects sequences will be storyboarded long before shooting begins. A storyboard can be as simple as a rough stick figure drawing of each shot with it's accompanying audio.

MOTHER HOLDS BOX. DAUGHTER TAKES
OUT SUNRINSE SHEET, PUTS IT IN DRYER.

ANNCR VO:
Now when you...

MOTHER TURNS ON DRYER.

turn on your dryer...

SPECIAL EFFECTS START. SUNLIGHT SEEPS
OUT OF DRYER DOOR.

Turn on the sunshine.

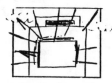

THE BASEMENT BACKGROUND BECOMES THE
OUTDOORS.

Turn on the freshness.

DRYER BECOMES TRANSPARENT AS WE
MOVE IN ON SUNRISE BOX.

ANNCR VO: New SunRinse Downy dryer
sheets!

KEEP MOVING IN AS WE PAN DOWN TO SHOW
CLOTHES AND A BRILLIANT SHEET TUMBLING
IN THE AIR.

So airy light...

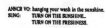

CONTINUE MOVING IN ON SHEET TILL IT
BECOMES A SUNBURST.

so sunny-fresh, it's like...

REVEAL THE CLOTHES NOW MAGICALLY HUNG
ON A LAUNDRY LINE.

ANNCR VO: hanging your wash in the sunshine.
SUNG: TURN ON THE SUNSHINE...
            TURN ON THE FRESHNESS.

PRODUCT NAME PANS IN FROM RIGHT.

ANNCR VO: It's the new dryer sheet from...

PRODUCT NAME AND SUN BECOME BOX AND
LOGO.

SunRinse Downy, the fabric softener that...

MOM TAKES CLOTHES FROM DRYER AS
DAUGHTER ENTERS. (SNIFF)

gives you fluffier softness, too.

AS MOTHER AND DAUGHTER TOUCH AND
SMELL CLOTHES, BACKGROUND BECOMES
OUTDOORS.

SUNG: TURN ON THE SUNSHINE.
         TURN ON THE FRESHNESS.

MOM PUTS SWEATER ON DAUGHTER,
DAUGHTER HUGS HER.

ANNCR VO: SunRinse Dryer Sheets, New from
Downy.
SUNG: COME ON IN!

PRODUCTION WORKSHEETS

This category of production paperwork includes forms which make communications among those responsible for a program accurate and professional. Most of these forms have been used by the production teams in the design and execution stages of *Bergen*, *In the Valley*, and *The Company Responds*.

BREAKDOWN SHEET

PRODUCER:
TITLE:
DIRECTOR:

PAGE # ____ OF ____
SHOOT DATE:
TIMES:

SCENE #	PAGES	LOCATION	INT/ EXT.	DAY/ NIGHT	CAST	CREW	PROPS	NOTES

G. CREW ASSIGNMENT SHEET

CREW ASSIGNMENTS

PRODUCTION:
DIRECTOR:

WORK DATE:
UNIT MANAGER:

TIME IN	TIME OUT	NAME	POSITION	LOCATION AND COMMENTS (S=STUDIO/C=CONTROL/F=FIELD)

EDIT DECISION LIST

TITLE:
EDITOR:

PAGE # ____ of TOTAL ____

SHOT #	TAPE #	TRANSITION	DESCRIPTION	AUDIO	VIDEO	IN TIME	OUT TIME	NOTES

I. FACILITIES REQUEST FORM

FACILITIES REQUEST

PRODUCTION: DATE REQUESTED:
REQUESTED BY: DATE NEEDED:
PRODUCER: TIME PERIOD:
DIRECTOR: APPROVED BY:

Studio A [ ]   Control A [ ]
    Lights [ ]   Switcher [ ]
    Cam-1 [ ] QTV [ ]   Audio console [ ]
    Cam-2 [ ] QTV [ ]   Character generator [ ]
    Cam-3 [ ] QTV [ ]
    Cam-4 [ ] Type: _____
    Boom [ ]
    Crane [ ]

Studio B [ ]
    Lights [ ]   Control B [ ]
    Cam-1 [ ] QTV [ ]   Switcher [ ]
    Cam-2 [ ] QTV [ ]   Audio console [ ]
    Cam-3 [ ] QTV [ ]   Character generator [ ]
    Cam-4 [ ] Type: _____
    Boom [ ]
    Crane [ ]

Remote Van [ ]   Van control [ ]
    Cam-1 [ ]   Switcher [ ]
    Cam-2 [ ]   Audio console [ ]
    Cam-3 [ ]   Character generator [ ]
    Cam-4 [ ]

Master control [ ]
    VTR's [ ]
        Specify type and quantity: _____
                      _____
                      _____
                      _____
    TBC-1 [ ]
    TBC-2 [ ]
    Character generator [ ]
    Time code generation [ ]
    A-B roll [ ]

Microphones: Type   QUANTITY
          _____ _____
          _____ _____
          _____ _____
          _____ _____
          _____ _____

Special requests:
          _____ _____
          _____ _____
          _____ _____
          _____ _____
          _____ _____

Standard Release:

I hereby give my permission to _____
its agents, successors, assigns, clients and purchasers of its
services and/or products to use my photograph (whether still,
film or television) and recordings of my voice and my name in any
legal manner whatsoever.

Date:

_____

Signature:

_____

Parent or guardian (if under age):

_____

Address:

_____

_____

City:

_____

State and Zip:

_____

Phone:

_____

K. ROUTINE SHEET

ROUTINE SHEET

PRODUCER:

TITLE:

DIRECTOR:

PAGE # ____ OF ____

AIR DATE:

TIME:

SEG #	SEG. TIME	RUN TIME	SEGMENT DESCRIPTION	VIDEO	AUDIO

SHOT SHEET

CAMERA #:

PAGE #___ OF ____

SHOT #	CUE	SHOT DESCRIPTION

SIGHT SURVEY

PRODUCTION:

SURVEY BY: DATE OF SURVEY: _____

PRODUCER: DATE(S) OF PRODUCTION: _____

DIRECTOR: TIME PERIOD(S): _____

Location address: _____   APPROVED BY: _____

_____

Location contact 1: _____ Phone: ( )

Location contact 2: _____ Phone: ( )

Power: _____ 120V. _____ 220V. Available Amps within 700 ft.: _____

Location of main power box: _____

Nearest Telephone(s): _____

Microwave/satellite path notes: _____

_____

Contractural or inherent limitations: _____

_____

Alterations required: _____

_____

NOTES

_____

_____

_____

_____

_____

_____

_____

_____

_____

_____

SOUND MIX CUE SHEET

SCENE:
EDITOR:

PAGE #:   OF TOTAL:
PRODUCTION:

NOTES	ACTION	TRACK-1	TRACK-2	TRACK-3	TRACK-4

O. STUDIO FLOOR PLAN

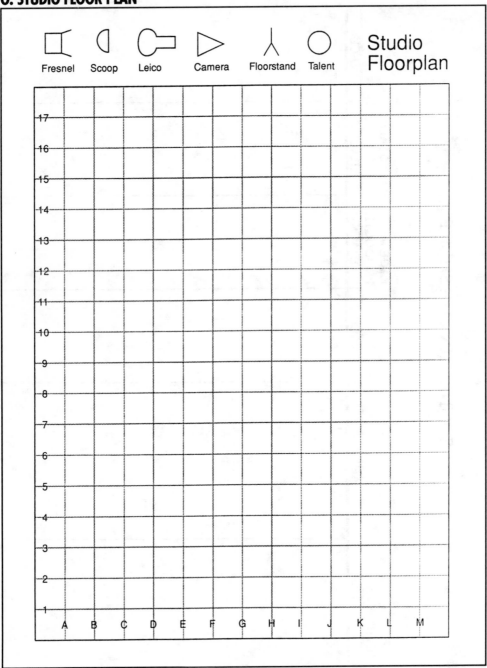

Fresnel   Scoop   Leico   Camera   Floorstand   Talent   Studio Floorplan

LIGHT BOARD PLOT

LIGHT	GRID #	INSTR./WATTAGE	INTENSITY	DIMMER	SUB	SCENE

TAPE LOG

TITLE:

SHOOTING DATE:

PAGE #:

OF TOTAL:

LOGGED BY:

DIRECTOR:

TAPE #	SHOT #	TIME START	TIME END	AUDIO	DESCRIPTION	STATUS

Appendix B

Learning Production

We offer this selected list of schools which teach television and film production. All of these colleges/universities have programs which lead to a masters degree.

Arizona State University
Cronkite School of Journalism & Telecommunications
Stauffer Hall 231
Tempe, AZ 85287-1305
602-965-5011

Boston University
College of Communication,
School of Broadcasting & Film
640 Commonwealth Avenue
Boston, MA 02215
617-353-3543

Brigham Young University
Department of Communication
E-509 HFAC
Provo, UT 84602
801-378-2077

Brooklyn College
Department of Television and Radio
Brooklyn, NY 11210
718-780-5555

California State University, Fresno
Department of Telecommunications
Fresno, CA 93740-0046
209-294-2628

California State University, Fullerton
Dept. of Comm./Radio/TV/Film Sequence
P. O. Box 34080
Fullerton, CA 92634-4080
714-773-2627

California State University, Northridge
Radio-TV-Film Department
18111 Nordhoff St.
Northridge, CA 91330
818-885-3192

Central Michigan University
Broadcast & Cinematic Arts Department
340 Moore Hall
Central Michigan University
Mt. Pleasant MI 48859
517-774-3851

Columbia University
Graduate School of Journalism
116th Street & Broadway
Journalism Building
New York City, NY 10027
212-654-3849

Emerson College
Division of Mass Communication
100 Beacon St.
Boston, MA 02116
617-578-8800

Florida State University
Department of Communication
356 Diffenbaugh Hall
Tallahassee, FL 32306-4021
904-644-5034

Howard University
School of Communications
Department of Radio, Television & Film
525 Bryant St. N.W.
Washington, DC 20059
202-636-7690

Indiana State University
Radio-TV-Film Area
Department of Communication
Terre Haute, IN 47809
812-237-3242

Indiana University
Department of Telecommunications
R-TV Building Room 101
Bloomington, IN 47405
812-855-6895

Kansas State University
A.Q. Miller School of Journalism
and Mass Communication
104 Kedzie Hall
Manhattan, KS 66506-1501
913-532-7645

Loyola Marymount University
Communication Arts
Loyola Blvd. at West 80th St.
Los Angeles, CA 90045
213-642-3033

Marquette University
Broadcast & Electronic Communication
1131 W. Wisconsin Avenue
Milwaukee, WI 53233
414-288-5129

Miami University
Department of Communications
Oxford, OH 45056
513-529-7472

Michigan State University
Department of Telecommunication
409 Communication Arts Bldg.
East Lansing, MI 48824
517-355-8372

Morehead State University
Department of Communications
Breckinridge Hall
Morehead, KY 40351-1689
606-783-2134

Northwestern University
Department of Radio/Television/Film
Evanston, IL 60208
708-491-7315

Ohio University
E.W. Scripps School of Journalism
College of Communication
Athens, OH 45701
614-593-2590

Oklahoma State University
School of Journalism and Broadcasting
206 Paul Miller Bldg.
Stillwater, OK 74078-0195
405-744-6354

Pennsylvania State University
School of Communications
123 S. Burrows St.
University Park, PA 16802
814-863-1484

Pepperdine University
Communication Division
24225 Pacific Coast Highway
Malibu, CA 90263
213-456-4211

San Diego State University
Department of Telecommunications & Film
5300 Campanile Drive
San Diego, CA 92182-0417
619-594-6575

San Francisco State University
Broadcast Communication Arts
1600 Holloway Avenue
San Francisco, CA 94132
415-338-1787

Southern Illinois University
Radio-Television Department
1056 Communications Building
Carbondale IL 62901 618-536-7555

Syracuse University
Television/Radio/Film Department
Newhouse School of Public Communications
215 University Place
Syracuse, NY 13244-2100
315-443-4315

Temple University
Department of Radio-Television-Film
Annenberg Hall
Philadelphia, PA 19122
215-787-8423

Texas Christian University
Department of Radio-TV-Film
Box 30793
Fort Worth, TX 76129
817-921-7630

The University of Michigan
Department of Communication
2020 Frieze Building
Ann Arbor MI 48109
313-764-0420

The University of Texas at Austin
Department of Radio/Television/Film
Austin, TX 78712
512-471-4071

The University of West Florida
Communication Arts Department
11000 University Parkway
Pensacola, FL 32514
904-474-2874

University of Alabama
Telecommunication and Film Department
P. O. Box 870152
Tuscaloosa, AL 35487-0152
205-348-6350

University of Colorado
School of Journalism and Mass Commu.
Campus Box 287
Boulder, CO 80309
303-492-4364

University of Denver
Department of Mass Communications
2490 S. Gaylord
Denver, CO 80208
303-871-2166

University of Florida
Department of Telecommunication
2088 Weimer Hall
College of Journalism and Communication
Gainesville, FL 32601
904-392-0463

University of Georgia
Department of Telecommunications
College of Journalism
Athens, GA 30602
404-542-3785

University of Iowa
Communication Studies
Iowa City, IA 52242
319-335-0575

University of Kansas
Radio-TV, Journalism
Robert Dole Building
Lawrence, KS 66045
913-864-3991

University of Kentucky
Department of Telecommunications
218 Grehan Bldg.
Lexington, KY 40506-0042
606-257-1730

University of Maryland
Department of Radio-Television-Film
Tawes Fine Arts Building
University of Maryland
College Park, MD 20742
301-454-2541

University of Miami
School of Communication
P. O. Box 248127
Coral Gables FL 33124
305-284-2265

University of Minnesota
Department of Speech-Communication
460 Folwell Hall
9 Pleasant Street S.E.
Minneapolis, MN 55455
612-624-5800

University of Nevada, Las Vegas
Greenspun School of Communication
4505 S. Maryland Parkway
Las Vegas, NV 89154
702-739-3325

University of North Carolina at Chapel Hill
Department of Radio, Television and Motion
Pictures
200A Swain Hall, CB# 6235
Chapel Hill NC 27599
919-962-2311

University of Oklahoma
School of Journalism and Mass Comm.
860 Van Vleet Oval
Norman, OK 73019
405-325-2721

University of South Carolina
College of Journalism and Mass Comm.
Columbia, SC 29208
803-777-4104

University of South Dakota
Mass Communication Department
414 East Clark Street
Telecom Center 108
Vermillion, SD 57069
605-677-5477

University of Southern California
University Park
Los Angeles, CA 90089-1695
213-743-2391

University of Tennessee at Knoxville
Department of Broadcasting
295 Communication
Knoxville, TN 37996
615-974-4291

University of Utah
Department of Communication
LeRoy Colwes Building, 204
Salt Lake City, UT 84112
801-581-6888

University of Wisconsin at Madison
Dept. of Communication Arts
821 University Avenue
Madison, WI 53706
608-262-2543

University of Wisconsin at Milwaukee
Mass Communication Department
POB #413
Milwaukee, WI 53201
414-229-4436

Washington State University
Department of Communications
Pullman, WA 99164-2520
509-335-1556

Wayne State University
Radio-TV-Film Area
Department of Communication
585 Mandogian Bldg.
Detroit, MI 48202
313-577-4163

Wichita State University
Elliott School of Communication
Campus Box 31
Wichita, KS 67208-1595
316-689-3185

Glossary

A-B editing A category of editing which incorporates two source machines. The editing is done through an electronic mixing board. This allows the inclusion of dissolves, wipes, and other special effects.

Above-the-line Production costs relating to the creative and performing personnel as well as the resources they need; such as offices and administrative costs. Above-the-line costs are those which must be negotiated and are not set by a rate card or contract. (see *Below-the-line*)

Account Executive An employee of an advertising agency who acts as a liaison with the client and production personnel.

AD See *Assistant Director*.

Affiliates Local stations that have contractual arrangement to re-transmit a network's programming.

Agent Represents actors, writers, directors, etc. Negotiates contracts for them.

Ambient sound Sounds such as crickets or traffic noises which add to the reality of a scene. (see *Room tone*)

Aspect ratio A mathematical formula which expresses the height to width ratio of an image. In television the ratio is three units (high) to four units (wide).

Assembly edit A category of editing used for copying tapes or dubbing sections of programs. (see *Insert editing*)

Assistant Director (AD) In studio productions this is often the person responsible for timing a program and giving preparatory commands to technicians who operate cameras, audio consoles, electronic graphics, and videotape machines. In single camera production, the assistant director performs tasks such as supervising extras and technicians.

Atmosphere shots Shots used to establish mood, theme, and setting.

Audio cassette A plastic housing containing 1/8 inch magnetic tape on two cores one for tape feed and one for take up.

Audio channel A section of magnetic media allocated for sound information.

Audition A trial performance in which members of the production team have the opportunity to assess actors and actresses.

Available light The light that exists naturally in a setting—the sun, a table lamp, a skylight, a candle, etc..

Back light An element of four-point lighting which illuminates the subject from behind and highlights his/her shoulders and hair.

Background light An element of four-point lighting which illuminates the background.

Barn door Adjustable flaps on a lighting instrument which control the throw of light.

Bass roll-off filters Microphone accessory which neutralizes distortions such as those resulting from placing a microphone too close to a sound source.

Below-the-line All expenses in a budget which are not negotiable; they are set by contract and rate card. (see *Above-the-line*)

Bi-directional A type of microphone sensitive to sounds from two discrete directions.

Black A video signal which contains a sync pulse or control track but no visual information. (see *Blacking a tape*)

Blacking a tape The process of preparing a videotape for insert editing by laying down a control track.

Blast filters A microphone accessory which helps screen out unwanted pops.

Blocking Planning and executing the movement and placement of actors and/or cameras in a performance space.

Boom A pole onto which a microphone is attached to keep the microphone out of view of the camera.

Boom operator The person responsible for holding, adjusting, or operating the boom.

Bottom line The total cost of a production above-the-line plus below-the-line costs.

Bounce Diffusing a light source by literally "bouncing" light off a wall, white card, or white umbrella.

Break-away A prop or set piece (window, door, table) designed to shatter on impact.

Breaks Time periods within a program where commercials or other announcements are placed.

Broad A lighting instrument which produces very diffuse, soft light.

Budget An outline of expenses anticipated for a production.

Burnt-in time code Superimposition of time code onto the visual portion of a video image. (see *Time code*)

C-SPAN Cable Satellite Programming Network. A public service network sponsored by the cable television industry. Its programming includes government functions (such as congressional debates) and other political coverage.

Cable television A technology which delivers to the consumer a variety of services program distribution, interactive video, home shopping, home security, and so on.

Cameo The appearance in one or two scene of a program by an actor or actors. Also, a lighting effect in which the subject appears within a totally neutral (usually white) background.

Camera originals First generation picture and/or sound.

Cardioid microphone A microphone with a heart-shaped pick-up pattern.

Casting Director The person responsible for selecting and hiring actors and actresses.

Character generator A computer system which produces titles and other graphic effects.

CDs Compact Disks. The disks used for high fidelity recording and playback.

Character sketches A synopsis of a character in a script.

Chromakey An electronic matting effect in which a specific color (usually blue or green) is used to "cut out" and replace portions of an image.

Cinematographer The person responsible for operating a film camera. (see *Videographer*)

Clients Individuals or institutions which hire production teams to write, design, and produce programs.

Close-up A picture composition which features a small part of a subject. For human subjects, a close-up is a composition that shows only the head and shoulders.

Co-produce When two or more parties join to participate in the financing of a production.

Color temperature Light color expressed in degrees Kelvin (k). Artificial, tungsten lights have a color temperature of about 3200k. Daylight is approximately 5400k.

Composite sound track A completed sound track in which music, dialogue, voice-overs, and sound effects are properly balanced and mixed together.

Condenser microphone A type of microphone containing two parallel metal plates. Sound waves move the diaphragm and alter the electronic charge between the two plates. This type of design is very durable and suited for "rugged" recording situations.

Contingency plans Alternative arrangements. For example, when a scene is planned to be shot outside, contingency plans are made in case it rains or snows.

Continuity Creating the impression that scenes shot out of sequence appear in sequence.

Contract A written legal agreement between two or more parties.

Contrast The range of brightness from the lightest highlight to the darkest shadow.

Control track A portion of a video signal which keeps tape running at a constant speed.

Corporate/Institutional Television Programs for organizations that are often produced and distributed "in house."

Costume Designer The person responsible for designing, selecting, and creating clothing for subjects in a production.

Costume Mistress Person responsible for maintaining costumes during production.

Count down The numbers which appear on the screen before the first frame of video. Usually a count of ten seconds.

Craning shots Moving the camera mount vertically up or down.

Credits The names of all members of the production team responsible for a film or television program.

Crew assignment sheets A list of crew members and their assigned jobs.

Cross shoot A technique of shooting scenes and interviews with two cameras.

Cyclorama (cyc) A large curtain which provides a neutral background in a studio.

Dailies Unedited film or video footage.

Day for night A photographic technique of shooting a night time scene during the day.

Depth of field The area in which objects are in focus. Varying aperture settings and focal lengths will change the depth of field.

Dialogue Spoken words.

Diaphragm An element of a microphone which vibrates when attacked by sound waves.

Diffuse light Light which is filtered, bounced or reflected. Diffuse light cannot be controlled. (see *Direct light*)

Dimmer board Equipment to which lighting instruments are connected. Dimmer boards make it possible to vary the intensity of light.

Direct light Light which is projected at a subject from a hard light source.

Director's script A script prepared by the director, sometimes called a technical script. For multicamera production, director's scripts are normally split page. For singlecamera shoots, director's scripts are normally singlecolumn scripts organized into scenes or shots.

Dissolve The simultaneous fading out of one picture or sound and fading in of another.

Distribution The stage of program making in which the production team and/or its client are concerned with delivering a program to its intended audience.

Documentary A type of program which appears to document reality.

Dolly A wheeled device on which a camera is mounted to allow smooth-moving shoots.

Drop out A flaw in an electronic signal.

Durability A term applied to equipment designed to withstand shocks and harsh treatment. Often used with microphones.

Dynamic microphone One in which a moving wire coil is attached to a diaphragm suspended in a magnetic field.

Edit decision list A list of the individual shots and sounds of a program and their location on "camera originals."

Editing console A computer controlled unit which allows two or more videotape machines to be "rolled" in unison for precise editing.

Editor The person responsible for selecting and ordering pictures and sounds in a program.

Effects make-up Special make-up which dramatically alters the way an actor or actress appears. For example, a young actor may be made to appear extremely old.

Electronic graphics Graphics produced by a character generator or other type of computer with video output.

Episode A single installment in a program series.

Equalizing A signal modifying technique that selectively increases or decreases specific sound frequencies.

Essential area The part of the television frame (inner 80 percent) that will not be cropped when broadcast.

Extra An actor or actress with few spoken lines of dialogue who plays a minor role in a program.

F-stop A number which indicates the relative diameter of a lens opening. The larger the f-stop number, the smaller the opening or aperture of the lens.

Facility requisition A form used to reserve production space (studio, editing room, folly sound studio, etc.) and/or production equipment (cameras, editing consoles, lights, etc.).

Fade Increase or decrease of sound volume or picture brightness.

Fall off The graduation of light intensity from light to dark. Fast fall off describes light which changes from light to dark abruptly. Slow fall off describes light which changes from light to dark gradually.

Fill light An element of four point lighting which is used to "fill in" or "model" shadows created by the key light.

Film magazine A unit of the motion picture camera which houses film. During shooting, film passes from the magazine through the camera and back to the magazine where it is collected onto a take-up core.

First generation Programs or program segments edited directly from the camera originals.

First run The initial showing of a film or program.

Fixed expenses Costs in a production which are set by contract or rate cards.

Flags Cardboard or metal panels used to deflect light from the camera lens or a section of the set.

Flood light A lamp with a parabolic reflector which produces a diffuse light. It "floods" the scene with light.

Focusing Altering the distance between the lens and the video chip or pick-up tube (or in film, the film plane) until a sharp image is obtained.

Footage Uncut film or videotape.

Four point lighting A standard model of film and television lighting consisting of a key light, a fill light, a back light, and a background light.

Frame The smallest unit of motion picture film and video. There are 24 frames per second in motion picture film and 30 frames in video.

Freelance Working on a shortterm contract basis.

Freeze frame An effect in which the action is paused or "frozen."

Fresnel A lighting instrument with a step lens and barn doors that produces direct light which can easily be controlled.

Funding agencies Public or private organizations which provide support for film and video productions.

Gaffer A member of the production crew whose job is to set up and adjust lighting instruments.

Gel Short for gelatin a translucent material placed in front of lighting instruments which changes the color or color temperature of a light.

General Manager The job title of the person responsible for the operation of a television station.

Gopher The title of the person in a production crew who "goes for" everything—from coffee to actors waiting at the airport.

Graphic Artist The person responsible for the design of graphics.

Graphic cards Cardboard cards onto which graphics are fixed.

Graphics Printed, drawn, or electronically generated letters and symbols.

Green room A lounge usually adjacent to a studio or stage for actors, program guests, and production staff.

Grips A member of the crew who assists in the set-up and operation of props and scenic elements.

Hair Designer The person responsible for making sure a subject's hair or hairdo matches the requirements of the script.

Hair light A light which highlights a subject's hair. Often the backlight produces this effect.

Hand held Shooting a scene with the camera mounted on the shoulder of the camera operator.

Head set Part of a two-way communication system which allows the production team to communicate with the technical crew during rehearsal and shooting.

High 8 A video system that has the potential to produce broadcast quality picture and sound recorded on 8mm video-tape.

High key A style of lighting or a "look" in which the overall illumination is very bright.

Highly directional A type of microphone with a very narrow pick-up pattern.

Highly produced A program with an expensive appearance or look.

Hot spots Portions of an image which are overexposed or have a washed out quality.

Hyper A prefix meaning "extremely" hypercardioid microphones are instruments with an extremely narrow cardioid pick-up pattern.

In the can A term meaning finished, complete "The program is in the can."

In-house A term used to describe equipment and personnel which are owned and employed by institutions which make their own programs.

Independent stations A television (or radio) station which is not affiliated with a major network.

Industrial quality A description of equipment used for corporate/institutional and other types of nonbroadcast television.

Insert A segment of video and/or audio which is edited into a program.

Intercut Inserting a shot into a scene.

Interiors Scenes that are shot indoors.

Interlock When two or more pieces of equipment are electronically or mechanically synchronized.

Intro Short for introduction.

Iris The element of the lens that controls the amount of light that enters a camera.

Jib A piece of equipment with a teeter-totter like design. A camera is mounted on one end and a counterweight is on the other. This allows for smooth craning shots.

Kelvin Unit used to measure the color temperature of a light source.

Key light An element of four point lighting which represents the primary source of light in a scene.

Kickers Small lights used to "punch up" or add light to isolated portions of a set.

Kinescope A process used in the 1940s and 1950s in which live broadcasts were filmed directly from television screens.

Lavaliere microphone A small microphone hung from a subject's neck or attached to the chest. Also called "tie tacs."

Level A relative term used to define the strength of an audio or video signal.

Light board plot A document which indicates the lighting instruments used in a production and the functions of the dimmer board to which these instruments are connected.

Light meter A device which measures the amount of light reflected off or projected onto a subject.

Lighting Director The person responsible for the creative decisions concerning light.

Line items The specific items in a budget.

Live-on-tape A program produced multi camera, on video-tape without post production editing, as if it were broadcast "live."

Local station A television (or radio) station broadcasting on one terrestrial transmitter serving one community or "market."

Location Scout Person who seeks out a place to record a scene which matches the requirements of the script.

Logging Listing individual shots and sounds of a reel of videotape or film.

Logo Short for logotype. A trade mark or symbol used to identify an organization, program or individual.

Long shot A shot from a wide angle which shows the overall scene.

Low key A style of lighting which has high contrast and shadows.

Made-for-television movie A fictional program shot on film or videotape that uses the syntax and style of film intended for television.

Mark A spot on the floor "marked" for the placement of equipment or talent.

Master shot A shot containing a view of all the action of a scene.

Matte A physical or electronic mask which blocks off part of an image in a camera or visual mixer.

Mic Microphone.

Millimeter A metric unit used in film and videotape (35mm, 16mm film, 8mm video).

Moles A small, highly directional light used on location.

Monitor Television sets used in editing and production.

Montage The French word for editing. It is also a term used to describe fast paced sequences without synchronous dialogue.

Multicamera A production technique using two or more cameras. In most instances multicamera productions are edited as they are recorded or produced.

Multi-track A recording which contains two or more channels of information; usually used in reference to sound recorders.

Network Two or more stations which are connected by wire, microwave or satellite. The three major commercial networks ABC, NBC and CBS are made up of six owned and operated stations and hundreds of affiliates.

Non-broadcast Programming that is intended for distribution on video cassette or other closed circuit systems.

Numbers An informal term for ratings "The show is doing great, the numbers are terrific."

Off-camera (O.C.) Action or dialogue which takes places out of view of the camera.

Off-line editing A stage in the editing process when "rough cuts" are produced—usually performed on inexpensive, "straight cut" editing equipment.

Off-mic A sound source which is outside the pick-up pattern of a microphone.

Omni A portable lighting instrument which produces diffuse light.

Omni-directional A microphone pickup pattern sensitive to sounds from all directions.

On-line editing A stage in the editing process in which final or "fine cuts" are produced on relatively expensive equipment.

Outro Final or closing element of a program or program segment.

PA See production assistant.

Pan A lighting instrument used both on location and in studios which produces diffuse, soft light. Also a camera movement in which the camera mimics the human motion of turning one's head left or right from a fixed position.

PBS Public Broadcasting Service. The network of public, non-commercial television stations.

Peak meter A device that responds to loudness "peaks" in an audio signal.

Photomation A sequence of still photographs that are given the appearance of animation with camera movement, transitions, and editing.

Pick-up pattern A term used to describe a microphone's optimum area of sensitivity.

Pick-up shots Shots which are usually not planned in a script but which are "picked-up" or "collected" during production.

Pilot A sample or test program.

Pitch A term describing a presentation in which producers "sell" their concept to potential backers.

Pop A distortion in a recording resulting from a sudden and loud burst of noise.

Post production house A facility specializing in on-line editing.

Prime time The hours from 7:30-11:00 in the evening, when there is the largest audience watching television.

Producer The person ultimately responsible for the program.

Production Assistant (PA) A member of the production staff who usually performs tasks like photocopying, making coffee, and assisting the producer and director.

Production Manager The person in charge of the logistical elements of a production. Also, at a television or radio station, the person in charge of production.

Program Manager The person at a television or cable station in charge of program selection and scheduling.

Public Television Non-commercial broadcast television partially funded by federal and state taxes.

PZM A microphone used to pick up sounds which resonate through the surfaces on which they are placed.

Q-TV See *Teleprompter*

Rate card A price list for the rental of equipment and studio space, the salaries of production personnel and commercial air time.

Ratings A measurement representing the percent of the total audience tuned to a specific program.

Readying cameras Moving a camera into position and framing it for an upcoming shot.

Ribbon microphone A microphone with a metal ribbon diaphragm which produces a rich, mellow sound. It "travels" poorly because it is not very durable.

Rim light See *Back light*

Roll In multi camera production, "roll" is a command usually spoken by the assistant director or director to playback a film, video or audiotape. In single camera production, "roll" is a command to begin recording picture or sound.

Roll in A segment of a program which is added while the program is being produced.

Room noise The natural sounds in a room—refrigerator hum, the buzz of florescent light fixtures, etc..

Room tone Another term for room noise.

Rough cut The final stage of off-line editing when a program is assembled to determine if the program "works."

Run through The last phase of rehearsal before filming or taping.

Rundown sheets The technical script used for sound mixing.

Rushes See *Dailies*

Safe area See *Essential area*

Satellites Television relay stations in space capable of receiving signals and retransmitting them to earth receiving stations.

Scene A unit of a program, usually a series of shots, that are related to a common theme.

Scenic Designer The person responsible for selecting or designing the setting in which a scene takes place.

Scoop A light fixture which produces reflective, diffuse light with slow fall off.

Scout locations The process of selecting locations and making sure they are appropriate and that they have adequate power and are accessible to production personnel and equipment.

Scratch mix A practice sound mix or a "rough cut" sound mix.

Scrim Spun glass material or metal screens placed in front of light fixtures to diffuse light.

Shading Adjusting the contrast and color balance of a video camera.

Shooting ratio The ratio of film or videotape shot to the amount used in the final product. A 30 minute program that is made from 5 hours of original videotape has a shooting ratio of 10 to 1.

Shot sheets A list of the shots assigned to a camera operator in multi-camera production.

Shotgun A highly directional microphone.

Sight survey The document used to report the results of scouting a location.

Silhouette A lighting design in which the background is lit and the foreground is dark.

Single camera A style of production in which sound and images are collected one shot at a time and combined into a program during post production editing.

Sitcom Situation comedy, a popular type of television program.

Slate The identification of a shot used by the production staff. In film it is also called clap-board.

SMPTE Society of Motion Picture and Television Engineers.

SMPTE Time Code Eight digit numbering system used to identify each videotape frame by hour, minute, second and frame. (There are thirty frames per second.)

Sound level The relative signal strength of an audio source.

Sound mixing Combining different elements of a sound track into a composite sound track.

Sound on Tape (SOT) Sound on tape, existing sound on an audio console line, usually sent from a video or film program insert..

Sound stage A sound proof studio.

Speed After a director requests filming or videotaping to begin, this term is used by camera and sound operators to verify that their equipment is running and "up to speed."

Spike A sharp peak on a waveform monitor which indicates that there is a bright spot in a picture.

Split screen A technique in which the screen is literally split into two or more sections.

Sponsor Individuals or institutions which directly or indirectly fund programs.

Spots Radio or television commercial announcements.

Sprocket holes Holes along the edge of motion picture film which keeps the film running at a constant speed. (see *Control track*)

Standard release form A signed agreement that gives a producer or a producing institution the legal right to use an image and/or sound.

Steadycam A stabilizing system used in hand-held camera shots which allows movement to be smooth.

Storyboard A series of sketches representing how a script is to be shot and edited.

Straight cut A term used to describe moving directly from one image to another.

Strip light A lighting instrument containing a series of soft, diffuse lights.

Stripped script A term used to describe a script prepared for shooting in the singlecamera style. In most instances this means reordering shots to efficiently use staff, production staff, equipment and personnel.

Super station Local broadcast station which has expanded its viewing area to a national level through satellite/cable distribution.

Supercardioid Unidirectional microphone with a slightly narrower pick up pattern than a cardioid microphone.

Superimposition An effect where one image is placed on top of another.

Sweeten A term used to describe improving the sound track of a program by adding sound effects. The term is also used to describe equalizing the sound track, or enhancement through other signal-processing procedures.

Sync sound (synchronous sound) The sound that is recorded at the same time as its corresponding picture.

Take In the singlecamera style of production, "take" is used to describe a single shot. In multicamera, it is a command to cut from one camera or video source to another.

Talent A term used to describe actors, hosts, commentators, and other performers on television.

Tape log A list of the content and location of program material on a videotape.

TD (Technical Director) In multi camera production, the crew member responsible for operation of the video mixer/switcher.

Telepromptor A device which allows talent to read his or her script while appearing to look directly into the camera. Also referred to as Q-TV.

35mm film Professional motion picture film. Often used in television production, especially for dramas, made-for-TV movies, and commercials. However, its high cost compared to videotape restricts its application in many circumstances.

Tie tac See *Lavaliere microphone*.

Time code synchronizer reader A device which stabilizes the operating speeds of two or more electronic devices (videotape recorders, multi-track audio recorders).

Transition The way one shot or sound element changes to another. The most common visual transitions are fades, wipes, dissolves and cuts.

Travelling matte An optical effect that creates the illusion that a stationary object or person is moving. For example, a jet flying through the cement canyons of a city may actually be a model airplane matted over moving shots of New York skyscrapers.

Treatment A general description/summary of an intended program organized into scenes or sequences.

Tripod An adjustable three-legged stand onto which a camera is mounted.

Tungsten light The type of light produced by most light fixtures used in production. Also, the type of light produced by household light bulbs. Tungsten light is "warm" or orange-ish; it is usually 3200 degrees Kelvin as compared to daylight which is "cool" or blue-ish and 5600 degrees Kelvin.

Turn-around-time The time it takes to complete a production from conception to distribution.

Two-shot A shot which shows two subjects.

Unidirectional A term used to describe a type of microphone which is sensitive in only one direction (as opposed to bi-directional).

Video switcher The visual mixing board. Also, the person responsible for operating the visual mixing board. He/she is often called the "technical director."

Videographer A term used to describe a video camera operator.

Videotape Library Record Sheet A form used for archival purposes to list the contents of a videotape.

VO (Voice Over) Words spoken over visual material by an announcer, actor, actress, or subject who is not seen.

Walk through A term used to describe a rehearsal without cameras, costumes, and lights.

Waveform monitor A piece of equipment that graphically displays a video signal.

Wind screen A filter usually placed over a microphone to reduce the sound of wind.

Wipe A transition in which one picture replaces another by cutting a pattern (a circle, square, a series of dots, etc.) into the first picture.

Wireless body mic A small microphone attached to a subject's clothing that transmits sound through a "closed circuit" FM radio transmitter to a "closed circuit" receiver.

Working title A temporary name given to a program during development, scripting and/or production. It usually is not the title of the finished program.

Zoom-in/out Increasing/decreasing the size of a subject by increasing the focal length of a zoom lens or by magnifying the subject.

Selected Bibliography

This list of books, periodicals, journals, directories, guides and computer software covers all of the aspects of television production discussed in this book; everything from planning, writing and designing to budgeting and execution. We have selected items published in the last ten years.

BOOKS Alkin, E. G. M. *Sound Techniques for Video and TV*. 2nd ed. London: Focal Press, 1989.

Alten, Stanley. *Audio in Media*. 2nd ed.. Belmont, CA: Wadsworth, 1990.

Armer, Alan A. *Writing the Screenplay: TV and Film*. Belmont: CA: Wadsworth Co, 1988.

Blank, Ben. *Professional Video Graphic Design*. New York: Prentice Hall, 1986.

Blumenthal, Howard J. *Television Producing & Directing*, 1st ed. New York: Barnes & Noble Books, 1987.

Brady, Ben. *The Understructure of Writing For Film & Television*, 1st ed. Austin: University of Texas Press, 1988.

Broughton, Irv. *Producers On Producing: The Making Of Film And Television*. Jefferson, N.C.: McFarland, 1986.

Browne, Steven, E. *Videotape Editing; A Postproduction Primer*. Boston: Focal Press, 1989.

Burrows, Thomas D., Donald N. Wood and Lynne Schafer Cross. *Television Production: Disciplines And Techniques*. 4th ed. Dubuque, Iowa: W. C. Brown, 1989.

Cantor, Muriel G. *The Hollywood TV Producer: His Work and His Audience*. New Brunswick: NJ: Transaction Books, 1988.

Cartwright, Steve R. *Training with Video: Designing and Producing Video Training Programs*. White Plains, NY: Knowledge Industry Publications, 1986.

Compaine, Benjamin M. *Understanding New Media: Trends and Issues In Electronic Distribution Of Information*. Cambridge, Mass: Ballinger, 1984.

Fielding, Ken. *Introduction to Television Production*. White Plains, New York: Longman, 1989.

Gayeski, Diane. *Corporate and Instructional Video*. Englewood Cliffs, NJ: Prentice Hall, 1983.

Greenberger, Martin. *Electronic Publishing Plus: Media For A Technological Future*. Washington, D.C: Washington Program—Annenberg School Of Communications, 1985.

Gross, Lynne S. and Larry Ward. *Electronic Movie Making*. Belmont, CA: Wadsworth, 1990.

Hausman, Carl. *Institutional Video, Planning, Budgeting, Production and Evaluation*. Belmont, CA: Wadsworth, 1991.

Hilliard, Robert L. *Writing for Television and Radio 5th edition*. Belmont, CA: Wadsworth, 1991.

Hoffman, E. Kenneth. *The Impact of Television Production on Motion Picture Production*. New York: New York University, 1982.

Iuppa, Nicholas V. *Advanced Interactive Video Design*. Stoneham, Mass: Focal Press, 1988.

Karentnikova, Inga. *How Scripts are Made*. Carbondale: Southern Illinois University Press, 1990.

Katsh, M. Ethan. *The Electronic Media and the Transformation of Law*. New York: Oxford University Press, 1989.

Kessler, Lauren. *Mastering the Message: Media Writing With Substance and Style*. Belmont, CA: Wadsworth, 1989.

Kuney, Jack. *Take One: Television Directors on Directing*. New York: Greenwood Press, 1990.

Lovejoy, Margot. *Postmodern Currents: Art and Artists in the Age of Electronic Media*. Ann Arbor: UMI Research Press, 1989.

Lukas, Christopher. *Directing for Film and Television: A Guide to the Craft*. New York: Anchor Books, 1985.

Madsen, Roy. *Working Cinema: Learning from the Masters*. Belmont, CA: Wadsworth, 1990.

Mathias, Harry and Richard, Patterson. *Electronic Cinematography*. Belmont, CA: Wadsworth, 1985.

Matrazzo, Donna. *The Corporate Scriptwriting Book*. 2nd ed. Portland, Oreg.: Communicom Publishing Co., 1985.

Mcquillin, Lon B. *Computers in Video Production*. White Plains, NY: Knowledge Industry Publications, 1986.

Miller, Lynn F. *The Hand That Holds the Camera: Interviews With Women Film and Video Directors*. New York: Garland, 1988.

Millerson, Gerald. *The Technique of Television Production*. 12th ed. London: Focal Press, 1990.

Millerson, Gerald. *TV Lighting Methods*. Stoneham, Mass: Focal Press, 1982.

Newcomb, Horace. *The Producer's Medium: Conversations With Creators of American TV*. New York: Oxford University Press, 1983.

Newsom, Doug. *Media Writing: Preparing Information For the Mass Media*. 2nd ed. Belmont, CA: Wadsworth, 1988.

Rabiger, Michael. *Directing: Film Techniques and Aesthetics*. Boston: Focal Press, 1989.

Rosenthal, Alan. *Writing Directing and Producing Documentary Films*. Carbondale: Southern Illinois University Press, 1990.

Rowlands, Avril. *The Production Assistant in TV and Video*. Boston: Focal Press, 1987.

Russo, John. *Making Movies*. New York: Dell Books, 1989.

Sayles, John. *Thinking in Pictures: The Making of the Movie Matawan*. Boston: Houghton Mifflin Co., 1987.

Shapiro, George H. *New Program Opportunities in the Electronic Media*. New York: Practising Law Institute, 1983.

Shook, Frederick. *Television Field Production and Reporting*. New York: Longman, 1989.

Swain, Dwight. *Film Scriptwriting; a Pracitical Manual*. Boston: Focal Press, 1988.

Taylor, Margaret H. *Planning for Video: A Guide to Making Effective Training Videotapes*. London: Kogan Page, 1988.

Weis, Elisabeth and John Belton. *Theory and Practice of Film Sound*. New York: Columbia University Press, 1989.

Wershing, Stephen and Paul Singer. *Computer Graphics and Animation for Corporate Video*. White Plains, NY: Knowledge Industry Publications, 1988.

Wiese, Michael. *Film and Video Budgets*. Stoneham, Mass.: Focal Press, 1984.

Wiese, Michael. *Home Video: Producing for the Home Market*. Michael Wiese Film/Video: Westport, Conn., 1986.

Wurtzel, Alan and Stephen Acker. *Television Production*. 3rd ed. New York: McGraw-Hill, 1989.

Zettl, Herbert. *Sight Sound Motion: Applied Media Aesthetics*. Belmont, CA: Wadsworth, 1990.

Zettl, Herbert. *Television Production Handbook*. 4th ed. Belmont, CA: Wadsworth, 1984.

American Cinematographer. Hollywood, CA: ASC Holding Corp. Monthly.

Audio-Visual Communications. New York: Media-Horizons. Monthly.

**PERIODICALS &
JOURNALS**

AV Video.Torrence, CA: Montage Publishing. Monthly.

Broadcasting. Washington, D.C.: Broadcasting Publications. Weekly.

Cinema Canada. Montreal: Cinema Canada Magazine Foundation. Monthly.

Cinema Journal. Champaign: University of Illinois Press. Quarterly.

Corporate Television. New York: ITVA (International Television Association). Monthly.

Electronic Media. Chicago: Crain Communications. Weekly.

Film Quarterly. Berkeley, CA: University of California Press. Quarterly.

Films and Filming. London: Arbrose Press. Monthly.

Journal of Broadcasting & Electronic Media. Washington, D.C.: Broadcast Education Association. Quarterly.

Journal of Film and Video. Chicago: University Film and Video Association. Quarterly.

Millimeter. New York: Millimeter Magazine. Monthly.

TV Communications. Englewood, Colo.: Communications Pub. Corp. Monthly.

Video Systems. Overland Park, Kans.: Intertect Publishing Corp. Quarterly.

Video Times. Hollywood, CA: The MPCS Video Center. Quarterly.

Videography. New York: Media Horizons. Quarterly.

Most popular word processing programs can be used to type scripts. But there are some programs which have special formatting functions to help you create professional looking single or multi-column scripts.

AVScriptor 3.6 by Tom Schroeppel, 4705 Bay View Avenue, Tampa, FL 33611.

Movie Master 3.07, Comprehensive Video Supply Corporation, 148 Veterans Dr., Northvale, NH 07647.

ScreenWright Professional 5.1, Paul D. Nalder Associates, 338 Prospect Place, #4C, Brooklyn, NY 11238.

Scriptor 2.9d, Screenplay Systems, 150 E. Olive/Suite 305, Burbank, CA 91502.

ShowScape for WordPerfect 5.1, Lake Compuframes, Inc., P.O. Box 890, Briarcliff Manor, NY 10510.

SplitScriptor 1.1, Ixion, Inc., 1335 N. Northlake Way, Suite 102, Seattle, WA 98103.

WordPerfect 5.1, WordPerfect Corporation, 1555 N. Technology Way, Orem, UT 84057.

SCRIPTWRITING SOFTWARE

Index

In-house media specialists, 85
Inky-dinkies, 146
Inserts, 183-184
Institutional/corporate (industrial) TV, 85
Institutional programming, 20-24
Interviews, 209-212
Invisible interviews, 210

Kinescope, 13
Kickers, 146
Key lights, 147-148, *illus.* 147

Language, visual, 41-53
Lenses, 139-140
Library sheets, 216, *illus.* 216
Light, bouncing of, 147, *illus.* 147
Light board plot, *illus.* 195, 305
Light doubling, *illus.* 149
Lighting, 48, 190, 195-197, *illus.* 195; cameras
    and, 139-141; design of, 144-151;
    equipment, 144-147; four point, 147-150,
    illus. 147
Lighting console, 228, *illus.* 228
Lighting designer, 228
Line items, 92
Location scout, 251
Location shooting, 143
Location video taping, 189-200
Logging tapes, 218-219, *illus.* 219

MacNeil/Lehrer Newshour, 43-44, 71
McLuhan, Marshall, 5
Microphones, 156-163; durability of, 162-163;
    frequency response of, 161; uses of, 159-160,
    illus. 160
Mixing, 269-273; editing and, 262-273; sound,
    154-155, 185-186
Moles, 146
Monitor, with spike, 191, *illus.* 191
Movement: camera, 58-62; in frame, 62-63
Multi-camera script, 289, *illus.* 290
Multi-camera television style, 9
Music, 70, 165; source of, 265-268

Narration, 69
Negotiable budget items, 91
Networks: cable, 17-18; commercial, 18-20

News departments, 14
News programs, 43-44

Off-camera mics, 160, *illus.* 160
Off-camera/off-mic interviews, 209-210
Off-camera/on-mic interviews, 210
Off-line editing, 183-185, *illus.* 183
Omnis, 146
Omnidirectional pickup pattern, 158, *illus.* 158
On-camera interviews, 210-211
On-camera mics, 160
On-line editing, 185
"Out of house" production companies, 172

Page slug or header, 289
Panning, 60
Pans, 146, *illus.* 146
Paperwork, production, 279-306
Peak meters, 227, *illus.* 227
Pedestalling, 59
Perspective, and camera movement, 61-62
Pickup patterns, of mics, 157-159, *illus.* 158, 159
"Pick up" shots, 194
Picture editing, 63-65
Pop filters, 161
Portable light fixtures, 146, 147
Producers, 80; role of, 34. *See also* Treatments
    and scripts
Producer/writer. *See* Treatments and scripts
Production: of commercial programs, 241-277; of
    documentary, 207-221; evolution of, 7-16;
    execution stage, 179-239; paperwork for,
    279-306; studio segment, 221-239
Production assistants (PAs), 253
Production budgets, 90-93
Production process, 75; commitment stage of,
    77-100; design stage of, 103-176; execution
    stage of, 179-277
Production schedules, 88-90, 181-182, *illus.* 182
Production team, 33-38
Production worksheets, 294, *illus.* 295-306
Program line, 224
Programming categories, 18-32; cassette TV,
    24-28; commercial TV, 18-20; corporate/
    institutional, 20-24; public/educational TV,
    28-32
Promotion, 274